50 Most Significant Jamaican Musical Artists Past To Present

Roger Grant

Organic Base Books

© 2014 Roger Grant

Contact organicrecordsus@yahoo.com

Table of Contents

6	*Author's Note*
11	*Introduction*

Book I

14	*Seven of Merit*
43	*Tribute to Sly & Robbie*

Book II

50 Most Significant Jamaican Musical Artists – Past to Present

56	*Augustus Pablo*
60	*Brigadier Jerry*
63	*Jah Cure*
73	*Vybz Kartel*
83	*Mavado*
89	*Jacob Miller*
100	*Mutabaruka*
105	*Damian Marley*
109	*Delroy Wilson*
113	*Byron Lee*
122	*Luciano*
127	*Ernie Ranglin*
131	*Judy Mowatt*

137	*Ninja Man*
144	*Capleton*
151	*Lady Saw*
158	*Sizzla*
169	*Bounty Killer*
179	*Beenie Man*
187	*Sister Nancy*
192	*Super Cat*
198	*Grace Jones*
204	*Garnett Silk*
210	*Hortense Ellis*
215	*John Holt*
221	*Big Youth*
228	*Sugar Minott*
235	*Freddie McGregor*
241	*Buju Banton*
253	*Sean Paul*
261	*Ziggy Marley*
267	*Lee Scratch Perry*
274	*Beres Hammond*
285	*Barrington Levy*
293	*Yellowman*
303	*Louise Bennett*
310	*Bunny Wailer*
319	*Desmond Dekker*
330	*Alton Ellis*
337	*Burning Spear*
346	*Shaggy*
362	*U-Roy*

370	*Shabba Ranks*
384	*Marcia Griffiths*
394	*Gregory Issacs*
402	*Toots Hibbert*
412	*Dennis Brown*
424	*Peter Tosh*
440	*Jimmy Cliff*
452	*Bob Marley*
477	DEDICATION & THANKS
478	AUTHOR'S BIO/CONTACT INFO

Author's Note

Jamaican music is at its nadir. If not for the weight of history and the proven fact that reggae has its place as a mainstream genre, it could be said that reggae's continued potency is tenuous. Standards have seen a steep decline in recent years after gradual erosion, beginning in the 80s. The dominance of the dancehall and dancehall performers has led to the decimation of bands. Musicians have found it less and less feasible to make a living at their craft, while the beat programmers have taken over. Today's practitioners have steadily undone music's great surge from the 70s. This began almost immediately following the death of the genre's greatest superstar, Bob Marley, in 1981. The most popular artist to emerge post-Marley was a foul-mouthed toaster called Yellowman.

This was the herald of the *'Dark Age of Reggae'* when the very ingredients that made it irresistible to the world, its spiritual attributes, were exchanged for minimalism and vulgarity. But even so, they were still others who were a counter balance to this new wave. In the 80s and into the 90s at least, there was a choice. As many slack DJs there were, one could still find cultural alternatives.

But today, even the singers are running behind the DJs, while songwriting is a lost art and musicianship rare. In addition, there is a famine of personnel in the form of managers, booking agents, real promoters and musical directors necessary for a vibrant industry.

The lack of government support over the years and the pervasiveness of ignorance shown by those active in the field have scared off intelligent people from entering. The blame for this overall collapse in standards is a collective one. In 1964, the Jamaican government sponsored local musicians to attend a trade fair in New York that brought exposure to future legends Jimmy Cliff and Toots and, in subsequent years, supported others at Midem in France. A return to showing interest and actively subsidizing the cultural export is still necessary.

Thirty years ago radio was not so myopic, although the selections offered a wider variety of music. At that time the charts reflected a broader palette with bands like Lloyd Parkes and We The People, 7th Extension, Bare Essentials, Fab Five, Chalice and Third World. Reggae artists at the peak of their careers, most of them in the 70s, played to stadiums and arenas. In contrast, today's top acts can barely fill a club. The stars of yesteryear saw the need for touring; today's pretenders have shunned the practice.

The Recording Industry Association of America's (RIAA) sales figures for 2012 showed the top artists out of Jamaica barely moving 1000 copies of their new releases. The only ones to register significant numbers were Jimmy Cliff, with his Grammy winning album Rebirth, and Bob Marley, who still remains a multimillion-dollar earner thirty years after his passing. One of the two biggest stars for the last several years out of Jamaica, the first being Mavado, has not had an international hit. The other, Vybz Kartel, had the lowest selling debut album of all time and currently resides in prison serving a thirty year sentence after being convicted for murder. Something is really rotten in Kingston.

The music has had a tremendous influence on foreign performers such as Maroon Five and Bruno Mars. They are the ones pushing the creative envelope for reggae. Locals seem to have taken what they have for granted, falsely believing that just because they are Jamaican anything will do. That is not the way Peter Tosh, Bob Marley, Jimmy Cliff, Burning Spear and others of this caliber saw it. At the same time, we must give kudos to the living legends that are still making us proud, but wonder when they depart who will carry the torch.

Younger, aspiring performers must become keener students of the music's history. They must realize that the genre has a great legacy, which they are obligated to uphold. The "pull ups" on stage and the absence of rehearsals smacks of laziness and at worst contempt for the paying public who attend the shows. To be a world star takes hard work and sustained focus. To stand out you cannot run behind every fad you must be original. Today's artists must leave fashion out of their craft and get back to the basics. Every great record begins with a great song. The other pieces of the puzzle are good musicians, a great producer, a visionary engineer and a properly managed record label.

The blueprint is there in the form of Bob Marley's work, but the singers and DJs of today are building a shabby house without one. The disgrace of fellow entertainers fighting each other is killing the music. Focusing on negativity is a creative burden that hampers growth and productivity. The pioneers were interested in the world, sought knowledge and had an insatiable curiosity that allowed them to move beyond the confinement of their native shore. This new generation must take a page out of the elders' books and embrace learning, while having big dreams. They must begin to take back the music and save it from ridicule and from becoming irrelevant. The efforts of our musical heroes must not appear as if it were in vain. Reggae music and the Jamaicans who placed it on the international stage have changed the world.

I hope that reading this book will awaken something in readers, especially those who are musical artists. *50 Most Significant Jamaican Musical Artists Past to Present* (50 Most) is my small contribution to a mission with which we must keep faith.

Introduction

Jamaica is a world power. Not economically or militarily, but indeed culturally. Many Jamaican artists are world-renowned and this book will tell you why. In the space of around ten years, beginning in the early 50s when a tangible music industry took shape that was indigenous to the island, it began to impact beyond its shores. In 1964 Millie Small's hit *My Boy Lollipop* was the first of many. Then there was Desmond Dekker, Jimmy Cliff, Toots Hibbert, Peter Tosh, Shabba Ranks, Shaggy and, of course, Bob Marley. Several Jamaican artists, at least a handful, have transcended the reggae genre becoming as big and influential as their British or North American counterparts. These few notables are even legends in their own right. The spirit, sound and words of this once parochial music has spread like a virus across the globe and has had a sort of colonizing effect, whereby anywhere it invaded it took root. It is a fact that there is a reggae scene of whatever size in almost every country in the world. There are artists of all races and ethnicity that are actively playing, recording and performing it and, in many cases, have adopted the religious practices closely associated with it: Rastafarianism. Reggae is seminal to many other genres such as punk, rap, and dance music that have morphed from it. The music made the island into a geographical star and people of the world are drawn to its physical beauty, robust people and unique culture. All this came through the labors of the artists that make up the illustrious list in this book.

50 Most summarizes the life and work of each artist. This anthology of sorts further provides the reader with heretofore little known facts about them, including the back-stories to their rise and, in some individual cases, subsequent downfall. You will become aware of some of the colorful personalities behind the scenes and their part in shaping the lives of the main subjects. It will educate and enlighten and, for some, it will be like a stroll down memory lane. Most importantly it is a document that puts the spotlight on the achievements of those who have dedicated themselves to something that has helped to enrich the lives of others. Some who did not make the list of 50 are featured in the opening bonus section, *"Seven of Merit"*, which also contains a tribute to Sly & Robbie. ***50 Most*** mainly focuses on solo performers, although some of their works overlap with groups to which they belonged. Many of the artists here will never have a singular biography that may be worth writing, but here they can receive their due. Above all, ***50 Most*** is a testament of men and women from humble backgrounds who persisted and triumphed over adversity.

Book I
Seven of Merit

Elephant Man

Christened: O'Neil Bryan
Born: September 11, 1975

Court Jester

Dancehall star Elephant Man has exceeded all expectations of how successful he could be. In an age of the poorly defined artist, with no discerning image, the DJ remained focused and determined. As a result, he created a unique niche in the competitive arena of dancehall. This was accomplished by sticking to one main formula: putting back the dance into dancehall.

Growing up in the Kingston ghetto of Seaview Gardens, he was aware of two others from his community who had become major artists: Shabba Ranks and, soon to be mentor, Bounty Killer.

In the mid-nineties a dancehall fad centered on the formation of crews took root. So Bryan hooked up with Donovan Stewart, aka Boom Dandimite; Andrew Reid, aka Nitty Kutchie; and Patrick Jackson, aka Harry Toddler, to create the Seaview Family. When Bounty Killer became involved with the outfit he renamed them Scare Dem Crew.

Being under the wings of one of the hottest stars of the time had its benefits. Killer had the group record on his label and gave them priceless exposure by allowing them to be booked on most of the shows he was on. They gained instant popularity with their debut single *Pure Gal*.

The crew was an entertaining lot and their somewhat noisy and clown like banter, both live and on records, proved extremely infectious amongst Jamaica's youth. The group then followed their first hit with a number of other songs that became favorites, *Nuh Dress Like Girl* and *Many Many*. Of the four, Harry Toddler and Elephant Man dominated and went on to have notable solo careers.

By the close of the 90s, the group had disintegrated, though not before seeing their album *Scared From The Crypt* getting a major release on **TVT/Interscope**. By this time however, the unity was already in tatters. Harry Toddler had the first solo hit with *Dance The Angel* (**Shocking Vibes**), but it was Bryan who would rocket to stardom in a few short years, while Toddler's early promise faded. Elephant

Man possessed what the others didn't: a ferocious work ethic and huge ambitions.

He was fully solo by 1999 and voiced liked a maniac, working with various producers. Hundreds of singles came on the market. His hard work finally paid off in 2000 through a combination with DJ Delly Ranks. The single *Headache* was the first major breakthrough. Elephant Man's success did not sit well with his former group mates and in a fit of jealousy was even attacked by Nitty Kutchie at a concert in 2001, which put any notion of regrouping to rest.

As a member of Scare Dem, Elephant Man was mainly a noisy, off-key mediocre toaster. He apparently dedicated himself to self-improvement and by 2001 showed all the signs of being ready for the big time. He kept the high-energy delivery but, this time, had his vocals under control, exhibiting a wider range so much that he could do his own background harmonies.

Incorporating influences from rap *ala* Mystical, as well as the hard edge of Bounty Killer, Elephant Man developed an exciting style and look of his own. His signature included a high-energy stage act and he dressed in outrageous costumes. He not only wanted to just make it. He also wanted to be number one and was willing to do what it took to achieve that goal. The workaholic Bryan, who is credited with over 600 singles, put his shoulders to the wheel and outworked everybody. With the massive hit *Log On*, he moved closer to becoming an A-list artist. Thereafter, the hits came pouring in.

He knew that to reach number one, he would have to get pass the feuding pair - his mentor Bounty Killer and archrival Beenie Man. This rivalry was blocking the way for many artists like him. Bryan's strategy was to change course by going in the opposite direction. Instead of joining the fray he went around it by honing his own image. This he achieved by becoming the best entertainer of them all, packaging himself as a dancehall dance act that would take all the popular moves being practiced by Jamaican street dancers and turning them into songs. Along the way he also created many dances of his own. Sidestepping the prevailing negativity, he further infused the scene with humor and fun. By 2003, Bryan was as big as, or perhaps even bigger than, both counterparts. For a space of around three years, he dominated the dancehall.

Elephant's list of hits is exhaustive; however, the biggest are: *Log On, Jamaica, Bad Man A Bad*

Man, Elephant Message, Signal De Plane, Jook Gal (US # 57) and *Pon De River Pon De Bank* (US # 86).

Naturally, being the hottest artist in this period, the majors called and after having his first three albums released by UK indie **Greensleeves**, his fourth came out in 2003 under **VP/Atlantic**. His hot streak took him way into 2007 and Sean "Puff Daddy" Comb's **Bad Boy** eventually picked up album number five, *Let's Get Physical*. The collaborations also came with the territory, while his growing international profile paved the way for pairings with Wyclef, Chris Brown, Lil Jon, Mariah Carey, Busta Rhymes and the Dominican sensation, Kat De Luna, on the US top 30 hit *Wine Up*.

His high profile image made him one of the highest paid entertainers that even the Jamaican government targeted him, along with a few others, for unpaid taxes.

Many would like to dismiss him as a joke, but Elephant Man never made any claim to the contrary. He lived up to his comical name and persona. He was a dance sensation, from a foreign country, rapping in a foreign dialect, and making inroads in to the US market long before the 2012 monster breakout of South Korea's Psy. He is the Court Jester of reggae and knows what he is good at.

His popularity has since waned in the last couple of years. Yet still, to ignore his impact, with dance music now being the most popular brand and the fact that he spearheaded that movement, would be an act of criminal negligence.

Ken Boothe

Christened: Kenneth Boothe
Born: March 22, 1948

Mr. Nice Guy

Mr. Ken Boothe is a significant artist who came of age during the rocksteady era, and is widely respected by other Jamaican entertainers young and old. He is one of few Jamaican acts to top an international chart, with the UK number one hit *Everything I Own*, and is still active after nearly five decades in the business.

Boothe came from a musical family, hailing from Denham Town, close to the heart of downtown Kingston. He got his first break as one half of the duo Stranger and Ken, with Wilburn Stranger Cole. Around 1964 the duo's first hit was *World's Fair* for Coxsone and they soon followed with others like *Artibella* and *Hush*.

By 1966 Boothe went fully solo, and by 1971 Cole migrated to Canada, eventually fading from view. Boothe became a certifiable star with the singles, *You're No Good* and *Train Is Coming* and emerged as one of the great stylists of the era, with a seductive low-tone voice loaded with sex appeal. This combined with matinee-idol good looks gave him a distinct edge over his competitors and the top star of the period Alton Ellis raced to out record him to stave off his growing popularity. The 60s were his most prolific period as a hit maker and they rained down in the form of *I Don't Want To See You Cry*, *Just Another Girl*, *Moving Away*, *Mustang Sally* and *Puppet On A String*. Although he scored his biggest hit in the 70s he would never again be in such fine form as he was in the previous decade.

In the 70s he flew the coop and ventured out away from Coxsone's label Studio One and sang for other notable producers of the time like Leslie Kong, Sonia Pottinger, and a young rising star on the scene, Winston Niney Holness. With them came the chart toppers *Freedom Street*, *Why Baby Why* and *Silver Words*.

In 1974 he teamed up with producer Lloyd Charmers and covered MOR American group Bread's song, *Everything I Own*. When released by Trojan, it went all the way to number one in the UK. The album of the same name also had respectable sales. Although giving Trojan one of its biggest hits, they did not control the song's publishing and, due to financial problems, the label was unable to further invest in Boothe's growing international career. Boothe, possibly because of lack of proper management, was unable to capitalize on his earlier successes. By the late 70s, into the 80s, he struggled to keep his footing in the ever-changing landscape of his industry.

The 80s saw the decline of the singers and the rise of the dancehall DJs. Singers who could not adapt to the newer sounds became anachronistic. Boothe kept recording, though mostly remakes of his past hits. The singer's decline could also be attributed to financial problems and a drug habit. While others like Dennis Brown, Gregory Issacs and John Holt on the singer's side, refused to back down in the face of the DJ onslaught, Boothe was indifferent and could not find a hit to save his life.

In the mid-90s he was thrown a lifeline by reggae superstar Shaggy with a revamped version of his 1965 hit *Train Is Coming*. The song featured him along with the high-riding Shaggy. This joint effort was part of a soundtrack for the hit movie *Money Train*, starring Wesley Snipes and Woody Harrelson. Released on **Virgin Records** with a glossy video, the single also appeared on Shaggy's multi-platinum Boombastic album. The royalties from the song vastly improved Boothe's financial position and a nicer guy it could not have happened to.

The singer at this time was apparently sober. With substance abuse problems behind him, he caught a second wind and returned to performing and recording. Being the showman and professional type, he again saw the bookings rolling in.

As late as 2010, he released an album called *Love Is The Ultimate*. And in 2013 teamed up with legendary group Inner Circle for a remake of Mr. Mister's *Broken Wings*, released on the Dubets various artists compilation. Also in 2013, Boothe celebrated 50 years in the music business with a brand new album *Journey* and remarked, "fifty years in any business is an accomplishment in itself".

Though mainly regarded as a nostalgia act, Ken Boothe was still awarded the Order Of Distinction by the Jamaican government for his achievements. This honor reminds us of how much Ken Boothe is still regarded as one of Jamaica's true national treasures.

Papa San

Christened: Tyrone Thompson
Born: July 1, 1966

Gospel Reggae Star

Save for legendary Jamaican gospel music group The Grace Thrillers, the only other international Jamaican gospel act is Papa San.

Papa San came to national recognition in the late 80s and went on to establish himself as one of the top DJs in dancehall. Years later when he switched lanes to gospel music, he became the one with the highest profile. Signing to **Gospocentric**, the same label as gospel superstar Kirk Franklin, San cemented himself as a headliner amongst a host of artists from Jamaica that had moved away from secular music.

The young Tyrone grew up in Jamaica's first capital Spanish Town and hails from the tough community known as Dela Vega. He loved to hang around the sound systems at big dances held in the heart of Spanish Town at the infamous Prison Oval. This experience was like a second school to the youngster.

He started out on *hi fi's*, Lees Unlimited, Black Scorpio and Kilamanjaro. Due to his slanted eyes, which made him look oriental, he was nicknamed Papa San.

His style stood out since, instead of rapping slow like most of his forbearers, he chose to develop a rapid-fire delivery akin to UK DJs like Papa Levi and Smiley Culture. Others such as Major Worries and Daddy Freddy would try this style of toasting, which came to be known as speed rapid, but Papa San was the best at this technique. Even before his stint as a known recording artist, he would become one of the most feared sound system DJs. In this atmosphere, where the competition was fierce, he built a reputation as a superior lyricist and marathon performer. In those days, cassette tapes were the primary source on which live dances were captured and his recorded performances became a crowd favorite. He was literally a star even before getting a hit record.

From around 1983, his first set of singles appeared on the market though none made any dent in the hit parade. In 1988 he finally scored with *Style & Fashion* for **Black Scorpio** and

Round Table Talk a duet with female DJ Lady G for producer Gussie Clarke. This was the advent of video in Jamaica and the humorous *Round Table Talk* short was popular with TV viewers. Other outstanding tunes showed his full range of storytelling, originality and humor, *Perdominent*, *DJ Business*, *Animal Party* and *Maddy Maddy Cry*.

As the new decade began San rose to the very pinnacle of the dancehall and was on the frontline of stars alongside Ninja Man and Shabba Ranks. In 1991 he had the chart toppers *I Will Survive* and *Strange*. He also seriously broke into the overseas markets when the demand for dancehall was at its peak, delivering a pair of hits *Dancehall Good To Me* featuring JC Lodge and *Gonna Get Along Without You* featuring Chevelle Franklin. San, it seemed, had a special chemistry teaming up with the leading female artists at the time with solid results.

Benefiting from a contract with US based independent Pow Wow Records; he seeped into the underground and was heavily played in New York, as well as the rest of the Tri-State area. In 1993 he exploded onto the surface with two number one singles on the Billboard dance charts on major label Mercury Records, combining with top house DJ David Morales on *Program*, which also featured singer Stanryk and *Gimme Luv*. At the time, Papa San was enjoying a very lucrative career, one continuously on an upward trajectory. He had all the makings of being a breakout on the international scene, but something else was beckoning.

His brother Patrick Thompson was also a DJ. He was active on the scene from around 1989, having a breakout year in 1992 with the smash *Hot Dis Year* for producer Bobby Digital. The following year during Christmas time Thompson, popularly known as Dirtsman, was murdered in his hometown. In the wake of this event, San constantly began travelling with a gun. In 1994 the law caught up with him. He was arrested and charged for the weapon for which he had no legal permit and had to fight lustily in court and narrowly escaped prison.

The tragedy of losing his brother, who was only a year younger, and his subsequent brushes with the law triggered a period of soul searching. He was a top dancehall artist but the lifestyle that accompanied it was wearing thin. In 1996 his last major performance as a secular artist was a clash with fellow DJ Lt. Stitichie on Reggae Sunsplash, which got very ugly. At this point he had enough.

In the following year he announced his departure from dancehall and began a new chapter. Papa San was now a born again Christian and would only record gospel music.

He subsequently signed to Kirk Franklin's **Gospocentric** and the *Victory* album on the subsidiary, **B-Rite Music**, was released in 1999. San's delivery on the album proved just as potent in the new genre as he was before in the dancehall.

There were also other high profile conversions around this time by more popular artists, namely Chevelle Franklin, Carlene Davis, Junior Tucker and Lt. Stitchie, but there was no doubt that San's contract with a major gospel label in the US set him apart from the pack. He has held his position as the top act in this field for many years and recorded strong follow-up albums, *God & I* and *Real and Personal*.

Papa San now lives in Florida with his family where he is an ordained minister, while enjoying a healthy demand for his services on the concert market.

Sanchez

Christened: Kevin Jackson
Born: November 30, 1964

The Voice

If you don't write your own material and was born with a voice of gold, what do you do? You do what Sanchez has done: interpretations of other people's compositions. After all, he's done it successfully and consistently for over twenty years.

From the minute you heard *Loneliness* (**Technique**) in 1988, you knew at once that a special talent had arrived. From then on the hits kept coming and for the artist who honed his chops by singing in the church, there was an endless well of songs he could pull from.

What Sanchez did, as well as covering the classics both local and international, was sing whatever song was on top of the American R&B charts at any given time. Were it not for him, many American songs would have gone unnoticed, since many of his followers sometimes thought that his version was the original. His famous covers included *One In A Million, If I Ever Fall, Old Friends, Lady In Red, I Care For You* and *Loving Pauper*.

Many in the wake of his success would live off the same formula, though with lesser results. Artists such as Wayne Wonder, Singing Melody and a host of others would sometimes do the same songs as Sanchez. Each version would battle with the other, but Sanchez's always came out on top. Frequently in a zealous effort to first other singers, racing to cover the latest soul hit from the US, he would occasionally botch the lyrics. Even still Sanchez was able to hold the listener's attention with his superior vocal gifts.

Later on in his career he managed, with the help of the guitarist in his band, to pen some originals which also became hits namely *Brown Eye Girl* and *Neva Dis De Man*.

Sanchez, by virtue of his longevity with over 30 albums under his belt and a long standing relationship with US reggae label VP Records, has been able to deliver products on a consistent and timely manner. As a result, he has stayed relevant over the years.

Now managed by his wife, he is still a

dependable and bankable act on the live reggae music circuit. He earns special recognition for the way he has effortlessly held Jamaican ladies captive over the span of his long and ongoing career, which still appears to have a lot left in it. This is an achievement not easily duplicated by his contemporaries.

Tanya Stephens

Christened: Vivienne Stephenson
Born: July 2, 1973

Dancehall Feminist

Tanya Stephens is lyrically clever, with a unique voice and style that's all her own. These factors have made her special in the crowded marketplace of Jamaican artists.

Stephens came to prominence in the latter part of the 90s with a slew of man bashing songs, the most popular being *You Nuh Ready Fi Dis Yet*, *Goggle* and *Handle Di Ride*. Breaking out a full three years after Lady Saw, Stephens presented an alternate viewpoint to her colleague's sexually charged and raucous output. Saw became like one of the boys and was at the very top, but Stephens's put down of her male counterpart and her frank discussions on relationship woes seemed closer to the reality of the female experience.

Both Tanya Stephens and Lady Saw were champions of the female cause, with very different approaches. Unfortunately Stephens was not as driven and focused, leading her to opt out of dancehall altogether. After three albums – *Too Hype* (VP), *Work Out* (Joe Gibbs) and *Rough Rider* (VP) – released in 1997 and 1998, she quit the local scene.

Around 1999 she went M.I.A. for about three years, moving to Sweden after signing with **Warner Bros** (Sweden). This was an effort to cross over into the European pop market. The album *Sintoxicated* came in 2001. This however proved to be a misadventure, with the album failing to ignite either commercially or critically. It also eroded her popularity in Jamaica and allowed Lady Saw to reign unchallenged as the lone female dancehall star.

Stephens came to her senses and returned home in 2003, embarking on a campaign of non-stop voicing for a plethora of producers. This allowed her to regain some old fans and win some new ones as well.

Her output this time was tunes that were more thoughtful than her previous efforts. Numbers like *These Streets*, *It's a Pity* and the acoustic folk ditty *Mr. Prime Minister*, showed a more mature side of her. Stephens also bridged the disconnect by picking up where she left off, again chiding the opposite sex for their shortcomings, and meting out punishment on new hits: *Way Back* and *Tek Him Back*.

In 2004 the hit album *Gangsta Blues* cemented her comeback. *Rebelution* came in 2006, when she delved into her penchant for experimentation, while remaining connected to her fan base. This strategy allowed Stephens to have her cake and eat it too.

She has since then backslid, somewhat into a low profile stance. At the same time however, she keeps her fans happy, especially in Europe, with appearances at one-off shows and on festivals.

Overall Tanya Stephens has failed to, or maybe chosen not to, become a super star. Her shortcomings are a lack of charisma, image problems, poor management and inconsistency. She has however, done enough to have had an influence on a lot of aspiring female artists because of her unmistakable vocal style and lyrical wit.

Tony Rebel

Christened: Patrick Barrett
Born: January 15, 1962

New Roots

Tony Rebel was one of many to spearhead the roots revival in the early 90s. When everyone had believed that the era of the conscious DJs was over for good, Rebel emerged. He led a mini revolution of sorts, which the French press dubbed Nouveau Roots or New Roots.

Patrick Barrett came from the central Jamaican parish of Manchester. By the 80s he made his way to Kingston in an effort to advance his music career.

He made an eventful stop at the "dancehall godfather" Sugar Minott and saw the release of an early single *Casino*. Making rounds as many artists did when seeking the spotlight, he voiced for several labels but failed to register until making connection with Donovan Germaine of **Penthouse Records**. Germaine was one of the hottest producers around and had one of the biggest artists on his roster Cutty Ranks. But the label was about to get even hotter at the beginning of the 90s, as he would break both Rebel and, a young star that became one of reggae's superstars, Buju Banton.

Barrett channeled the two great proponents of Rasta's dancehall foundation U-Roy and Big Youth. He flowed as a singer would, though not quite singing and staying away from the normal topics that prevailed amongst DJs – mainly celebrating guns and sex. He showed his potential with the 1990 release *Mandela Story*. Ultimately, he broke out a year later with the melodic sing along love tune *Fresh Vegetable*, with the chorus line putting his name on the lips of everyone: "*Love you like a fresh vegetable, tell me if you love Tony Rebel*".

The country boy with good old fashion work ethic immediately capitalized on his hit single. He worked to put himself in the line of A-list artists, and in that same year had a bunch of popular tunes: *Defend My Own*, *Hush*, and *Armour*. His hot streak continued into the following year with a slew of combination singles alongside top **Penthouse Records** artists: Beres Hammond, Marcia Griffiths, Cutty Ranks and Buju Banton. Barrett's rise was so phenomenal that by 1993 he signed to **Chaos/ Columbia Records**. His major label album, *Vibe Of The Time*, contained some of his local hits like *Chatty Chatty* and *One Day*, but it didn't yield an international hit single. He was however, intelligent enough to put himself in the right position, by cultivating important relationships and working hard at his craft.

His success would help draw others, from his home parish to aspire for the same. This became evident by the emergence of Garnett Silk, Kulcha Knox, Uton Green and others. It seemed that Rebel had reignited the flames of a cultural movement of young roots artists that could counter the dominance of the slack DJs. This advancement would pave the way for others to develop as major stars of New Roots such as Capleton, Anthony B and Sizzla. Before their careers eclipsed his own however, Barrett kept getting bigger scoring with more significant hits, including *Just Friends* and the classic *If Jah*.

In later years, he launched his own label **Flames**. This venture brought many young artists to recognition with the release of the *Lalabella* collection. The album served to expose several new culture type acts and remains, one of the top selling, various artists reggae albums of all time. As a result, artists such as Everton Blender, Ras Shiloh, Aaron Silk and the duo Sugar Blacks and

Lebanchulah came into public view.

Barrett subsequently became more than just an artist, and is now a full-blown public figure, enjoying a respectable standing in Jamaican society. This he achieved by being a musical ambassador, businessman, (promoting his annual show, **Rebel Salute**), running his record label and managing the hottest female roots artist, Queen Ifrica.

Tony Rebel continues to record and tour alongside his entrepreneurial activities. He may not be the highest profile artist, but must be remembered for changing the tide of the music at a very critical juncture in its history.

Ernie Smith

Christened: Glenroy Smith
Born: May 1, 1945

The Tunesmith

A lot of Jamaican music today is alluring because of the attitude it conveys; though woefully short on penmanship and depth of musical arrangement.

That missing link can be found in the contributions of reggae luminaire Ernie Smith. Reaching back into Ernie's musical archive, one has to wonder what went wrong between now and then. In today's reggae scene we have an emphasis on beats and aggressive presentation, but the current practitioners would do well in checking out Mr. Smith to tap his creative genius.

Smith is a lyricist and musical composer of the first order, capable of delivering songs with ease and grace as found mostly in country and blues. Presenting himself at first to producers as a songwriter, but after being unable to find many takers, he was forced into becoming a recording artist. Introducing himself with the 1967 classic *I*

Can't Take It, he gained additional popularity through his first hit *Bend Down*, followed by others such as *Ride On Sammy*, *Duppy Gunman*, *One Dream*, *Pitta Patta* and the ubiquitous *Life Is Just For Living*. It was *Life Is Just For Living* that earned him the top prize in a Japanese song competition in 1972. Then in 1973 he was awarded the Badge of Honor by the Jamaican government; the first artist to be recognized at the state level.

Ernie Smith is primarily a storyteller who sings in a style that unpretentiously does not get in the way of what he wants to relate. His songs are arranged in a light optimistic style with hooks made in pop heaven. It is not an exaggeration to say that Abba or the Beatles had nothing on Ernie Smith. Moreover, when Johnny Nash redid one of Smith's songs *I Can't Take It* as *Tears On My Pillow* it made it to the 5th spot on the British charts.

Playing the guitar as his first instrument, Smith's knack for melodies and big sing along choruses came from having a love and appreciation for all styles of music. Two critically acclaimed and commercially successful albums *Life Is For Living* (1974) and *Pitta Patta* (1975) are Jamaican classics. In 2008 he also released a collection of his best works titled: *After 30 Years: Life Is Just For Living* (**VP**).

Artists like Ernie Smith are often overlooked, owing to the fact that international stardom has eluded him and his music is more appreciated for its academic value. He is also a somewhat weak vocalist, as his voice is usually carried along with the songs and not the other way around. A thirteen-year exile in Canada, beginning in 1976, was also a major contributing factor in his relative anonymity amongst the younger generation.

Ernie's music however represents a more articulate and refined reggae product. It's similar to a middle of the road approach. The bigger stars are usually more unpolished, lending credence to the argument that Jamaican music is more revered for its bravado, and accompanying penchant for protest. But Ernie is a reminder that Jamaican music has many sides. He represents the best of those alternatives.

Tribute To Sly & Robbie

Christened: Lowell Dunbar
Born: May 10, 1952

Christened: Robert Shakespeare
Born: September 27, 1953

The next two noteworthy mentions are architects of modern Jamaican music and the island's two most celebrated musicians.

Becoming significant songwriters, producers and artists in their own right, they have been the go to guys for creating many international hits for Jamaican artists. Many top stars from around the world have chased after the duo, in search of the island's distinct sound. They are legends. They are Sly & Robbie.

They rose from being small time session musicians from playing in nightclubs, moving on to live touring and eventually blossoming into producers and entrepreneurs. They started their own label, the legendary **Taxi** imprint and their footprints are all over the landscape travelled by Jamaican music on its way to international recognition. Their vision and innovativeness helped to propel the music into the modern era and kept it on the cutting edge of the changing trends in musical tastes.

Their biggest achievement though, is an enduring partnership, which stems from the suppression of individual egos, the admirable simplicity of mutual respect and the love that the two have for each other. Evidently, these points came first and the music second. Part of their true legacy is clear that through the absence of arrogance greatness can be attained.

Lowell Dunbar was born in Kingston and grew up in several neighborhoods, including

Waterhouse and parts of western Kingston. One of the schools he attended was Trench Town Comprehensive in a violence-riddled community known as Jungle. He knew where his talents lie when he would use scraps of wood to bang on paint cans and garbage pans. It is fair to say that Dunbar was somewhat of a child prodigy, and entered the music business very early. One of his first gigs was playing drums on a television show called **Top Ten Tunes** in the 60s, with bandleader Tommy McCook.

Dunbar hung around musicians on a daily basis and quit school, seeing it as irrelevant to his plans. Sitting at the feet of drummers like Lloyd Knibbs, Ansell Collins and studying the legendary Carlton Barrett, he started to imitate them and strove to emulate their skills as he developed his craft.

It was Ansell Collins who eventually gave him his first studio session at age 15, playing on *Night Doctor*. The following year, he played on the first of many songs that would be million sellers, starting out with *Double Barrel* by Dave and Ansell Collins. It ultimately became a number one song in the UK.

His workman-like nature and restlessness led

him to play in several bands early on such as *The Rainbow Temple Healing Invincibles* (which included Lloyd Parkes), *The Volcanoes* and *Skin Flesh and Bones*. While he was barely into his teens, it was with *Skin Flesh and Bones* that he had a residency in a lounge called *Tit For Tat* on Red Hills Road. This part of town was a strip littered with nightclubs and sort of a red light district in the making. Playing across the street at another joint called *Evil People* was a young bassist, Robert Shakespeare.

Robert Shakespeare hailed from East Kingston, which spans the entire length of Windward Road, with many communities branching off. He was fortunate to have an older brother Lloyd who sang with a group called The Emotions. They used their home as a rehearsal spot. Being around all this musical activity awakened his own desires, as he sat in on rehearsals and became friendly with the many singers and musicians in attendance.

Several acoustic, or what is known in Jamaica as *box guitars,* were lying around the house so one day Robert picked one up, fooling around with the strings to get a feel of it. He discovered that he had a knack and developed a serious passion for playing the instrument.

One of the most important figures in his life, bass player Aston "Family Man" Barrett, was a regular visitor. From the minute Robert heard him play he was smitten. Barrett made him want to become a bass player and also helped him to become one.

According to the story Barrett came to Shakespeare's home for rehearsals and to buy weed. Aston was also just coming into his own as a bass player, being a part of a group called the Hippy Boys. Robert stayed close to his side and drank in everything he could.

Robert also hung around Aston as well as his brother, drummer Carlton Barrett. The two, who would later become the legendary riddim section for Bob Marley's, band The Wailers. Shakespeare jumped right into the action, carrying their instruments for them, allowing him access to the studio. These musicians were the rising stars of session-men. Shakespeare then proved his worth by practicing his craft assiduously and injecting himself into the scene. It wasn't long before he was getting gigs on his own. Not being lazy, he juggled session work with, playing in at least three different bands.

One evening in the early 70s, playing at *Evil People* club on Red Hills Road alongside keyboard player Bernard Harvey, Bernard told Shakespeare that he was going across the street to check out a drummer friend called Sly. The coincidence would prove to be destiny's call. Robert was not only taken by Dunbar's ability to play, but also his calm and affable demeanor. They soon became friends.

At the time Robert was doing a lot of session work for producer Bunny Lee, as a member of a unit called The Aggrovators. Robert told him about the "bad likkle drummer" he met. Lee assented and told Robert to bring Dunbar to the next session. The history making event was described by Shakespeare himself: "*The minute the red light in the studio came on and we stroked up the first sounds everyone started to jump up and down in the studio*". Sly & Robbie were conceived.

The two complimented each other and filled in the spaces lacking on either side. Dunbar was mild mannered and Shakespeare was acerbic, having a reputation as a tough guy. Sly was small and looked rather frail, which belied his amazing athleticism as a drummer. Robbie was solidly built. One was the brain, while the other was the muscle, but both were workaholics. Robbie was naturally the leader. His aggressive nature and out-there personality got those most of the work. Sly was personable, non-confrontational and readily followed his partner's lead. It was a *marriage* made in heaven.

In the meantime, they continued to build their reputations individually. Sly played on many records including the two top spots in the 1976 *Festival Song Competition*, Freddie McKay's *Dance This Ya Festival* and Jacob Miller's *All Night Till Daylight*. Robbie did work with Bunny Wailer as a solo artist and, when Bunny's group, The Wailers, made their first album for **Island**, *Catch A Fire*, Shakespeare played bass on two enduring classics: *Stir It Up* and *Concrete Jungle*.

As a pair they worked on Peter Tosh's sophomore album for **Columbia Records** – *Equal Rights*. Peter was putting together his backing band for touring, which he called *Word Sound and Power* and Robbie told Peter that he wanted Sly on drums.

Being on the road together strengthened their friendship and cemented their partnership. The rigors of touring and its relatively small rewards though, made them start to plan their next moves.

Not that they disliked being on the road but, because ambition would not allow them to settle for less. They aspired to be more than workhorses of the industry and began to make the necessary sacrifices to go further.

On tour they would employ creative ways to save their wages. They refused to go on shopping sprees like other musicians and would collect unwanted food to take to their hotel rooms to avoid room service. Sly and Robbie had a plan.

This plan came to fruition in 1979 with the launch of their label – **Taxi**. The name came about because Sly, who did not drive, mainly travelled by cabs and usually the most beaten up, unreliable ones. Robbie previously had his own label, **Bar Bells**, but set it aside to concentrate on their new joint venture.

From the gate it was an overwhelming success, scoring a bumper crop of hits. They enlisted the services of some of Jamaica's premier vocal talents and also some newcomers. **Taxi** ruled the charts in 1979, with top singles such as *Soon Forward* (Gregory Issacs), *Sitting and Watching* (Dennis Brown), *General Penitentiary* (Black Uhuru), *Fort Agustus* (Junior Delgado), *Sweet Sugar Plum* (Wailing Souls), *My Woman's Love*

(Jimmy Riley) and *Drunken Master* (General Echo).

They ended up taking the vocal group Black Uhuru under their wings and worked on an album, *Sensimellia*, which they licensed and released on **Island Records** in 1980. Black Uhuru opened the doors for the duo as international producers. This was also the beginning of a working relationship that would be enjoyed for years with Chris Blackwell, **Island's** founder. Blackwell was so taken with the sound and style of production that Sly & Robbie employed on Black Uhuru's records, he hinted at them using it for some of his other acts. One such person was their fellow Jamaican, Grace Jones, whom **Island** previously marketed as more of a disco act with some degree of success.

Blackwell had studios down in the Bahamas the now infamous **Compass Point Studios** and flew the newly nicknamed "Riddim Twins" in to work on material with Jones. The chemistry was instantaneous. Grace craved their tracks like an addict needing a fix. These sessions also featured musicians Franklin Waul, Wally Badarou and engineer Alex Sadkin. The work yielded some big hits: *Pull Up To The Bumper*, *Nipple To The Bottle* and *Private Life*. The sound was edgy, futuristic and would propel both Jones and Black Uhuru to greater heights.

Sly & Robbie achieved exactly what they aspired to, which was escaping the unrewarding and at times mundane existence of just being mere musicians. Their heightened profile led to widespread recognition and worldwide notoriety and work with names as big as or even bigger than Grace Jones followed. The pair's services extended to the likes of Eric Clapton, Joe Cocker, Bob Dylan, Serge Gainbourge and The Rolling Stones, just to name a few.

They also continued to have success back in Jamaica with a plethora of artists on **Taxi**. And by 1985 they were actual members of Black Uhuru, as well as cowriters and producers on the album *Anthem*. This was the first reggae album to win the United States' biggest musical award, the Grammy.

Sly& Robbie also emerged as artists in their own right with an impressive seventy-four albums and at least two top 15 singles on the UK Charts – *Boops* (Here To Go) and *Night Nurse* (featuring Simply Red). They have seen their works released on big labels such as **Virgin**, **East West Records**, **Island** and **4th & Broadway**.

Their output is staggering with many sources indicating that they have played on and produced over 200,000 songs. An insatiable appetite for exploration of all styles of music while embracing technology kept them on top, and on the cutting edge of modern music.

On top of all this, they are the first choice of the major labels to spearhead production for newly signed Jamaican and international solo artists, as well as groups wanting to capture the island's sound.

The evidence is their involvement in creating the most significant hits for Grace Jones, Gwen Guthrie, Black Uhuru, Chaka Demus and Pliers, Maxi Priest and, most recently, a pair of platinum singles for American rock band No Doubt. It is probably easier to highlight whom they have not worked with instead of the other way around, which a simple phrase would suffice: "everyone that mattered".

They have continuously pushed the envelope and have done as much to colonize the world with reggae just as Bob Marley, Jimmy Cliff, Peter Tosh and the other great ones.

Sly & Robbie are national heroes of Jamaica. They deserve more recognition than they have been given but, knowing Sly & Robbie, the journey has been its own reward. They have never practiced the habit of tooting their own horns. All descriptions apply: *legends, pioneers, innovators,* and *originators*. This is their tribute.

Book II

50 Most Significant Jamaican Musical Artists Past to Present

50. Augustus Pablo

Christened: Horace Swaby
Born 21, June 1953
Deceased: May 18, 1999

Dub Pioneer

Far away from the shores of Jamaica there is a sub-genre of reggae called dub. This style is alive and well, with a rabid following. The worldwide practice and acceptance of dub music came out of a creative explosion in 1970s Jamaica. We have Augustus Pablo to thank for its emergence alongside significant others.

Augustus Pablo must be considered as one of Jamaica's finest products. He built a career, not as a singer but as an instrumentalist. Playing the melodica, an instrument used at the time to teach music in schools, he forged a style and sound of his own soloing his way to success and dub immortality.

Debuting in 1969 on Aquarius Records with the single *Iggy Iggy*, he would go on to leave an indelible mark on a sound that was growing stale and one-dimensional. Pablo brought out the mystique that Jamaican music is known to cast over the world, by uncannily drawing from Middle Eastern and East Asian musical influences. His break came with the 1972 hit *Java*, establishing him as an artist in his own right. His instrumentals were hypnotic, infectious and soon became quite popular.

His dub versions drew artists searching for a new sound so Pablo naturally evolved into an artist/producer. He flourished in this role, forming a label with his brother called **Rockers**

International. With the label they collectively had a hand in the success of many others.

His body of work, buttressed by a partnership with the legendary engineer King Tubby, would become a part of the sounds of the seventies, which was roots-dub music, more popularly called rockers. Teaming up with fine musicians such as Sly & Robbie, the rockers phenomenon dominated the period. This advancement even led to a movie of the same name, which starred popular drummer Leroy "Horsemouth" Wallace.

Many classic Jamaican songs came from artists produced by Pablo, most notably: Jacob Miller's *Keep On Knocking*, John Holt's *My Desire* and Hugh Mundell's roots anthem *Africa Must be Free by 1983*. The **Rockers** discography also included material from the likes of Dillinger, Junior Delgado, I Roy, Fred Locks and the Heptones.

Meanwhile his own albums were ground breaking like the brilliant *East of River Nile* (1978) and the classic *King Tubby Meets Rockers Uptown* (1976). They contained material that was so far ahead of the time and became the blueprint for the future establishing of dub culture, a branch of reggae by itself.

Dub music now has its own market and fan base separate and apart from what prevails in today's Kingston. Its growth has contributed significantly to modern music, being the forerunner of genres such as dubstep, drum and bass, garage and electronica.

Swaby, the rail-thin Rastaman with oriental features would see a decline in his local popularity at the start of the 1980s, which was the advent of the dancehall era. But in Europe and Japan he was still revered, continuing to record and tour way into the 90s. He also still maintained his record label and added a retail outlet to his many enterprises.

In the late 90s he began to have health issues that worsened as the years progressed. The diagnosis was nerve disorder and severe bronchitis. After a prolonged battle, the beloved musician, the man known as the greatest out of Jamaica to have played the melodica, died in 1999 of a collapsed lung.

49. Brigadier Jerry

Christened: Robert Russell
Born: September 28, 1957

Well-Respected

Even though this artist may be considered a one hit wonder with the early eighties chart topper *Pain*, it can be argued that Brigadier Jerry is a well-respected figure, from an historical perspective, of the dancehall.

His clout comes from the ethos of being a purist militant and a vocal stylist. His DJ career was used more as a pulpit rather than as a springboard towards fame and fortune.

Starting out in 1975, the freckle-faced Jerry was taught at the feet of the "Teacher" U-Roy. He further served his apprenticeship on U-Roy's sound system **King Stur Gav**.

The devout member of The Twelve Tribes of Israel Rastafarian movement saw his mission as one to spread its teachings. He avoided the more sordid topics of dancehall, like gangster-life and sex. Jerry would frequently quote whole passages from the Bible and through an uncompromising viewpoint carved out a niche of his own.

After leaving **King Stur Gav,** he established himself as the resident DJ on **Jah Love Muzic** using scorching oratory, hitting out against Babylon (nickname for the establishment) with marathon all night long performances. This enabled him to amass a loyal fan base, especially amongst young Rasta's and disaffected youth.

Brigadier Jerry, in the new school post-U-Roy, was the influential catalyst, in terms of sound-style and substance, which artist like Josey Wales, Charlie Chaplin and Burro Banton rode to success. Even current dancehall star Beenie Man, cites Briggy, (as he is affectionately known) as one of his main influences. This makes Brigadier Jerry a sort of icon of his fraternity.

He never gained the type of popularity similar to his peers, but his dedication to his art and mastery of the DJ craft, which he continues to exhibit up to this very day, has put him in a class by himself.

48. Jah Cure

Christened: Siccaturie Alcock
Born: October 11, 1978

The Resurrection

Even though Jamaica, thanks to Vybz Kartel and Mavado, is caught in the grips of a new breed of deranged characters, we have to be grateful for Jah Cure.

What is more remarkable is that his string of

hits started while he was in prison, serving a 15-year sentence for rape. He is the first reggae act to score several number one hits from a jail cell. A career that was dead was literally resurrected from "hell".

His epic story began in a little village called Cascade Smithfield, in the quiet parish of Hanover. He was born to Pansita Campbell and a father he would barely know. Little is known about his schooling but along with, his mother and his siblings on his mother's side, soon moved to the Flankers area in the tourist capital and Jamaica's second city Montego Bay.

The young Siccaturie, in later interviews, admitted to being a difficult and ill-tempered child who was always getting into fights. His reputation amongst the town people was one of a troublemaker. In spite of being a very small boy, he was fierce and fought with stones, or any weapon he could get his hands on. His home situation was not stable and his mom struggled to support her four children while living with his stepfather who according to Siccature was "very abusive". Most of what he learnt was from the streets. In his life, this kind of knowledge would prove to be a double-edged sword.

He loved to sing, and had his first taste of success when he won a talent show at age 11. By age 15 he made his way to Kingston, where he soon fell in with other aspiring artists that were distinctly a part of the Rastafarian faith. Chief among them was Miguel Collins, who became known as Sizzla and they fed off each other as iron sharpened iron.

As the journey continued he began his professional singing career under the name of Little Melody, him being an admirer of popular singer Singing Melody. But his Rasta colleagues would have none of it and members of a group known as the David House Krew, led by firebrand singjay Capleton, instigated a name change. "Jah Cure" was the result.

He stood out among a crowd of aspiring singers because of his unique vocal gifts. Coming at a time shortly after the death of Garnett Silk and during the emergence of roots singer Luciano, he became a part of a resurgence in roots music and began to record for some of the top producers. Some early singles thrust him into the role of contender for the roots crown. Numbers like *Trod In The Valley* (X-Terminator), *Like A Mountain* (feat. Sizzla, Greensleeves) and *Sunny Day* (321 Strong).

It wasn't long before he came to the attention of Jamaica's premier singer Beres Hammond. The veteran kind of adopted Cure and became his musical father, grooming and developing his talents as a vocalists and songwriter. For Hammond he delivered more musical explosions in the form of *Run Come Love Me* (feat. Jah Mason) and *King In The Jungle* (aka *Divide and Rule* feat. Sizzla).

But instead of focusing on his growing musical career that was now paying financial dividends with earnings from tours, where he was the opening act for Beres Hammond, Cure was needlessly going back and forth to Montego Bay. These trips were not only to visit his relatives but to show off to his childhood friends that he was making it. In an effort to play the role as some sort of don the singer apparently became swell-headed, basking in his early success in an unruly manner. Lacking the maturity to handle his burgeoning popularity, he was also indulging with behavior of associates of unsavory character. What happened near the close of 1998 would swiftly bring him back to earth.

It was a Sunday night, November 8, 1998 when Suzanne Ferguson, her aunt and some male companions, was walking home after a night out at a club called The Flamingo in Montego Bay. According to Ms. Ferguson, a car pulled up and two men alighted from it brandishing guns. They ordered the males to run and hustled the two females into the car. As the story goes, the women were taken to a deserted area where they were raped at gunpoint. Ms. Ferguson alleges to have been the victim of Jah Cure and her aunt by the other man.

On November 16th at around 1am in Montego Bay, Jah Cure was driving. He was pulled over by the police and questioned of his whereabouts during the previous week. When he asked the police if he was free to go they said no and waited while others arrived. Among those that came to the scene was Suzanne Ferguson, who identified the artist as her abuser not by facial recognition but incredulously by the sound of his voice. The singer was then taken into custody and subsequently charged with robbery, rape and illegal possession of a firearm.

At his first court appearance he was granted bail in the sum of J$20,000 and released. It is not clear if the terms of his bail were violated or due to incompetence on the part of his attorney Roy Flairclough, but at another court appearance he was remanded in custody. A trial without jury commenced and on April 15th 1999 Siccaturie Alcock aka Jah Cure was sentenced to 15 years in prison. The sentenced was appealed but the best outcome was a reduction of the time to 12 years. Thus the artist began a new life in the notorious St Catherine Correction Center in Spanish Town. He was only 20 years old.

Jah Cure, when he began to serve his long prison term was not yet a household name. He had also just received a visa for the United States to go on tour with Hammond and it was swiftly cancelled. His career appeared to be over.

But forgettable he was not. Before then, he had recorded prolifically; the material was potent and coming from a rare talent. His songs were uncommonly resilient and his incarceration galvanized a small but rabid following, making him into a sort of folk hero wronged by the system.

In the aftermath it is said that desperate attempts were made by the imprisoned artist, his relatives and friends to bribe Suzanne Ferguson to make statements exonerating him. Ms. Ferguson also complained of being harassed by members of the public and intimidated by anonymous callers. The "Free Jah Cure" movement gathered steam while Ms. Ferguson was branded as a liar.

In 2005 Ms. Ferguson went public in an interview in The Jamaica Gleaner written by staff reporter Glenroy Sinclair. In it she says that hearing the name of the singer brought back bitter memories for her and that she had no desire for monetary compensation and that it would be enough for Jah Cure to admit to his wrongdoing and make a public apology. Neither came. The artist throughout has insisted on his innocence.

The years came and went and Jah Cure naturally went through all the stages one suffers when facing a crisis of this magnitude: disbelief, despair and finally acceptance all under the umbrella of deep depression. He described the experience as "the worst thing that has happened to me".

On the outside, producers for whom the artist recorded prior to his imprisonment kept on releasing singles. Around 2004 brand new recordings started to pop up making it evident that the artist was working from behind bars. It seemed that Cure had very influential friends. The artist later admitted that the recording equipment was "donated" to the prison by an outfit called Danger Zone, a record label based in Florida.

It was unheard of for convicted felons to be allowed to resume their careers while still in the system, but Cure and his friends pulled it off. In late 2004 one of Jamaica's leading producers Donovan Don "Carleone" Bennett released *Longing For*, which historically became Jah Cures first number one single and the first for a prisoner recorded behind bars. The following year Cure sang a composition written by fellow artist Duane Stephenson called *Reflections*. The song on its release by the Downsound label immediately shot to number one. *Reflections* allowed the artist to do what he had failed to do while he was free, achieve mainstream success.

In *Reflections*, Cure is almost crying and exorcising all his demons. It sounded like a confession as well as a cry of remorse. After listening to that song everyone knew that this was the voice of a changed man. Now it became clear that guilty or innocent, whatever path Jah Cure was on before, was redirected by his jail time.

On July 28th 2007 after spending 8yrs and three months in prison, Jah Cure was released. The people who afforded him the privileges of working from jail, owners of Danger Zone records, were waiting in the wings for their payback and scooped him up by becoming his management. The artist came out in a rare position of financial stability, as his back royalties and licensing fee percentages were piling up, waiting to be collected.

Like Nelson Mandela and the Biblical patriarch Joseph, Jah Cure came straight from the jail cell to kingship. He became an A-list artist while still in prison and on his release stepped right into the role without missing a beat. Since then the hits have rained down on a market otherwise dominated by the dancehall DJs that have descended into a demon like cauldron increasingly spewing out one outrage after the other.

An obvious change in the artist's persona is his choice of material post incarceration. Gone is the fiery *"Burn Babylon"* Jah Cure of the 90s, now replaced by the smooth ladies' man. Singles indicative of this *Unconditional Love, Call On Me* and *Find That Girl* are his biggest hits since his release. In a recent sit-down with the media, he remarked in a poignant moment that "it is because of woman that I went to prison so it is women that I am aiming to win over".

Jah Cure is currently the biggest roots singer

out of Jamaica. He sits on top a pile of stars- Taurus Riley, Chronixx, Romaine Virgo and Christopher Martin being the ones in main contention. Cure's reach is only hampered by the fact that he is unable to work in the United States and Britain, countries that won't admit him due to his status as a convicted sex offender.

In continental Europe, Africa, Asia and Latin America however, he is pulling sizable crowds at his concerts, and is seen as one of the few remaining great hopes of a genre in deep trouble.

47. Vybz Kartel

Christened: Adidja Palmer
Born: January 7, 1976

Uncle Demon

In the post-Beenie Man/Bounty Killer era, dancehall hegemony belongs to Vybz Kartel and rival Mavado. But of the two Kartel has held the spotlight, in a more sustained manner.

He has incited a near media frenzy with his extracurricular habits that include intense skin lightening, known in Jamaican vernacular as *bleaching*. Dubbing himself as Michael "cake soap" Jackson.

His big break, despite of his musical talents, dates back to an attack against Ninja Man in 2003 at the Sting Concert. His career has since thrived on the subsequent feuding with Mavado, in the much-publicized Gully and Gaza sideshow.

His celebrity comes from bizarre habits as much as from his prolific musical tendencies. The press, from his coming into national recognition, has been riveted with stories about him of secret sex tapes and allegations of involvement with the occult.

There is little doubt however, that the former expelled student of Calabar High School, is well read, articulate, shrewd and above all else extremely manipulative. He possesses a brain attested to in his interviews, with "above average intelligence". Moreover, his star could have been one of the brightest in the firmament if not for his moral failings.

Palmer arrived at the name Vybz Kartel, as it was the name of a crew that he was once a part of. He formally went by the moniker Addi Banton but later claimed the group's name as his own. Another famous personality who went by the nickname Adi was none other than the German dictator Adolph Hitler.

Much like his archrival Mavado, Kartel was brought to the fore under the patronage of dancehall star Bounty Killer, for whom the young talent served as a writer. The collaborative single with Killer, *Gal Clown*, and a separate solo effort were intros to popularity. But the assault of the Ninja was the catalyst towards national attention; stunts like these were instrumental strategies, to be used in the coming years to maximum effect. In his own words he would later declare, "everything I do is done with an ulterior motive".

He shrewdly built his home base in Portmore, specifically in the community of Waterford. This strategy was spearheaded by a fast talking emcee known as Nuffy. It helped Kartel to win over Portmore, a municipality with a population of close to one million, way before gaining national notoriety.

Bounty Killer was his blueprint and he would emulate the veteran by using popular catch phrases to gain a following. Using slangs such as "it's Kartel" and "up to the time", this new find quickly became the talk on the streets. His first big hit was the R-rated single *Tek Buddy Gal*, following not-so-popular numbers such as *Most High* and *New Millennium* with singer Wayne Marshall.

Kartel ushered in his own era in dancehall. Beenie Man and Bounty Killer were the last two holdovers of a bygone age that could be considered DJs in the traditional sense. Kartel an ardent fan of American rap music became a new kind of dancehall artist a sort of Rap-J rather than the conventional DJ. In the ten years prior to his arrival, Kingston had witnessed a total take over by hip-hop. Kartel caught and rode the wave. He proceeded to mirror his North American cousins in both style and substance with a rapid-fire delivery, and where lyrically, sex and bling are his main points of interest.

From 2005 onwards a rapid amount of hit singles caused his popularity to eclipse that of his patron Bounty Killa and he became a top draw in his own right. This led to a bidding war between reggae indie giants **VP Records** and **Greensleeves** with the latter prevailing. The company issued two albums but they were not big sellers. His albums suffered because of the overwhelming amount of singles he unleashed on a tiny marketplace.

While not being able to boast about album sales, over the course of five years, he was able to command major fees for live performances and in turn, made a small fortune in the process.

Major controversy surrounding Vybz concerning the Alliance movement, a set of artists under Killa's leadership, and the management of promoter Sharon Burke then arose. Kartel was a part of the group but would soon acrimoniously depart, as in his own words he refused to be a "follower".

According to observers, The Alliance was seen as Bounty trying to prolong his "dying" career by using the members (Mavado, Busy Signal, Aidonia and Vybz) as props. Kartel's departure erupted into a full-scale feud and a subsequent media circus. This also was the precursor to the later Gully/ Gaza civil unrest. Vybz Kartel's ambitions would not permit him to remain under the thumb of anyone. Shortly after the Alliance affair he and Mavado rode the coat tails of conflict to stardom and put the entire dancehall fraternity into a two-man strangle hold.

A 2008 Kartel-Mavado Sting clash drew a

bumper-crowd, but was also a low point for dancehall. What was supposed to be a lyrical confrontation became personal with both artists verbally assailing each other. In an unprecedented outrage, even in the mudslinging atmosphere of Sting, they proceeded to do the unthinkable which was to trade insults about each other's mothers.

Many entertainment insiders referred to this showdown as the official death of dancehall. It seemed that the negative forces had totally taken over the music for good. Consequently, in the aftermath came a plethora of diss tracks traded back and forth, leading to fanatical factions and violent incidents.

Kartel, intent on dancehall domination, teamed up with producer Ainsley "Notnice" Morris and assembled his own camp of artists under the moniker of the Portmore Empire. They recorded and released singles at a breakneck pace. This was the beginning of a takeover and The Empire was sometimes collectively responsible for nearly fifty percent of what was on the local charts at any given time. Dancehall sound systems playlists and radio play were hijacked and held hostage by their repertoire. In the process Kartel brought to public notice new names such as Black Ryhno, Jahvinci, Lisa Hype, Gaza Slim, Merital Family, Russian and Popcaan.

But trouble in the camp surfaced and as fast as "The Teacher" bussed them they were also jettisoned upon any form of disagreement, weather egregious or petty. The hits from the Empire nonetheless came fast and furious with top takes being *My Money*, *Dumper Truck*, *Cake Soap* and *Clarks*. The Portmore Empire artists were all marginal talents and a lot of their material mediocre, but the flood of product emanating from the camp was hard to ignore

That's it for the musical side. Another picture would be brought out of the family closet and it would not be a pretty sight.

Coming into view was now a gush of media grabbing stunts and controversies surrounding the artist such as, questionable shootings credited to his associates, fire bombings of his enemy's property, and brushes with the police. Then several cases of him being a no-show on events for which he was booked. This he confessed to top radio personality Richard Burgess was due to a "fear of flying". He also underwent a complete physical transformation in the form of heavy tattooing, skin bleaching and body piercing. These things he stridently defended in his interviews.

Other rumors bordered on the outrageous: that he drinks blood and has sold his soul to the devil.

It seemed as if Vybz at least as it appeared, was overtly courting the dark forces. Many cited as proof of this, a song he recorded and released titled *Daddy Devil*. Another indication is that one of his protégées Tommy Lee who has confessed eternal allegiance to him and seems to be his most dedicated disciple took what his mentor was allegedly been accused of to another level.

Lee rose to prominence with a Kartel-style delivery but more stark in demonic references both in his appearance and lyrics. He described his style of dancehall as *gothic* and has shocked the music fraternity with macabre and disturbing compositions and their accompanying videos. Leading his repertoire are songs like *Psycho* and *Uncle Demon*.

As for Kartel himself, the one Lee unwittingly refers to as Uncle Demon and himself as Nephew Demon, in several interviews apparently corroborated this viewpoint by denouncing Christ and flashing what looked like a freemason ring.

Upcoming events however would humble the once mighty DJ who was riding high while enjoying being the number one artist in Jamaica. Adding to his profile as well was his business success as a rum distributor and having several other enterprises in the works. The artist, along with business partner and manger Corey Todd, was adopting the business model of branding – attaching his image to a plethora of products, including at least one major Kingston nightclub.

The first sign of trouble came with a falling out between himself and Todd, which the ex-manager took public by saying that his life was under threat. Kartel in turn went to the media, denying the claims while at the same time displaying arrogance personified by statements such as "I am the puppet master and the people are the puppets". Vybz Kartel, as a major talent, seemed unstoppable but was being exposed as a megalomaniac, infused with delusions of grandeur.

In 2011 everything fell apart for the self-styled "World Boss" when Jamaican police arrested him in a hotel room on drugs and weapons charges. This proved to be a bait to detain him on more serious crimes that were being investigated.

While in custody the news broke like a

bombshell. Vybz Kartel, Jamaica's number one artist was charged with two counts of murder.

The artist in these affairs was implicated to be the mastermind behind the murders of Clive Williams and Barrington Burton both occurring in 2011. It became apparent that the artist allegedly had a parallel career as a gang boss alongside his musical one.

Both cases went to trial. Kartel was acquitted in the matter concerning Burton after the prosecution's case collapsed for lack of sufficient evidence. For Clive Williams aka Lizard however, the case proceeded and held the nation's attention for three years while Kartel's supporters screamed for his release.

On April 3rd 2014, the most dominant Jamaican entertainer in recent times was found guilty and bludgeoned with a life sentence. One wonders if dancehall, by the episode, has been dealt a serious blow or given a new lease on life as in a remarkable feat of persistence, even while incarcerated Vybz Kartel continues to dominate the dancehall with both old and new songs

46. Mavado

Christened: David Brooks
Born: November 30, 1981

Gully King

A teaspoon of Michael Rose
A pinch of Garnett Silk.
A shake of Sizzla and an ounce of Bounty Killer.
Mix it all together and you get Mavado.
The hottest star in dancehall.

Mavado carries the qualities of someone with huge potential as an international prospect. His style has already drawn the attention of many leading hip-hop artists, professing glowing admiration for his skills as a mc.

The artist himself has cited late rap star Tupac Shakur as a major influence and indeed there are many similarities: above average talent, charisma, prolific and a persona that pits him against law enforcement. Mavado, much like Sizzla, jumped onto the scene with a sound so refreshing that upon gaining popularity with his first hit, *Real McCoy*, he swept over the competition like a tidal wave.

He too was also a protégé of dancehall veteran Bounty Killer and followed his mentor's playbook to the tee. Much in the same way Bounty Killer rose to success and stayed there by battling his nemesis Beenie Man. Mavado dove headlong into his own conflict by locking horns with Vybz Kartel. Much like Bounty he also cultivated an aura of danger, with the all black sinister style of dress and a repertoire of gun tunes.

Another early break out song *Wha Dem A Do* is the perfect example, in which he talks about buying guns and killing his enemies execution style. He even announces himself with the catch phrase *gangster fi life*, so there is no mistake as to what he stands for.

In the initial stages of his popularity, he was under the shadowy group of Bountyites called The Alliance, which he later outgrew.

After hooking up with the Harrisingh brothers' owners of a production house called **Daseca**, his material took on a more poignant undertone. His single for them *Dying* spoke of his late-father, who was claimed by the streets, and Mavado's own fears of heading for a similar fate. The video had the artist sitting in a jail cell bearing his soul with self-revelatory lyrics. The song drew a lot of attention internationally to this fresh voice of the dancehall.

On the heels of a stockpile of hits, the *Gangsta For Life* (**VP**) album was released in 2007. On this album though was one musical anomaly, which was the inclusion of the spiritually inclined single *Amazing Grace* drowning amidst a sea of songs talking about guns, gangs and girls. Two years later the album *Mr. Brooks A Better Tomorrow* expanded his audience, covering autobiographical and inspirational themes. On it were songs like *Every Situation, So Blessed, Don't Worry, Overcome* and the monster single *On The Rock*. This latter album tipped the scales in Mavado's favor in the ongoing race against Vybes Kartel as his originality and depth came to the fore in ways that went beyond targeting hardcore fans. Another single, *So Special*, off of it hit number one on all reggae charts and was picked up by **VP**. A remix with Jay Z and glossy video was produced for Black Entertainment Television (BET) consumption. This however had middling success and was trumped by another song on the same riddim, Serani's *No Games*, which was a top fifty hit (respectable for a dancehall song) on the US Pop charts.

In the meantime, his intense rivalry with Vybes Kartel was becoming increasingly vicious, taking on the makings of a tribal war. Troublemakers affiliated with both artists started to beat each other up, even, with mysterious shootings occurring at the homes of the main principals. Sound system operators at the height of the conflict even had to adhere to a policy of parity, which is to play an equal amount of songs from both sides. The alternative would've been to risk being beaten up or having their equipment destroyed.

The ongoing feud dominated the daily headlines and the warlords were summoned to a meeting by the then Jamaican Prime Minister Bruce Golding, in order to restore sanity to the situation.

Both Mavado and Vybz Kartel were also starting to reap the bitter fruits of their actions with travel bans from neighboring Caribbean countries, multiple show cancellations, detention by the police and having their US Visas revoked.

In subsequent years Mavado has fared better than his archrival, eventually having his visa reinstated; while, Kartel's life reached its nadir with him being arrested and jailed to answer several counts of murder.

All in all, with Kartel serving a 35 year prison sentence, Mavado is the top dancehall act coming out of Jamaica. He has achieved this with a machine-like pace, churning out hit singles like bees making honey. Another factor to his credit is a toning down of his gangster image in favor of becoming the new dancehall sex symbol with songs like *Mad Over* and *Pon the House Top*.

His quest for a wider acceptance beyond his native shores has landed him in the arms of DJ

Khaled's Miami based **We The Best** label. When Khaled's label was bought out by the most successful imprint in hip-hop **Cash Money** Mavado became part of a company rubbing shoulders with hip–hop royalty, celebrities like Little Wayne and Drake.

Now residing in Florida, he is striving to gain a foothold in the US market that has so far proven unsuccessful.

45. Jacob Miller

Christened: Jacob Miller
Born: May 4, 1952
Deceased: March 23, 1980

Destiny Halted

There was a time in the 1970s when one of the biggest stars in Jamaica was Jacob Miller. He enjoyed a very successful solo career while fronting one of the biggest bands at the time, Inner Circle.

Miller was on the threshold of international stardom when, in early 1980, he lost control of his automobile while driving and rammed into a utility pole. Succumbing to his injuries as he was on his way to the hospital, he left a stunned populace to mourn. He was only 27 years old.

Jacob Miller was born in the rural hamlet of New Green, in the central Jamaican parish of Manchester. His mother, Joan Ashman, dispatched him to the city to live with relatives. He ended up at Rosseau Road in Kingston, about a half mile from Radio Jamaica. There he lived in a little house where there were more buildings that were small motels.

Not much is known about his schooling but by the time he became a teenager, he was showing up at Brentford Road at Studio One, owned by Coxsone Dodd. He hung around hoping to be noticed by the legendary record man. In the process he became friends with singer Al Campbell, who later had hits like *Gee Baby* and *Talk About Love*. Miller would harmonize on some of Campbell's recordings as a way to get his foot in the door and soon would get his turn.

In 1968, at the age of 16, his maiden recording for Coxsone was a single called *Love Is the Message*, but it flopped and Dodd lost interest in Miller. It would be six more years before anything significant happened in Jacobs's nearly doomed career.

In 1972, Horace Swaby (aka Agustus Pablo), known for his instrumental recordings along with his brother Garth, launched a label called **Rockers International**. The label was located on Orange Street, downtown Kingston and conceived as a home for Pablo's own recordings, but soon expanded to working with vocal talents.

From the outset, Jacob had a voice that no one could ignore. Like Dennis Brown, he oozed with natural talent, the kind that other singers would readily give up a body part to obtain. His high tenor sound would be at home in any opera house, if he had been born in Europe, since he simply could out sing anyone. Miller was a chubby adolescent and carried an equally big voice akin to legendary big men like Pavarotti, Barry White or Luther Vandross.

Producer Augustus Pablo and King Tubby were pioneers of the reggae sub-genre known as dub where they experimented with version cuts of live recordings adding a lot of echo and reverb. Miller was one of the young talents that the label placed an early bet on. The result was a slew of singles with *Keep On Knocking* being released in 1974, one of their first hits. Again like Brown, Jamaica fell immediately in love with Miller's voice. It was so mellow and irresistible, having the capacity to carry any tune in any style.

From the moment Jacob came to national attention he operated like the proverbial *young man in a hurry*. His work pace was frenetic and his appetite for stardom voracious. While Marley and Tosh were out conquering the world, artists such as Miller and Brown owned Jamaica in the 70s.

He made Rockers into one of the hottest labels around by following up with hit after hit. The most prominent of those releases were *Baby I Love You So*, *Who Sey Jah No Dread*, *Each One Teach One* and *Girl Named Pat*.

Miller however, eyed Marley and coveted the international fame that he was achieving. This quest would lead him to the progressive looking outfit Inner Circle that he joined as lead vocalist in 1976.

Inner Circle was formed in 1968 by a pair of corpulent siblings, Roger and Ian Lewis. Also in it were Ibo Cooper, Stephen Coore and Richard Daley. They operated as a lounge-band, playing on the tourist circuit in hotels. This was one of the first bands that drew members from both the lower and upper class of Jamaican society

(Coore's father, David, later became the Deputy Prime Minister).

In 1973 Coore, Cooper, and Daley left to form Third World with Prilly Hamilton, Irvine Jarrett and William Stewart. Third World would go on to legendary status, in its own right after, William Bunny Rugs Clarke replaced Hamilton on lead vocals. Inner Circle soldiered on by adding Bernard Harvey, Charles Farqurson and Rasheed McKenzie.

In 1975 Inner Circle was under contract with **Trojan**, having a minor hit with the single *I See You*. In the **Trojan** years, the band mainly recorded covers and imitated soul groups; a formula which was not getting them much traction. Things finally started looking more hopeful when Miller took the reins, coming in with the clout of already having a successful solo career and adding the potency of his songwriting ability. With Miller came more socially conscious output and a more robustly *rootsy* instrumental sound. The same year the star came on board, and through the guidance of manager Thomas Tommy Cowan, the group inked a deal with **Capitol Records**.

The album *Reggae Thing* released in 1976

was musically more like reggae fusion where the group was really playing other styles of music with a reggae slant. The two strongest cuts were the ones that adhered to the basic sound like *Tired Fi Lick Weed In A Bush* and *80,000 Careless Ethiopians*. *Ready For The World* the following year was much of the same and wasted Miller's talents in lightweight pop, imitating American music instead of building on the hard roots sound that made him famous in the first place.

Inner Circle's **Capitol** years taught that you should not try to crossover; moreover, that being yourself and sticking to what you're good at will bring the market to you. After all, Marley, Tosh and Burning Spear proved the point. But Inner Circle's main driving force, the Lewis brothers it seemed, were deeply infatuated with soul music and in the group it was them and not Miller who called the shots.

On the other hand, Miller carried on a parallel solo career in Jamaica, alongside the international one with Inner Circle and by himself he was wildly successful. *The Tenement Yard* album released in the same year as *Reggae Thing* was as potent as the overseas release was the opposite.

Tenement Yard was the result of a production

outfit called **ABC,** which had heavy involvement from their manager, Tommy Cowan and fellow members of Inner Circle and brought out the best Miller had to offer. This package was laden with hits that ruled the airwaves: *All Night Till Daylight, Suzy Wong, Forward Jah Jah Children, Tired Fi Lick Weed In A Bush* and the classic title track, *Tenement Yard.* And then, in 1978 came the *Wanted* album. This was another brilliant collection, featuring *Healing Of The Nation* and the stylish *Peace Treaty Special.*

At this time, Kingston was ablaze with political violence and when a truce was called, Miller sang, "peace treaty is going on to raa to raa". It showed an artist on top of the times. His end of year Christmas album "A Natty Christmas", featuring toaster Ray I, showed Miller's populist streak as most of the great reggae artists stayed clear of this "Babylon" holiday. That same year he co-headlined the One Love Concert with Bob Marley and in a fit of youthful exuberance, lit up a marijuana joint on stage and then taunted the police much to the delight of the crowd.

A new contract from **Island Records** gave Miller and Inner Circle another shot at international acceptance. *Everything Is Great,* under this renewed effort, came in 1979. The album was recorded in Jamaica but mixed at Blackwell's Compass Point studios in The Bahamas.

Blackwell was still unable to reign in the group's penchant for experimenting with myriad musical styles; nevertheless, he had better results than **Capitol**. The title track, a disco number that could easily be mistaken for soul group the O'Jays, made the UK Top 20 and topped other charts in Europe. Other minor hits were the psychedelic sounding ode to marijuana, *Mary Mary*, and *Stop Breaking My Heart*.

On **Island**, Miller was Marley's label mate and good friend. Apparently, he was also in Blackwell's good graces and was being eyed by the **Island** boss to be groomed as the next star to follow. He even travelled with them to Brazil in 1979 to take part in the opening of a new office in Rio De Janerio. Blackwell at one time remarked that, "If there was anybody at the time who could be the next big thing, it would have been Jacob Miller...he just had that presence".

Jacob had all the ingredients: raw talent, irreverence and rebelliousness. He was also hardworking and extremely charismatic. In spite of his weight, he often times performed shirtless in a maniacal fashion and was a rock star in the making.

However, this was not to be.

On Sunday March 23 1980, two months shy of his 28th birthday, Miller was driving his Mercedes Benz with his three children on Hope Road in Kingston. According to some accounts he was eating a piece of sugar cane while behind the wheel and apparently driving way too fast. Other sources claimed that he was on his way to an album launch for Third World as their special guest and was late; hence he was rushing to get there. Whatever the case, at the intersection of Hope and Trafalgar Road, he careened off and hit a light pole. He died on his way to University Hospital in Papine, while being transported in a police vehicle.

Miller's funeral was a packed affair at the National Arena, where thousands paid their respects to the beloved artist. Amongst the mourners was Minister Of National Security Dudley Thompson, while Miller's manager read the eulogy.

A large procession then made way to lay the

showman to rest at Dovecot Memorial, Park in St Catherine, 27 miles out of the city. He joined the so-called "cursed 27 club" of famous artist to have died at that age which includes Janis Joplin, Jimmy Hendrix, and Jim Morrison. In later years, Amy Winehouse and Kurt Cobain would follow suit.

In just five short years Jacob "Killer" Miller worked harder than most. Yet he lives on through a treasure chest of classic recordings. It is a shame how this unsung hero of reggae is almost forgotten by the Jamaican media.

In the year of his passing another brilliant album, *Mixed Up Moods*, came out. It brandished more classic hits such as *Jolly Joseph, Once Upon A Time* and *Chapter A Day*.

It is not beyond the realms of probability that Miller could have been as big as Marley. His versatility was evident by his cover of Tom Jones's *Delilah* and a live recording of *Disciplined Child* send chills up the spine.

Jacob's untimely passing was a huge lost to the momentum of the reggae movement and preceded Bob Marley's own death by only a year.

Inner Circle, devastated by the tragedy, disbanded but recovered years later. They have managed to keep Miller's legacy alive.

44. Mutabaruka

Christened: Allan Hope
Born: December 26, 1952

Celebrity Poet

There is one name synonymous with dub poetry, one of reggae's sub genres. That name belongs to a man called Mutabaruka.

At the beginning of the 80s while surrounded

by some of the best young musicians in Jamaica, Muta emerged from the recording studio with his debut album *Check It* (Alligator). On the strength of this album Mutabaruka became a genre unto himself.

The album offered a potent mixture of hardcore dub, mixed with a pinch of dancehall and pop references in which even Michael Jackson's *Billy Jean* was sampled. *Check It* took spoken word, an art form, normally something of only academic interest to radical college students and leftist scholarly types, as close to the mainstream as possible.

Muta became and remains the only star of dub poetry. This he achieved through an uncommon courage and a refusal to conform to the norms of the presiding musical scene.

Mutabaruka formerly known as Allan Hope was a telephone technician in the early 70s and a regular at The Creative Arts Centre in Kingston, where he and a small group of poets, including names like Michael Smith and Orlando Wong aka Oku Onuru, participated in readings before a captive audience.

Michael Smith was an early influence and

leading figure in the emerging movement with the popular recording *Mi Cyaan Believe It*, but was stoned to death outside a political rally in 1983. This emboldened Hope to carry on his friend's legacy.

While most poets were purists and frowned upon the idea of recording their works, Mutabaruka actively pursued a recording career knowing the reward would be a platform from which he could propagate his ideas. He was determined to have a voice in the affairs of his country and the world. He knew that having a hit record would help.

He saw an opportunity when he hooked up with guitar maverick Earl China Smith, who ran a label and record retail store called **High Times**, and it was Earl Smith who subsequently produced *Check It*.

The groundbreaking collection was released on the heels of the single *Every Time I Ear De Soun*, and capitalized on the strength of it. *Every Time I Ear The Soun* excited a local audience that never experienced poetry in this format before. Thoughtful and stimulating it was but most importantly extremely entertaining. Furthermore the song presented a fresh, unique ideology, being one of the first records of its kind to be in regular rotation on Jamaican radio and ultimately became a hit.

Many albums followed as Muta built on his initial success, doing deals with several US based labels like Shanachie and Heartbeat. The most notable of these releases came in 1985 with *Outcry*.

In 1986 he cemented his position as a top entertainer, rare for a dub poet, with the most coveted slot as the headliner at the legendary Reggae Sunsplash concert. He single handedly carried the genre from then on into the present time and opened doors for less successful beat poets such as Yasus Afari, Benjamin Zepaniah and the comical DYCR. But while they had their fifteen minutes in the spotlight Muta continued to thrive.

Mutabaruka embraced Rastafarianism from in his twenties. But it was a version according to his own viewpoint and this would follow him throughout his public life as his opinions are always out of step with what prevails in the mainstream. He blossomed into a full-fledged maverick: albeit a likable one and charmed his way into becoming a public figure.

The one constant theme he adheres to is an uncompromising stance of promoting a doctrine of Negro independence. He typifies the outsider by being a strict vegetarian and donning traditional African garbs. Topping it off, he refuses to wear shoes.

In his time as a popular recording artist, he has toured extensively and overtime proved his mettle as an intellect, possessing one of the best minds not only as a musical entertainer, but also as a thinker and philosopher. He parlayed the goodwill built by his musical career into a new one in journalism. He for many years has his own radio show *The Cutting Edge*, one that is widely listened to on Jamaica's number one radio station, Irie FM.

Mutabaruka has gained the respect of both the common man and of those in officialdom and mostly sees his present role as one to be a champion of the anti-establishment, while acting as a social and cultural provocateur.

43. Damian Marley

Christened: Damian Marley
Born: July 21, 1978

Junior Gong

Damian Marley, aka Junior Gong, makes the list as the son of Bob Marley with the most successful solo career of his siblings.

Damian has the highest profile of the other

Marley children in the business. Moreover, his ranking in respectability is on par with that of Marley's eldest son Ziggy Marley. The others including Kymani, Julian and Stephen all have respectable careers, but are not in the same class as these two.

Damian the last son sired by Bob Marley with former Miss World Cindy Breakspeare, unlike the other offspring's of Marley active in the music, DJ's in a dancehall style instead of singing and his vocal sound has more in common with dancehall icon Super Cat.

Performing from age 13 and releasing his first album *Mr. Marley* at 18, Damian has been a tireless worker in building a career of his own. Under the skillful guidance of his producer/artist brother Stephen, Damian has risen to become a force in his own right and not just his father's clone.

Hitting his stride with the 2001 release *Half Way Tree*, he never looked back. Hit singles like *Youth Dem Bawling, Karl Kani* and the combo with Capleton *It Was Written*, have established Junior Gong as a certified star coming out of Jamaica.

The follow up to *Half Way Tree*, *Welcome To Jamrock*, propelled him to a greater level of success with the title track being a worldwide smash and the album certified as gold by the Record Industry Association of America (RIAA), for sales of more than 500,000.

He also signaled to a lazy dancehall scene that he is not a regular reggae artist just willing to get by with playing it safe. So he surprised the industry when he embarked on the most ambitious and the riskiest project of his career, which resulted in the 2010 release of the *Distant Relatives* album with American rapper Nas. The album was a rare pairing of musical styles on which each track gave the listener reggae and rap in one serving. The move paid off immensely, winning him a legion of new fans.

Damian became the darling of his peers, on the international stage whom have invited him to do collaborations, big names like Mick Jagger, Bruno Mars, Rihanna and Gwen Stefani. His latest strategy has him teaming up with electronic dance music stars like Diplo and Skrillex, placing him on the cutting edge of the latest trend in the entertainment game.

As a live performer he is on another level in

comparison to his fellow Jamaicans. He delivers his set without flaw accompanied with a superior sound quality, distinct backdrop and a tailor made light show. His bookings are also mainly outside of the reggae circuit and he his regularly billed on major festivals covering multiple genres.

Damian is one of a few reggae artists as a solo act with three Grammy awards under their belts. And even with this level of success he keeps the pressure on, recording and releasing new material at a breakneck pace, while adhering to a hectic touring schedule.

There is an uncanny feeling that Damian has just begun as the world awaits his next move.

42. Delroy Wilson

Christened: Delroy Wilson
Born: October 5, 1948
Deceased: March 6, 1995

Mr. Soul

Amongst Jamaican vocalists that dominated the rock steady era, Delroy Wilson's legacy has been his influence on many other artists and a body of work that has had a lasting impact. He is one of the Princes of Jamaican music as it came into its own, alongside Alton Ellis and Ken Booth.

Blessed with a soulful voice reminiscent of rhythm and blues great Otis Redding, Wilson was a trailblazer who would influence the next generation of stars such as Dennis Brown and Beres Hammond.

His voice had a classical tilt; while at the same time it managed to retain a parochial essence, a quality that usually endears certain singers to the common people. His vocal style was sometimes jubilant, though most effective when melancholic.

His material was mainly bittersweet odes that hinted at a life plagued by complications and anxieties. Wilson possessed the stuff of all great singers: the believability factor. When he sang you felt what he was feeling.

Wilson was discovered in 1962 at the age of fourteen by Sir Clement Coxsone Dodd. He cut a set of unnoticeable singles before finally hitting with the song that is still regarded as his signature, 1966's *Dancing Mood*. He then racked up an impressive string of hits: *Riding For a Fall, Once Upon A Time, Rain from the Sky* and *Better Must Come,* among numerous others.

In the 1972 election *Better Must Come* became a part of Jamaican political history when campaign challenger, The Peoples National Party, successfully used it as a rallying cry to defeat the incumbent Jamaica Labor Party. The song's impact on the elections was huge, as it resonated with the poor. As a result Wilson became one of the early working class heroes and was the most loved artist, only to be overtaken in later years by Dennis Brown.

As the story went with most of Coxsone's artists, Wilson left in 1967 over money issues. He moved forward to work with several other producers, most notably Bunny Lee and Sonia Pottinger which produced stellar results, with the artist churning out one chart-topper after the other.

For reasons unknown, he went back to Coxsone before leaving again. This last time was for good, in order to start his own label called **W&C**, in partnership with Wilburn Strangah Cole and another which he named **Links.**

In 1970 he received valuable international exposure while touring the UK, even cutting a number of sides for **Trojan**. In 1976 he had another huge hit with Bob Marley's *I'm Still Waiting*.

Wilson was one of the most prolific hit-makers of his time, but managed his money poorly and suffered for lack of proper guidance. In spite of all his success, financial and personal problems persisted and he dealt with them by turning to alcohol.

By the 1980s, as the DJ era was gaining ground, Wilson's career started to wane. Even though he continued to record, Wilson was unable to regain the momentum of his glory days.

In 1994 he was honored with a plaque of merit by the Jamaican government for his contribution to the arts, as his health deteriorated. One year later on March 6th 1995, at the age of 46, the beloved artist succumbed to complications relating to cirrhosis of the liver.

41. Byron Lee

Christened: Byron Lee
Born: June 27, 1935
Deceased: November 4, 2008

Mr. Caribbean

Described at the time of his passing as a "great musical pioneer", Byron Lee was a musician, bandleader, visionary and entrepreneur. He was consequently one of the main players in shaping Jamaican and Caribbean musical history.

Lee was the son of a Jamaican mother and a Chinese immigrant father. The young Byron first lived in the parish of Manchester, where he attended Catholic School. By the time he was nine his parents moved to Kingston.

In his adolescent years his two great loves were music and soccer. For a time, the latter took precedence to the point where he made the Jamaican national squad. The music bug however, in time, like the proverbial tortoise, overtook the hare and he was soon playing both piano and bass proficiently.

At age 15, he started a band with childhood friend Carl Brady. After practicing for six years, the band, called The Dragonaires, started doing small gigs playing the early form of Jamaican music called mento. Being somewhat from a privileged background in pre-independent Jamaica, he was able to secure engagements with the island's hotels. By 1959 the group was Jamaica's premier band, and then naturally hired by local promoters to back top international stars with engagements on the island, like Harry Belafonte, Chuck Berry, Sam Cooke and Fats Domino.

In that same year Lee's band made their first record, produced by future Prime Minister Edward Seaga called *Dumplings*.

Byron Lee is also known to have been the first Jamaican musician to own and play an electric bass guitar which, when paired with the drums, would become the emphasis of the drum and bass sound of reggae in its embryonic stage.

In the meantime, mento gave way to another musical shift called ska and The Dragonaires was at its forefront. The band released numerous ska singles including *Fireflies*, *Mash Mr Lee* and *Joy Ride*. Lee, the entrepreneur, released their songs under his own **Dragon Breath** label. In 1962 they got their first major dose of international exposure when they lip synced Ernie Ranglin's compositions, in the James Bond film *Dr. No*.

In 1964 Edward Seaga, the Dragonaires' former manager, was a rising political star and became the head of The Department of Social Welfare and Economic Development. This afforded the band the opportunity to travel to New York to play at a business expo called the *World's Fair*, showcasing the island's music where they backed Jamaican stars such as The Maytals, Jimmy Cliff and Millie "My Boy Lollipop" Small.

In this period, lower class Jamaicans inhibited by poverty began moving away from the feel good vibes of ska. They would soon embrace the pre-reggae incarnation, rock-steady. Byron, who came from the other side of the economic fence, found a natural affinity to ska, in the form of Trinidadian calypso.

In 1964, he took his band to the Twin Island Republic for the first time and so began a lengthy love affair with what prevailed as the dominant form of music in the other parts of the Antilles. In 1974, after a decade of building a credible presence as a calypso band, the only serious one outside of Trinidad and Tobago, The Dragonaires made their debut at the mecca of calypso music, the *Trinidad Carnival*.

Byron Lee, the pioneer, led the way in building a bridge for Jamaicans to keep in touch with their Caribbean relatives, and on which they could do the same with their slightly different cultural cousin. Where regional political union had failed in the 1940s with the demise of the short-lived West Indian Federation, Lee achieved much more through his employment of culture as a form of integration.

Along the way he helped to break Jamaican singers like Tony Gregory and Ken Lazarus by offering them lead vocal duties in the band. In later years he also did the same for other Caribbean talents like Oscar Benjamin from Trinidad and Tobago and Guyanese Jomo Primo.

His legacy is twofold.

Lee's entrepreneurial side prompted him to make two pivotal moves back in 1965 that would help to provide some much needed infrastructure to the fledgling Jamaican music industry. One was the formation of Lee Enterprises, a show promotion entity, with partners Ronnie Nasralla and Victor Sampson. The other was the purchase of The WIRL recording studio and vinyl pressing plant, later to be renamed **Dynamic Sounds**.

The promotion company was responsible for setting up Byron Lee's Spectacular Show, which took top stars of the ska period such as The Maytals and Hortense Ellis on tours mainly through the Caribbean. The recording studio became the most equipped and professionally run in the island. In the 70s it would become the place of choice for many foreign acts wanting to capture the feel of reggae, which was fast becoming a genre of international significance. Those that called were the cream of the rock world, among them: The Rolling Stones, Paul Simon and The Clash. As for the pressing plant, it provided a means through which production of local records could keep pace with the demand that the music was garnering beyond its shores. In later years he would also become one of the founders of The Jamaica Federation of Musicians, a union representing the interest of the island's musical practitioners.

Another masterful move was forming a relationship with American major label **Atlantic Records**, who distributed his label's releases in the US and in return him theirs in the Caribbean.

Lee was among a group of Jamaicans of Chinese descent who became leaders in manufacturing, distribution, retail and record production with a somewhat love hate kind of relationship with the artists that were mainly of negro heritage. Throughout the island's musical history, allegations of exploitation of the latter by the former have been a familiar one but the fate of both have nonetheless became intertwined. Others in this class are names like Neville Lee **(Sonic Sounds)**, Vincent Chin **(Randy's and VP Records)**, Herman Chin Loy **(Aquarius**

Records), Leslie Kong (**Federal**) and record producer/musician Mikey Chung.

Lee's success as a businessman by no means diminishes his achievements as an artist, with no less than sixty albums credited to his group during his lifetime. This alone is enough evidence that the bassist was a prolific musician and composer. Within this huge discography are many classic hits such as *Mr. Walker, Shaving Cream, Wings Of A Dove, Fire Fire* and, the perennial favorite, *Tiney Winey*.

The single most important achievement for Lee, not only as an artist but also a visionary, is bringing carnival to Jamaica at the start of the 90s. Clannish upper-class Jamaicans, over prior years, had been holding their own versions of it in their walled-off circles. This pained Lee for what he saw as a disenfranchisement of the masses of music he had championed for decades. His business instincts also informed him that bringing Carnival downtown would not only help to bridge a class divide but could be enormously profitable.

He pooled resources together by exercising his organizational muscle. In 1990 the dream became reality when the first annual *Byron Lee Jamaica Carnival* took over the streets of Kingston with

Lee and his band jamming at center stage. An overjoyed Lee described the moment as *"the happiest day of my life"*.

This set off a chain reaction that helped the new offset of traditional calypso, that came to be known as soca, go mainstream in Jamaica. It was undoubtedly these developments that brought it and Jamaican dancehall closer. There was a point where the movement influenced dancehall and the sound textures of the two started to morph into one. In the 2000s the new sound that was born out of Lee's dancehall soca experiment of the 90s became the new sound of Jamaican music, helping the careers of Elephant Man, Kevin Lyttle (St Vincent), Bunji Garlin and soca star Machel Mantano (Trinidad). Not to be overlooked is his influence on other bands that followed in the footsteps of The Dragonaires, such as The Fabulous Five and The Bare Essentials.

After fifty straight years of performing with his band, even becoming now more than a band but an institution, the legend had to take a break as a result of treatment he had been receiving for bladder cancer.

In 2007 the national honor of Order of Distinction, which he initially received in 1982, was upgraded to Commander Class. This was for excellence and his overall contributions to Jamaican music and culture. The following year he succumbed to his illness and was given a state funeral.

40. Luciano

Christened: Jepther McClymont
Born: October 20, 1964

Messenger

There are times in a nation's cultural history

when a musical lifeline is needed. In the wake of Garnet Silk's passing, in December of 1994, the man who filled the void was roots star Luciano.

The healing began with a pair of singles released in the spring of 95. *It's Me Again Jah* and *Lord Give Me Strength* was sorely needed to compensate for a great loss to the music fraternity. The singles were also the foundation for a brilliant album *Where There Is Life* (**Island Jamaica**), now regarded as a reggae classic. The year 1995 became Luciano's. Every cut from the album was potent and could be heard ringing out in every hamlet and village across the island.

Luchi, as he is affectionately called, emerged three years earlier, though at the time was largely overshadowed by Silk's dominance. Offerings such as *Ebony & Ivory* (**Aquarius**), *One A Way Ticket* (**X-Terminator**) and *Shake It Up Tonight* (**Big Ship**) were early showings of his potential.

Here was a young artist with a rich vocal texture resembling that of Jamaica's most beloved singer Dennis Brown. Luciano's delivery was flawless and his diction superior to the other singers of the time. His style of singing was bombastic; hence the association with opera and the adoption of the European name, in tribute to opera star Luciano Pavarotti.

What Jamaica's Luciano has in common with Garnett Silk is that they both spearheaded a cultural renaissance. With the *Where There Is Life* album he was being looked upon like a sort of musical Moses leading the genre out of spiritual Egypt.

He followed up on his breakthrough album with ones equally strong, such as *Messenjah* (**VP**) and *Sweep Over My Soul* (**VP**) cementing his position as a top reggae star. Thereafter, he was a top draw, constantly touring and headlining most reggae festivals.

He cultivated the image of an artist whose mission was to deliver sermons to his fans. Often times with an evangelical zeal with Bible in hand. His act is delivered with a fiery intensity matching that of any preacher. Live he is electrifying, his performances exhibiting high energy kicks and cartwheels. To his fans the preaching is sometimes a bit too much but it still made him stand out from the pack. He dominated the latter half of the 90s and had a stellar run, until he split with his manager Phillip "Fattis" Burrell in 1999.

At this point, the cracks in his righteous amour

began to appear. What followed post Burrell was a career lacking focus. He proceeded to record for a plethora of inept producers, resulting in plummeting quality in his output.

His personal life also derailed when the police killed a known gunman at his house and took him into custody for harboring a fugitive. With the absence of a steady hand, his career never regained the strength it had in the mid-90s.

However, he has soldiered on and cannot be accused of being a sluggard, as he continues to record and perform with consistency. Because of these factors a career that should have had a marked, upward trajectory is one that has leveled off and cruising.

But the Rasta youth from Daveytown, Manchester is still regarded as one of the remaining bright spots in reggae, based mainly on his high level of talent and previous successes in a genre, which is currently adrift in mediocrity.

Luciano's relative high ranking as a reggae star is testament of what a few good albums can do for one's career and the fact that he remains a very hard working individual who continues to get work on a regular basis

39. Ernie Ranglin

Christened: Ernest Ranglin
Born: June 19, 1932

Founding Father

There was a song originally recorded by a fifteen-year-old American singer by the name of Barbie Gaye, which was a minor race record hit in 1957. Then there was a cover version of that same song which was a massive hit in 1964. The song was *My Boy Lollipop*, re-recorded by Jamaican singer Millie Small and rearranged by a Jamaican musical genius named Ernie Ranglin.

His significance is due to the fact that his arrangement of the song for a young entrepreneur called Chris Blackwell was the first Jamaican international hit and his overall contribution in shaping the sound of Jamaican music.

The song was done in the ska style, an ancestor of reggae, and conquered the charts on both sides of the Atlantic. It reached number two on the US and UK singles charts. It made millions for Blackwell's fledgling **Island Records** and made it possible for the label to bankroll other Jamaican artist's, enabling them to take their place on the international stage. This helped to make the islands music ubiquitous.

Ranglin was a child prodigy that made his first guitar from wood, strings and a sardine tin. By his early teens, he was playing jazz and blues that he would improvise to give birth to the distinctive Jamaican musical idioms of ska, and rocksteady. This, in no uncertain terms, makes him one of the founding fathers of Jamaican music.

He was the first to record for Chris Blackwell when the name of the label was **R & B**. This association led to the historical remake by Mille Small. Ranglin was later involved in composing many classical Jamaican songs and closely worked with Jimmy Cliff, Prince Buster, The Skatalites, The Wailers and Jamaican Jazz great Monty Alexander.

Ranglin recorded many solo albums mixing reggae with jazz in his pioneering style of Caribbean blend. These efforts were direct precursors to the modern surfer music popular in the United States on the west coast and Hawaii. Whenever you listen to any kind of record with an island sound, you are experiencing the fruits of Ranglin's labors.

Working closely over the years with **Island Records** and its offshoot **Palm Pictures**, he has composed movie soundtracks as well as offering services as a session player on many legendary recordings, including those of Bob Marley.

In 1973 he was given the Order of Distinction (OD), by the Government of Jamaica for his contributions to Jamaican music and the promotion of its culture.

Not to belabor the point though, one must wonder how well Jamaican music would have fared internationally, if it wasn't for the success of the reshaped version of the little known Barbie Gaye original.

38. Judy Mowatt

Christened: Judith Mowatt
Born: December 23, 1952

Black Woman

Judy Mowatt is one of the maternal figures in reggae music. She is respected by a whole generation of female singers that have followed in her footsteps.

Her place in Jamaican musical history and her

reputation as a spiritual person, first as a Rastafarian and now as a professing Christian, is admirable. This endears her to women singers who prefer the more traditional route to fame, rather than indulging in the more sordid side of the business.

Mowatt hails from Gordon Town, St Andrew. As a teenager she was already singing in the church and loved dancing. She joined a dance troupe and, while in it, met two young ladies – Beryl Lawson and Merle Clemenson. The three started a singing group the Gaylettes and in 1968 scored with the song *Silent River*, but broke up two years later

Following the group's demise she meandered around the edges of the business and wrote a few songs for Bunny Wailer. She also recorded sparingly under aliases such as Jean Watt and Julliane Mowatt. Singles released around 1973 by her included, *Mellow Moods*, *Way Over Yonder* and *Too Good For Me*.

Staying in play, she eventually fell in with other singers and writers. On one occasion she was asked to sing on a record that was being done by Marcia Griffiths, one of the most popular female stars at that time. From this opportunity she met another singer, Rita Marley, and began to harmonize with her backing Griffiths.

In 1974 Rita's husband, Bob Marley, was on the cusp of international stardom with his group The Wailers, when it suddenly broke apart. It is said that it was under the advice of producer Lee Perry that Bob asked Rita and her friends to sing on his first solo album *Natty Dread*. It worked out so well that in order to retain the homogeneity of sound, he took them on tour in support of the record. Judy thus became a part of musical history and one of the main ingredients in the greatest musical outfit to come out of the so-called third world.

Dubbed as The I Threes (Judy, Rita and Marcia) they set the standard for what harmonies should do on records. This was not only for coloring but also to improve the songs. That's what they did for Marley and on the ones they were featured, they helped to make, into masterpieces.

Mowatt was known for her pleasant personality, and seemingly got along well with everyone in Marley's contingent. She articulated well the position held by Marley and his musicians, in their advocacy of Rastafarianism and was sometimes even called upon by them in press conferences to clarify their beliefs to the media.

Judy, along with Rita and Griffiths, also made a good living touring with the reggae great. The women it seemed did better financially, more so than a lot of artists who had their own careers being out front.

In 1975 after Marley launched his own imprint **Tuff Gong**, one of his first projects was a solo album by Mowatt titled *Mellow Moods*. With the I Threes a permanent section of the legendary group, Mowatt recorded her own songs in between tours.

On her own she also started two record labels **Ashandan** and **Judy M Records** making sure that, as a solo act, she could maintain control over her artistic vision as well as her business affairs.

In 1977 she teamed up with one of Jamaica's great producers Geoffrey Chung on one of her greatest compositions, *Black Woman*. It was released on her own label. This became the title track for the 1979 album on **Grove Records/Island,** and was regarded as one of the greatest by a female reggae artist. She had a lot on her plate, but being a tireless worker she was able to juggle working with Marley, her solo career, and group work with the I Threes.

After Marley's death in 1981, The I Threes became more visible with an increasing amount of singles, albums and live appearances. Mowatt also put her solo work in high gear and, in 1982, inked a deal with Randy Grass's **Sanachie Records** based out of New Jersey, USA. The deal yielded four strong albums: *Only A Woman, Love Is Overdue, Working Wonders* and *Look At Love*. She stayed with them until 1991, and then made the switch to **Pow Wow Records** for the 1993 release *Rock Me*.

During these years Mowatt proved herself to be an artist of significance, delivering excellent songs that were never short on quality. In them she championed women's concerns regarding equality, dignity and praised motherhood as a worthwhile endeavor. (*Young female artists of today should reconnect and feed from her great legacy, instead of taking the music further down into the pit which it has sunken*). Not to be overlooked are her talents as a songwriter. The spirit of any woman would be lifted by the words she wrote in songs such as *Only A Woman, Black Woman, Working Wonders, Hush Baby Mother* and *Many Are Called.*

Starting out as a member of the Rastafarian sect *The Twelve Tribes Of Israel*, it is still unclear whether Mowatt held to the doctrine that regards Ethiopian Emperor, the late Haile Selassie, as a deity. In the liner notes on her **Sanachie** releases, she makes no reference to him at all.

Whatever doubts she had in her former beliefs seemed to have been resolved when she announced, in the 90s, that she had converted to Christianity. From then on she expressed herself musically through the gospel genre. The album *Something Old Something New* came with a mixture of the new gospel songs as well as some of her classics from the past.

She currently works the gospel circuit, and was even honored with the Order of Distinction by the Jamaican government for her contributions to arts and culture.

37. Ninja Man

Christened: Desmond Ballentine
Born: January 20, 1966

King of Stage

It is easy to overlook the impact of Ninja Man's role in helping to spread dancehall across the globe because of his many troubles with the law. But with closer observation it can be argued that he is one of, if not the most electrifying DJ ever to grace the stage. Many of the top performers of dancehall have copied him because of him setting the bar, in terms of style and overall showmanship. This puts him in a class by himself.

Desmond Ballentine was born in Annotto Bay, St. Mary and migrated to the city at age eleven. He grew up in the Kingston 11 ghetto of Mall Road, gravitating to the dancehall scene primarily as a dancer. In the dance yards of his community, one could witness his slender frame writhing with style in the center of a crowd. The DJ, in these early days, was learning what it took to excite an audience even before taking up the microphone. It hit him over time that it was not the record that the people came to hear but it was the performance they came to see. In the years to come only few could ignite a crowd the way he did.

As a youngster he did not have any formal schooling and, apart from hanging around the sound systems of the time like Black Culture, would spend the rest of the time engaging in small time criminality. Studying other entertainers in the community of Cockburn Pen like Early B and Super Cat, he began to inch his way closer towards the mike-stand, making brief performances of his own.

In 1980 he started an apprenticeship on the legendary Kilimanjaro Sound, under the moniker of Ugly Man, and in the process yearning to becoming a recording artist.

Legend has it that after recording a number of unremarkable singles in the mid-80s for various producers, he used the proceeds from a small heist to self-produce his first hit, *Protection*, a duet with singer Courtney Melody. After that there was no looking back and the DJ, now recording under a new name Ninja Man used the formula of pairing up with a singer to good effect. In 1988 he delivered two more hits, teaming up with festival icon Tinga Stewart for *Cover Me* and *Long Fi Release*.

As the 90s approached, he became one of the two biggest stars towering over a crowded field, the other being Shabba Ranks. One was for the girls and the other was more popular with a male following. At this time Shabba was unstoppable as the original "Lover Man" while Ninja held court as the bad man's artist.

Isaiah Laing's *Sting* concert, built on a model of clashes between top entertainers, would be Ninja's springboard into dancehall immortality becoming, Jamaica's clash superstar. On it he would prove himself to be the killer of giants. No one made an appearance more dramatic than him, entering the stage, always with a classic melody, then bursting into a lethal assault with opening lines like, *"mi have di license fi bury and the permit fi kill"*.

Ninja also held an edge over his competitors with his colorful costumes, often times looking like a kung fu master and the list of his casualties is the cream of dancehall: Shabba, Super Cat, Cobra, Papa San, and Flourgan.

Above all else his most dangerous weapon was his ability to create his lyrics on the spot, which trumped any amount of preparation undergone by his challengers. His ability to take the audiences temperature was unmatched and he never seemed to be in a hurry. He interspersed his vitriolic tirades with humor and, when it warranted, smatterings of social commentary. He could always sense when his audience was getting bored and would immediately switch gears. It is no exaggeration to say that he is a master of the stage.

Even though Ballentine thrived as a battle DJ, it must be mentioned that it was pure entertainment, done in light-hearted fun. His was not fashioned by personal attacks, or the physical confrontations that would eventually characterize the rivalries of the generation of DJs that would succeed his.

This new ugly face of dancehall was evident, when in 2003 at a Sting clash with the then-rising star Vybz Kartel, Ninja the veteran, was assaulted in a mob-style beat down by Kartel's entourage. The episode goes down as one of the most disgraceful in the annals of Jamaican music.

Ninja's recording career, on the other hand, was weak in comparison to the other stars of his time. Whilst Super Cat, Shabba Ranks and Cutty Ranks all secured international recording contracts based on numerous number one hits, Ninja remained largely a local hero, strong-live, but with a porous song catalog. One of his more famous hits after the initial success of the 80s was the single *Artical Don*, that became the title track for the **VP** released album in the early 90s. He however, was raking in large sums for live appearances as he held court as the king of stage.

Even with the talent that he possessed tough, the artist still found it hard to extricate himself from his colorful past. In the years to come his life played out like the worse tragic drama.

From his heyday as a top entertainer he dabbled with hard drugs, namely cocaine, and he eventually became fully addicted. His criminal past, also exacerbated by his chemical abuse, caught up with him. His demons led to a rebirth into a familiar world of lawlessness, with allegations of him marauding at night with known gunmen, committing nefarious acts. The murder of a taxi driver in 1996 led to his arrest, for which he was later acquitted after over a year in detention. Also in 2001 his brother in law seriously wounded him in a machete attack. This happened during a fight between Ninja and his common law wife. His attacker became furious when Ninja in the midst of the fracas hurled his own five-week-old daughter across a room, nearly killing the infant.

In the ensuing years he made some attempts to clean up his act, even having a sort of resurgence in popularity. In one brief period he even reinvented himself as a born again Christian. He then acted in films most notably *Third World Cop*, appeared on many TV talk shows and started recording again with the likes of reggae star Shaggy. He also resumed performing and clashing with the newer stars of the day.

But the battle with drug addiction and out of control behavior raged on.

In 2009 he hit rock bottom, when he was

arrested and charged jointly with his son for murder in the affair of a drive-by-type shooting incident. The beloved but troubled entertainer languished in prison for the better part of two years while awaiting trial. In 2012 he was granted bail.

In 2013 he signed to **Downsound Records**, owned by the enigmatic American millionaire Joe Bagdonovich. The label has been good for Ninja's career and his fortunes have since turned for the better. The association gave the veteran a new lease on life and much sought after financial stability. He is once again a media star and performing on shows like a man reborn.

36. Capleton

Christened: Clifton Bailey
Born: April 13, 1967

The Fireman

Capleton, like another top Jamaican DJ by the name of Buju Banton, started out as a "baldhead", putting himself on the map with pornographic lyrics.

He ultimately converted to Rastafarianism and in the second phase of his career became socially conscious, leading the New Roots movement.

Through the sheer force of his personality, he's been at the very top or stayed close to it. Tony Rebel may deserve credit for a wave at the beginning of the 90s described as New Roots but it was Capleton and Sizzla who became its biggest stars.

Coming from St Mary, notably the poorest parish in Jamaica, the artist adopted the name of Capleton. It was the surname of a popular lawyer with a practice in Islington, the community in which he grew up. The meaning of his alias he wears well, being very glib in his interviews and forceful in espousing his points of view.

From the very beginning, he possessed the rural work ethic. On his arrival into Kingston, on his musical quest for recognition, he worked ceaselessly to establish himself. In the early days, he voiced for different producers but most notably for Phillip "Fattis" Burrell, the man responsible for bringing Luciano and Sizzla to prominence.

At the advent of the 90s his ascent to the top started with hits like *Bumbo Red*, *Lotian Man*, *Number One Pon Di Look Good Chart* and *Buggering*. His style in these early days was not definitive, with him still searching for his own sound. These records saw him mimicking artists more prominent than himself like Ninja Man, Major Mackerel and Shabba Ranks.

Arriving on the scene at a time when artist-to-artist conflict was at a height, he won fans by weighing in as a sort of pacifist highlighted by a pair of songs, *Alms House* and *Music Is A Mission Not a Competition*. These singles pointed in the direction he was heading, while raising his level of respect within the fraternity. Around 1992 his conversion to Rastafarianism was already in progress, evident by his sprouting locks and a focus on more spiritual material.

In this same period he met, and subsequently developed a serious working relationship with producer/ sound system owner Stuart "African Star" Brown, who became his manager. Under Brown's guidance, he flourished, while his level of exposure grew with a growing number of overseas appearances.

It was for Brown whom Capleton recorded the song *Tour*. This song took him from the condemnation of local stardom into international recognition. A remix of the local version which was a hit in Jamaica by US based producers, The Dynamic Duo and Lil Jon, sampled Slick Ricks *Children Story*. It became the success story in the summer of 1995. Its addition to the play list of top New York stations like Hot 97 propelled the song onto the *Billboard Hip-Hop Charts*. Tour's success rewarded him with a major label contract from **Def Jam,** for which two albums *Prophecy* and *I-Testament* were released but with disappointing results.

His involvement with the American label had another effect on his career as this took him away from the local scene. Meanwhile Kingston moved on, embracing other acts who were coming into their own, most significantly the feuding pair of Beenie Man and Bounty Killer. But Capleton, the fierce competitor known for wearing very colorful outfits, regrouped and by 1998 launched a major offensive on an unsuspecting dancehall scene that needed more than the spectacle of artists at each other's throats.

A reenergized Capleton decorated his new campaign with one word that would be found in almost all of his new string of hits: *Fire*. In this incarnation, the DJ was like an arsonist, having a good time and proceeding to ignite the airwaves and stage shows with a barrage of new material. Big ones in rapid succession like *Dis Marcus, Slew Dem, Jah Jah City* and *Good In Har Clothes* put the Bobo Shanti back on top. He closed the

90s in fine style and his performance at the 1999 Reggae Sumfest concert was the most anticipated.

The early millennium was also a time that set off panic in Jamaican society, as youths attending Capleton's shows were taking his fire-burning message in a literal sense. Everywhere he performed, they armed themselves with spray cans, which were used as torches. Setting ablaze anything they could put their hands on.

The self-proclaimed "Fire Man" is a show stealer, and feared by his musical peers. He has a reputation for a high-energy act, employing classic call and response with heavy audience participation. His routine drains the crowd of their strength, leaving nothing for those billed to come after him.

Capleton as an artist though, when put under the microscope, has rightfully earned the ire of his critics with glaring contradictions in his conduct. Although maintaining a two-decade run, by having one of the best vocal deliveries and having a knack for penning songs with overpowering punch lines, his repertoire, at best, have been somewhat uneven.

Staunchly cultural songs such as *Jah, Jah City,*

Bad *Mind*, *That Day Will Come* and, the combo with Damian and Stephen Marley, *It Was Written* are like the proverbial oasis in a desert of otherwise lightweight crap. An apt description of him would be "Pop Star Rastaman". Capleton, even though overtly zealous for Rastafari, did not really abandon his old slack self. Attested to by risqué numbers such as *Tek Off* and *Bun Out The Chi Chi*. In his songs he mainly concentrated on catchy choruses while paying little attention to verses with thoughtful explanations. The verses in many cases are a string of rhymes, delivered in an irresistibly entertaining fashion, which is all that matters to the majority of his followers anyway.

From the mid-2000s his popularity waned, due to saturation and over-exposure. This in tandem with strong pushback by gay rights organizations (who refused to forgive him for his scathing attacks on their lifestyle in the early days of his career), slowed him down considerably. Negative press and show cancellations inflicted damage on his career.

However, Capleton in response made some pragmatic moves such as explaining his fire-burning stance, as well as signing the *Reggae Compassionate Act*, which forbids him from performing hate lyrics.

Capleton through consistency and non-stop activity has earned longevity in a very fickle and thankless profession. He is one of the most influential artists of the New Roots movement and his place in Jamaican musical history is firmly cemented.

These days he stays busy, touring, promoting new releases and staging his own annual show, *A St Mary Mi Come From*. Many artist in homage, have emulated his style and his influence is seen in the work of other roots stars such as, Anthony B, Jah Mason, Lutan Fire, Fantan Mojah and Munga Honorable.

35. Lady Saw

Christened: Marion Hall
Born: July 12, 1972

One of the boys

There are some people in life for which failure is not an option. Lady Saw is one of them. Her uninterrupted reign as the top female dancehall artist for the past twenty years is proof of this. She achieved this through sheer persistence and hard work. Moreover, she delivers when required and makes intelligent decisions.

The country girl from Galina, St Mary is a living vindication of the rural work ethic. Her journey began at the age of fifteen when sound systems like Romantics would play in the town square. Marion would start to introduce herself to the village crowd. First oriented as a singer from her upbringing, while attending services in The Seventh Day Adventist Church, she emulated the style of dancehall icon Tenor Saw, and was known at first as Female Saw.

Legend has it, that she came to Kingston on the back of a sound truck, which might be more folklore than fact. But surely she came to the city in the mid-80s in a musical environment that was hostile and not at all fit for a "lady".

Settling in the Kingston 13 area, she sought employment in the sweatshops of the Kingston Free Zone and was hired as a seamstress. In those days she worked long shifts in the factory to make ends meet. After work she moved around the city, making links with whomever she could to gain entry into the music industry.

Her efforts led her to an in-house producer at Castro Brown's **New Name Music**, Sagittarius Band's bass player Derrick Barnett. Barnett was the first to work with her on a serious level. The time at **New Name** was valuable in gaining studio experience, but it was not until meeting Garfield "Sampalue" Phillips of **Diamond Rush Records** that her big break came. Phillips, with whom it was rumored that Saw was also romantically involved, seemed to have provided the fodder for her first set of big hits.

In 1993 the song *Stab Out Di Meat* shocked an audience not used to hearing such sexually explicit talk from a woman. It scored big in the era of slackness, with its lyrics urging her partner to engage in rough sex. Another underground hit, *If Him Lef* boasted that her vagina was a trophy. With these songs she excavated a new kind of Jamaican female: one that was more aggressive in their pursuit of the opposite sex.

Her first number one record came in the summer of that same year. Probably inspired by drama in the relationship with her producer, who was also involved with another woman, the song resonated with the female public. *Send A Miracle* was her prayer for "a good man" and one that was not already taken. The single was her first song appropriate for airplay and made her into a household name.

Her rise also coincided with that of two other future legends of the dancehall: Bounty Killer and Beenie Man. All three became a bulwark of the new school of dancehall.

This period of music was marked by an intensification of rivalry between artists with no space left for ones with finer qualities. Saw, who often times in her youthful years suffered from the sting of gender confusion, been mistakenly taken for a boy, in the crucible of the rough and tumble world of entertainment, and operated like one. She quickly realized that there was no sophistry associated with the career of being a dancehall artist and that she had to match the crassness and naked aggression of her male counterparts in order to compete.

There were other female DJs like the pioneer Sister Nancy, as well as popular ones who came before like Lady G, but after Saw's arrival it was clear that she was cut from a different cloth. It was evident that her ability as a toaster was way above the average female. As a live performer her risqué and edgy act made her into a top class entertainer. Her career moves were calculated and her business acumen on point.

She quickly established a business relationship with reggae giant, US based, **VP Records**. The label released her 1994 debut album *Lover Girl* and all subsequent ones *Give Me A Reason* (96), *Passion* (97), *Raw the Best Of Lady Saw ,99Ways*

(98), and *Striptease* (2004) for the next decade and a half, while the artist stayed on top of the game. Her swan song album for the label, the aptly titled *Walk Out* came in 2007. Her string of hit singles includes *Sweet For My Sweet*, *Sycamore Tree*, *Healing* (featuring Beenie Man), *I've Got Your Man* and, the Dave Kelly produced, *Man A Di Least*.

Lady Saw ascended to a hill top that was inhabited by other top dancehall stars that were all men, while building a loyal fan-base both at home and abroad. Becoming one of the most sought after reggae stars, she have toured the globe and copped features on records with international acts. Earning for herself a gold disc for *Smile* with pop singer Vitamin C and going triple platinum on No Doubt's US top 5 single, *Underneath It All*. Also notable is *Since I Met You Baby*, with UK superstars UB40. There is also no question that her success had an influence on Caribbean born superstars: Barbados's Rihanna and Trinidad's Nicky Minaj.

For her however, success has been a bittersweet experience. A downside to her dominance is envy on the part of her female peers. Their inability to dethrone her led some of them to resort to personal attacks. One example is in making the most of the public knowledge of her miscarriages, which have robbed her of motherhood in the biological sense. Sadly she had to settle for adopting. Her other misgivings are maybe the private pain of not being able to claim the status of being, in the traditional sense, a role model for young girls. Her professional persona displayed through her records has pandered to the worse attributes associated with women such as promiscuous behavior, bitchiness, flirtatiousness and man-stealing. This was made more evident with a vulgar tracing match passed off as a musical clash between herself and Macka Diamond at a 2013 Sting concert.

Based on her level of talent, she is capable of much more than what she has offered. A lack of personal courage threatens her legacy. The international collaborations present another side that should have been developed. Also her gospel and country songs on some of her albums shed light on a range and depth never fully explored. Success, it seems, trapped her in a golden cage with her fans holding her hostage.

For better or for worse, she played the game by her own rules. Her numerous interviews, notwithstanding her colorful repertoire, reveal an intelligent woman who is in control and knows exactly what she is after.

Her confidence is the thing that sets her apart. Even as other female stars such as Cecile, Tanya Stephens, Spice and Macka Diamond came and made their own space they never posed a serious threat.

There is no official Queen of Reggae, but there *is* a Queen of Dancehall. This title is undisputedly Lady Saw's. There is no question that there has not been anyone the likes of her. She is the standard, in terms of durability, by which all other female DJs will be measured.

34. Sizzla

Christened: Miguel Collins
Born: April 17, 1975

The Real Sizzla?

Here is an artist so talented, so original and so prolific, yet still, so undisciplined, so complex, and enigmatic.

The artist known as Sizzla could have easily landed higher on this survey, instead he is maybe considered as one of reggae's biggest disappointments. If based on talent alone he would surely be top ten. Based on unfulfilled potential, he would top that list as well.

Born in Scotts Hall, St Mary and raised in various parts of Kingston he settled in the semi-rural ghetto of August Town. Miguel was a bright student who attended Seaward All Age and Dunoon Technical High. The gifted scholar is rumored to have passed eight subjects in the Caribbean Examination Council (CXC), which would make him exceptional in a field where most of his contemporaries rarely excel beyond a secondary level education.

His story is a tale of the two Sizzlas. One documents a young star that remade the landscape of roots-reggae mixed with dancehall that has come to be known by Europeans as New Roots. The other reveals a troubled and confused person reveling in the worst excesses of mediocrity. On top of this is also a litany of bad behavior and allegations of gang involvement.

But let's start with the good part.

In 1997 blaring through the speakers of your

radio was a song that sounded like it came straight from the motherland. The song was called *Black Woman and Child*. It was not lover's rock, nor was it dancehall. The artist was not toasting, nor was he singing and he did not sound like the typical Jamaican artist. This was Sizzla.

A few years before, the young "ras" was in school uniform and sweating around the Matilda's corner-based, Caveman Hi Fi. Under the tutelage of talent scout Homer Harris, Collins was introduced to Dean Fraser who, in turn, put the aspirant on to Phillip "Fattis" Burrell.

Burrell, a tall surly Rastafarian ran the **X-Terminator** label, renowned for his authoritarian style and rough street reputation. Fattis was just what the artist needed, as even at this entry level Sizzla was already a handful. At the time, the label was home to Luciano, the biggest roots singer. The young Miguel started to record for it and put to work on the road as an opening act.

His debut album for Burrell was released before he came to the public's attention. The 1995 *Burning Up* (**X-Terminator/ Ras Records**) revealed an artist that was yet to find his own sound, and most of the cuts bore an uncanny similarity to the vocals of dancehall star Terror

Fabulous.

However, the chemistry between Sizzla and another veteran producer Bobby "Digital" Dixon proved to be the winning formula, resulting in the breakout single *Black Woman and Child*. The single was also the title track of Sizzla's first successful album. This was an artist who emerged as a true original. Here was a trendsetter, with a style melodically and irresistibly refreshing to lead a new wave of young cultural lions that was unprecedented since the advent of roots reggae in the 70s.

The year 1997 partially belonged to Sizzla and was a good year for other emerging talent such as Sean Paul and Mr. Vegas. *The Black Woman and Child* album was a masterpiece. The artwork on the front cover cleverly had an illustration of the mother and child depiction inserted into the image of Africa, symbolically declaring the continent as the mother of all civilizations. The individual cuts all became favorites both on radio and on the street. Hits like *Guide Over Us*, *Give Them A Ride*, *One A Way* and *Love Devine* were instant classics.

Burrell, Sizzla's manager wasted no time in capitalizing on his newfound success by releasing an equally potent album in the same year, *Praise Ye Jah*, on his own label distributed by UK based **Jet Star**. No one knows for sure if the artist was a workaholic or a workhorse, but he kept up an incredulous recording schedule, which yielded both the *Good Ways* (**Digital B**), and *The Freedom Cry* (**VP**) albums in 1998. Also in 1998 were indications that Sizzla's handlers were not being prudent with his career, since within this twelve-month period there was also two more discs on the market *Kolonji* (**X-Terminator**) and *Reggae Max* (**Jet Star**), with tracks from all his previous releases and a splatter of a few new cuts.

Meanwhile on the streets of Kingston, as well as in the nooks and crannies of rural Jamaica, Sizzla was responsible for a seismic shift in the cultural landscape. Attracting a rabid following amongst the youth and leading to an unusual amount of new converts to Rastafarianism not seen since the days of Bob Marley, et al. Young dreads were springing up all over, painting his image on community walls and adorning fences and sidewalks in red green and gold – the colors of the Ethiopian flag. This scenery was not complete without CD players propped up against zinc fences and the sound of the artist's albums in continuous rotation.

This was happening not because Sizzla was a normal type entertainer, but because his radically articulate message began to punctuate the consciousness of the downtrodden Jamaican youth. He in this period was taken seriously and been looked upon as a sort of guru with the power to influence public opinion and enough charisma to attract followers beyond musical parameters.

This burden may have been too much for the twenty something Sizzla to carry. Buoyed on by initial success and, apparently lacking the maturity to temper his message, he was offending people left and right. A lot of his material was laced with ranting, going as far as naming names of high officials and uttering what many religious people in a heavily Christian Jamaican society, considered to be blasphemous statements in reference to Jesus Christ.

In the constituency that mattered to him the most though, which was amongst the younger segment of the population, he was still a folk hero and sat at the very top of the pile. His anti-establishment rhetoric was considered courageous and, for promoters, the artist who subscribed to the most radical faction of Rastafarians called Bobo Ashanti was a hot ticket.

But at the height of his popularity in the late 90s, Sizzla headlined on the premier music festival in Jamaica, Reggae Sumfest. During his set, he proceeded to offend many, including sponsors of the event with an unprofessional and coarse display. This led to him being subsequently blacklisted and passed over by many large promoters staging major events with heavy reliance on sponsorship dollars. His career suffered and went into a brief lull.

That was the first of the two faces of Sizzla.

The second face is likened to Jekyll, which lurked inside of Mr. Hyde. It started with a song laddered with expletives called *Pump Up*. In the **Troytan** produced single, same riddim as Sean Paul's *Gimme Di Light*, Sizzla undid the positive message of his breakthrough *Black Woman and Child*. On this song he demeaned women with graphic descriptions of the vagina and referencing how forcefully he was going to *"take her"* almost sounding like an endorsement of rape. Even though he continued to record at an alarming pace and releasing albums (over fifty), still delivering cultural ditties, he went from bad to worse.

Spiraling out of control he then got into fracas with other artists and fell into the mob mentality releasing new material: *Gi Dem* and *Get To The Point,* slack tunes and gun songs. Declarations like these were tolerated coming from hardcore DJs, but not from Sizzla, the man being hailed as reggae's next great hope.

Later albums like *Black History* and *Royal Son of Ethiopia* contained many songs worthy of the artist's past glory but Sizzla, by this time had become too big and unruly even for a man of Fattis's reputation, and was in full hustler mode recording for anybody with a fist full of cash.

Bewildered by his inconsistency as a cultural beacon, his international fans abandoned him for a resurgent Capleton and the original fire Bobo, Anthony B. Sizzla's local following in spite of the critics mainly remained intact .

But an artist of Sizzla's caliber does not go down for the count that easily, and for a few more years regained his footing with the Bobby Dixon produced 2002's *The Real Thing* (**VP**). This collection returned Sizzla to the peak and contained massive hits, *Just One Of Those Days*, *Thank You Mamma*, *Woman I Need You* and *Solid As A Rock*. Sizzla was again the man.

This momentum carried over into the brilliant

Rise To The Occasion album, produced by Donavan "Don Corleon" Bennett. The success of these two albums sparked a new found creativity within Sizzla and he proceeded to unleash material that rivaled anything and everything that was being offered by his peers.

The years 2003 and 2004 saw Sizzla's records dominating dances, clubs, bars and strip joints. The artist delivered culture, gun tunes, alternative songs and hardcore slackness as well. He ceased to be the leader of the cultural army. He became Sizzla- the pop star.

On another front a major weakness that plagued him throughout his career was poor stage presentation. He often times sang off key with no backing vocals and showed no real improvement as the years passed. In addition, his return to top form worsened his attitude and coarse mannerisms to the point of disrespecting the backing musicians during some of his live appearances.

After constructing a huge house in his community of August Town equipped with his own studio called Judgment Yard he established his own label **Kolonji Records**. Judgement Yard was more than a place to make music but also a haven for unsavory characters. His career and personal life, in a few short years after the success of the *Real Thing* album, would descend into chaos.

What followed were several scrapes with law enforcement and him being detained in relation to shootings in his area. He was also banned in many countries for his alleged homophobic lyrics. Other incidents were him engaging in violent confrontation with fellow artists and having one of his residences torched, allegedly by his enemies. On top of it all he had his US visa cancelled, apparently for amassing so much damning connections to so-called criminal elements. Just like the Biblical Samson, Sizzla's powers seemed to have abandoned him.

But his legacy remains strong owing to the fact that he possesses one of the largest cadres of hits of any artist in recent times. His influence is global with artists far and wide emulating him. New stars like I Octane, Bugle, Pressure (St Croix), Natural Black (Guyana), Lyricson (Benin) and Gentleman (Germany).

His massive catalog of hits ensures that he will not be forgotten and still brings him steady work. Many have prayed that he would still steady his hand and become one of the greats of reggae but at this point this seems to be just a distant hope.

Sizzla's state of affairs proves that talent alone is not enough. The true legends of the genre were able to gather the other pieces of the puzzle: strong management, consistency in quality, focus, good public relations and being driven by a higher purpose beyond personal popularity.

All is not lost, as he is still a young man and only time will tell. But for now his hopeful fans keep asking.

When will the real Sizzla stand up?

33. Bounty Killer

Christened: Rodney Pryce
Born: June 12, 1972

The Warlord

The third most influential dancehall DJ, bettered only by Shabba Ranks and Buju Banton, is Bounty Killer. He looms large over a scene he has dominated for close to two decades, and is the man responsible for mentoring and steering a set of artists who have replaced him at the top.

In the beginning, projecting the same hardcore credentials of his predecessors, Bounty sounded much like Shabba Ranks, but showed only little of what his voice was really capable of. After his first hit, 1992's *Coppershot*, it was evident that this new-find had an extensive vocal range and, in one phrase, could switch from a deep baritone to a high tenor.

From this point on, he was able to quickly establish his own sound, in the process becoming the king of Jamaican catch phrases. He made this work by twisting the English language to his own benefit: turning *yes yes* to *yea yeh* and *hello* to *yallo gallo*. Other popular taglines identified with the dancehall star are: "*lord ha mercy*", "*people ded*" and "*cross, angry and miserable*".

Pryce was born and raised in Seaview Gardens, a violent ghetto five miles outside of downtown Kingston. Seaview is hemmed in by other equally dangerous neighborhoods such as Riverton City and Waterhouse. Close by is also the city dump.

His mother was a travelling street vendor and, the young Pryce, in between attending school, also peddled newspapers and small household items to supplement the family's income. He proved himself to be a natural hustler who was very industrious. From the outset he was determined to lift himself and his family out of poverty. On realizing his musical talent, he seized all opportunities with an uncommon passion.

Observing the phenomenal success of Shabba Ranks who at one point briefly made Seaview his home, Pryce interned on several sound systems. The sound systems provided a solid training ground for many Jamaican stars pre-nineties, before the era of the specials dawned. Before then, aspiring DJs had to show their mettle by working live on the discos.

Pryce's appetite for the game led him to the famous studios of **King Jammy**, located in Waterhouse. After much hankering around, he was finally noticed by the brother of King Jammy, Uncle T. This resulted in the recording of *Coppershot*. It became, at least in the dancehall, a breakout hit during the Christmas of 1992. He followed with other songs that also glorified his violent surroundings, such as *Spy Fi Die*, *New Gun* and *Lodge*.

Bounty's rise fatefully coincided with the emergence of another DJ, a child prodigy, known as Beenie Man. Both were talented and extremely ambitious. Whether by coincidence or design, they set their sights on each other and became sworn enemies. There have been rivalries in Jamaica's musical history from as a far back as the feud between Sir Coxsone and Duke Reid, but the one that would soon develop between Bounty and Beenie would become legendary in its magnitude and scope, transfixing both the industry and fandom for more than a decade. Starting from 1993 and erupting into all-out war by 1995, both protagonists used it to establish hegemony over the dancehall.

In the meantime *Coppershot*, Killa's first hit, only gave him a presence in the dancehall. The 1993 hit *Intimate Woman*, a duet with singer Anthony Red Rose of *Tempo* fame, was radio friendly. It helped to ease Killa into the mainstream. Other singles like *Cellular Phone* and *Book Book Book* broadened his appeal. But Killa's audience, whom he fed on a staple of gunman tunes, would largely remain downtown and predominantly male.

While his archrival Beenie Man dubbed himself *"the girl's dem suga"*, Bounty wore the emblem of the *Warlord*, sort of The Jamaican Rolling Stones as opposed to the Beatles. As he held sway, he further established his credentials with ghetto anthems such as *Momma Is Not In A Good Mood* and *Poor People Fed Up*, adding another alias:"*The Poor Peoples Governor*".

To further distance himself from Beenie Man, a rather flamboyant character, he cultivated an image that was street wise and grimy. His attire characteristically was always all black and his promo pictures would always show him looking menacingly evil. He backed this up with catchwords that always referenced violence. Talk like "*bullet*", "*connect*", "*boung bang*" and celebrating morbidity with his opening line on entering the stage at his concerts "*people ded*". To top this off he behaved in an anti-social manner towards his fans, never smiling or signing autographs, which ironically made them love him even more.

At concerts Killa abused the sound engineers, balking at them to "*tun up the mike*" and refusing to perform unless the lights were turned off. At his peak, he had the most fanatical followers who went into frenzies whenever he took to the stage, and even knew his songs word for word.

The infamous Sting concerts, built over the years on artist rivalry, would prove the ultimate battleground for Beenie and Bounty. At this annual event, a years' worth of recorded works was put to the test in order to crown a champion. Year after year both artists became staples at Sting, while the spectacle became the most anticipated on the calendar. Suffice it to say, Beenie Man steadily gained an edge through bigger hits and a more polished stage act.

After several years in the spotlight, Killa met an American, a white street hustler and frequent visitor to Kingston known as Johnny Wonder. The foreigner became star struck by the artist, while at the same time spotting an opportunity to make some money off him. This association led to Johnny parlaying their relationship and his music biz connections into getting Bounty a recording contract in the US with **TVT Records**, distributed by Jimmy Iovine's **Interscope.** The resulting album, 1997s *My Xperience*, marked a creative and commercial milestone for the artist. It went on to move upwards of 250,000 units, a remarkable achievement for an underground act.

Around this same time the artist teamed up with dancehall wunderkind producer Dave Kelly, who gave Killa two monster hits in the form of *Look Into My Eyes* and *Anytime*. This period was when the Killa truly arrived as a certified dancehall megastar, at the cusp of international stardom.

Aiming for the US charts he combined his efforts with stars of the hip hop world, like The Fugees, Ghostface Killa, and Busta Rhymes. This led to several of his songs showing up on the Billboard charts. *The Next Millennium* album did not fare as well as its predecessor, for reasons that would soon become apparent.

According to insiders, the artist imploded under the duress of operating within the confines of the major label structure. They observed a display of arrogance and lack of discipline by not being punctual for anything. His refusal to tour virgin territories in front of meager crowds, robbed him of a chance for gaining new fans. This scenario was ripe in the absence of proper management, which Pryce did not have since departing from Clifton Dillon in the early 90s. As a result of this he was subsequently dropped by **TVT**.

Then as if lightning couldn't strike twice, it did. In the year 2000, Bounty was afforded another chance for acceptance beyond his domestic base when super producers Sly and Robbie summoned him for a feature on No

Doubt's *Hey Baby* single. The record became a global smash going platinum and winning a Grammy.

But true to himself, he again dropped the ball when his rival Beenie Man goaded him into a row about his appearance in the *Hey Baby* video. Bounty bit the bait. In it was a scene with No Doubt's drummer, Adrian Young, frolicking in the nude. Bounty, for his participation in it, according to Beenie Man and his camp, was endorsing homosexuality. Fearing a backlash from his core supporters he reacted by turning on No Doubt. He started to bad mouth the group, implying that he was tricked into doing the video and signaling a refusal to perform the song with them. After this, major labels would not touch him with a long pole and he would have to hereafter settle for simply being a local star.

Turning inward to the domestic market he would continue in his ways of keeping himself relevant through rivalries with not only Beenie Man, but with any artist he set his sights on.

In a Machiavellian bubble of his own existence, Killa frequently teamed up with artists and producers who would give him much-needed hits, then turning on them when perceived that they were no longer useful. Bounty as many in the industry came to realize had an aversion to sharing the spotlight. This included sharing it with his protégés who would move on to become famous such as Elephant Man, Vybz Kartel and Mavado. But in his penchant for self-promotion, was always quick to highlight his contribution to their success. You see, he had no problem with them becoming famous only with the prospect of them becoming more so than himself.

Nevertheless, through his consistency for more than a decade and a half of numerous number one records, legendary performances, and his endorsement of up and coming talent, he indeed became a *kingmaker*. Killa has matured into a sort of elder statesman of the dancehall, becoming a favorite on TV talk shows and doling out advice to aspiring artists.

He even achieved the ultimate prize of fame: celebrity status. But even this comes with a steep price. It guarantees that his many controversies and brushes with the law have been well documented in the local tabloids.

Arrested a number of times for abusing his baby mothers and girlfriends and violating obscenity laws at live shows have provided the press with much needed stories. Additionally, over the years he has met stiff opposition from gay rights groups for his anti-gay stance and, in recent times, have battled with the Jamaican government for allegedly not paying taxes. His notoriety and legal troubles may also have influenced the US State Department's decision to cancel his visa, severely affecting his ability to earn a living.

His lasting legacy is his mentoring and helping to create the other generation of stars that are now dominating a moribund dancehall scene.

Two of his so-called sons, Vybz Kartel and Mavado, would pick up where he and Beenie Man left off, plunging dancehall into it most disgusting phase.

He is undoubtedly one of the most naturally gifted DJs in the nation's history but his story; much like a lot of his peers is one of missed opportunities and severely unfulfilled potential.

32. Beenie Man

Christened: Anthony Davis
Born: August 22, 1973

The Entertainer

Beenie Man became huge for two reasons: by out working his competitors and shameless self-promotion. In the mid-2000s, in a Napoleonic move, he crowned himself the *King of the Dancehall,* and up to this day, still proclaims that it is so.

A child prodigy born in the Waterhouse section of Kingston, he claims to have started out at age five, when in fact he recorded his first album by age eleven for producer Bunny "Striker" Lee. Beenie's first single was *Too Fancy* for Henry Lawes, though in these early years he did not stand out in any particular way and was being upstaged by other young DJs such as Little Harry and Risto Benjie.

He gained invaluable experience toasting in Kingston dancehalls and from watching top line DJs such as Josey Wales, Brigadier Jerry and Burru Banton. He jumped into the arena as a kid and exhibited a drive and determination that, over the years, proved to be unmatched amongst his peers.

His bravado brought him to a pivotal moment in life when in 1991; the eighteen year old pushed his way onto the stage at the National Stadium. The crowd was about forty thousand strong and the occasion was the visit of the newly liberated South African freedom fighter Nelson Mandela. Frightened by the immense crowd, eager to please but overwhelmed by the occasion, the artist drew a lyric inappropriate for the historical gathering and was embarrassingly booed by the whole nation. The freestyle piece *Hey Green Arm*, a rip off of Pincher's *Bandelero* became the humiliation known in local folklore as *The*

Mandella Boo. It proved though that Beenie Man was not afraid of the big moment, and underneath possessed nerves of steel. In two short years after the infamous incident he would begin to redeem himself.

In 1993 he hit with the single *Wicked Man* and so began an ascent that would put him at the very peak. His association with future manager Patrick Roberts of the Shocking Vibes label dated back, as early as 1988. But five years later the relationship would blossom into hit singles and firm management. Numbers such as *Tear off Mi Garment*, *Modeling* and *Old Dawg* established him as one of the fastest rising artists.

By 1994 he won the title of *DJ of the Year* and started to lodge salvos at the head of the other top dog, namely Bounty Killer, who regarded Beenie Man as a threat to his own dominance. A defining trait that Beenie Man possessed was a talent for mimicking other artists, including his nemesis. This chameleon-like skill would become a primary weapon that he would employ to stay on top of an ever-changing musical landscape.

After a legendary clash between himself and Bounty at Sting 1995, so began a long and bitter rivalry between the two. In a titanic-like battle, they locked the gate on the rest of the fraternity. While Bounty touted the image of the rebel, Beenie dubbed himself *"the girls dem sugar"*, aiming straight for the female audience, which gave him a distinct advantage in this two-man race.

Under the guidance of Patrick Roberts, the artist thrived and became flamboyant in his choice of stage wear, even to the point of inviting criticism of sexual ambiguity. This was yet another irony as, along with a slew of girl tune hits, *Nuff Gal* and *Slam*, were also songs that were staunchly anti-gay.

Beenie Man racked up numerous number one songs locally, during the mid-90s. He cracked the international market in 1997 with the Jeremy Harding, produced *Who Am I* (more popularly called *Zim Zima*). The **VP Records** release containing the single, the album *Many Moods of Moses*, was a commercial and critical success, becoming one of the best-selling reggae albums for an indie label. This earned the artist several awards, including the ASCAP Reggae Songwriter of the Year in 1998.

The follow up to *Many Moods* 1999s *The Doctor*, on **Island Jamaica**, was a feeble attempt to capitalize on the momentum gained. On it were cuts like *Tell Me* (featuring Angie Martinez) and *Pride and Joy* (with Jon B), obvious attempts to cross over into the R&B market that backfired. The album however because of the collaborations helped to enhance his international profile and at least kept him hot in the clubs and the dancehall.

Around this time reggae-pop star Shaggy was having far greater success, and his 1995 *Bombastic* album on **Virgin Records** was a big seller. When Shaggy's next release for the label fell flat on its face, he was dropped from the labels roster. **Virgin** then decided to place their bets on Beenie Man, since he was dancehall's biggest star at the time.

The **Virgin** years saw the release of three albums: *Art and Life* (2000), *Tropical Storm* (2004) and *Undisputed* (2006). Beenie Man's tenure exposed all the limitations of the artist and his management.

Beenie Man, being Shocking Vibe's star act, in a camp of lesser names, was the main breadwinner. Increasingly, he became a law unto himself. When the artist signed to a major international label, his management was unable to reign in his appetite for engaging in confrontation with other local entertainers. This proved a distraction, along with a habit to write mostly mediocre songs that were merely pleasing his local fans, but unable to compete on an international level. One member of Beenie Man's backing band at the time remarked that the artist acts as if "he's God".

Instead of assembling a team of writers and musicians who could take the artist in a new direction, his management team stuck with the old formula of recycling old hits. Subsequently, all the albums were poor sellers. Even a duet with Janet Jackson, *Feel It Boy*, and another, *Girls Dem Sugar*, featuring Mya went nowhere.

Beenie Man's saving grace over the years has been his frenetic work pace and the indisputable fact that, as a live performer, his contemporaries cannot challenge him. He has proved himself not as a serious artist out to make a statement, but as an entertainer of the first order. It is as a performer that his genius lies.

Though he has attained international recognition, international stardom has somewhat eluded him because of the absence of a certified mega hit.

Nevertheless he has continued on his way, being one of the most consistent and prolific hit makers in the history of the Jamaican dancehall, racking up over one hundred number one singles. His longevity and a sustained high profile presence solidify his legend and celebrity status.

Beenie Man the workaholic continues to score hits and headline major concerts, remaining relevant throughout. Apart from his obvious love for his craft there is another explanation why he works so hard. It is because his numerous hits are not musically significant and have little publishing value.

In 2006, after 22 years, he severed ties with his longtime manager Patrick Roberts and his company Shocking Vibes. Since then he seemed to have somewhat lost his way. Moreover, his self-proclaimed title as *King of The Dancehall* rings a bit hollow, as Yellowman is widely regarded to be the holder of that crown.

Many of his off stage antics also makes him look like a publicity hound, trapped within his own fame, as he continues to feed the media with the many twists and turns in his life. His personal drama contains his time dating dancehall queen Carlene and getting married to Bounty Killer's ex-girlfriend D'Angel.

A long running feud with members of the gay community was somewhat laid to rest with a very public apology. But as far as entertainers go, *no news is bad news.* And there seems to be a kind of method to the madness that has worked in his favor at the end of it all.

From where he came, Beenie Man's career is still remarkable for its endurance. What it has lacked in musical substance has already been over compensated for by consistent hits, a likable personality and personal passion for his craft. Being on top of the game for close to two decades is no ordinary feat and places him in an elite group of Jamaican artists.

31. Sister Nancy

Christened: Ophlin Russell
Born: January 2, 1962

Female Pioneer

The history of Jamaican music has many turning points and pivotal moments. One of these game changing occurrences is the arrival of Sister Nancy. She was the first female DJ of prominence, which makes her a pioneer.

Another female toaster, Muma Lisa, came out a few years before her, but it was Sister Nancy who broke through the proverbial male glass ceiling becoming a top artist in her own right, and along the way winning the respect of her male peers. Another consideration that gives her a distinct edge over Lisa is that Lisa's fame came largely through being a minor talent who played sidekick in a partnership with Nigga Kojak, a DJ that was briefly in vogue from the late 70s into the early 80s.

Sister Nancy came out of a large family of fifteen siblings. One of them was Robert Russell, otherwise known as Brigadier Jerry. He was probably her main influence and the catalyst for her foray into the rough entertainment world. She cut her teeth on the **Stereophonic** sound system, holding her own in the company of the highly respected General Echo. She then burst into full stride alongside her brother on **Jahlove Music**.

Producer Winston Riley made the tentative move of recording her from as early as 1980, the result being the single *Papa Dean*, though he did not have the courage to release it until the following year. A confident Nancy however found a home on the producer's **Techniques** label, on which she had a number of hits: *One Two, Transport Connection* and the hugely popular *Bam Bam*.

Her style was typical of the time, which was a slow pedestrian like flow over old Studio One riddims. She toasted in the same pattern as the other popular emcees; a sound reminiscent of U-Roy's but, to her credit, she never attempted to sound like anyone. Instead, she used her natural tone which came across as distinctly feminine.

Being the younger sister of Brigadier Jerry, who at the time was the most cultural of all the artists, she was keen on staying clear of the increasing tide of slackness that was the main staple for most of her colleagues. The time of her ascent was not one that was remarkable for lyrical excellence across the board and Nancy did not raise the bar either. Nevertheless, the basic fact that a woman could command the attention she got was a milestone in itself.

As her career took off she achieved a number of firsts: first female DJ to tour internationally, making her debut stand in London at the Brixton Academy, first female DJ to release an album, *One Two* in 1982 and the first female DJ to perform on the legendary *Reggae Sunsplash Concert*.

In this era she stood as the lone representative of her gender, encircled by all the top artists of the day like Josie Wales, Yellowman, Charlie Chaplin, Jah Thomas, Peter Metro and Welton Irie. In 1982 she also copped the best Female DJ Award from **Rockers** magazine.

After her historic breakthrough, doors were opened for the entry of others in the mid to late 80s like Sister Charmaine, Lady Ann and Lady G. Because of this, Nancy has come to be addressed more appropriately as *"Muma Nancy"*. No one owes Nancy more gratitude than Marion Hall, aka Lady Saw, who would become the most successful female DJ ever. Others who walked the pathway cleared by the pioneering exploits of Nancy are, Angie Angel, Macka Diamond, Shelly Thundah, Lady Patra and her closest resemblance musically speaking, Sister Carol.

With the baton passed to a new generation of female DJs, she migrated to the US in 1996 and still did the occasional recording. She took a job in a bank in New Jersey and devoted the bulk of her time to family life.

Still she makes time in between to perform when the calls come in. This author had the pleasure of witnessing one such performance in Philadelphia in 2006. Lady Saw headlined, on a bill that also included Lady Ann, Sister Charmaine and Spice. Sister, no, Muma Nancy stole the show and was awesome by delivering a set that could not be matched by her fraternal daughters.

30. Super Cat

Christened: William Maragh
Born: June 25, 1963

Wild Apache

Super Cat's impact on Jamaican music is huge. His style of toasting was adopted by a younger group of artists, and has proven to be the most lucrative of Jamaica's cultural exports.

This specific sound of his, he acquired naturally, by virtue of his ethnicity. And those who didn't quite fit in with what was typical of the dancehall, in him, found an answer to their dilemma.

His mother is a Negro woman and his father is

a second generation East Indian, descending from indentured laborers, who came to Jamaica in the early 1900s. Cat's lyrics are definitely Kingston but his voice is unmistakably Bombay. He is the first and the only one of note, with his ethnic makeup, to dominate a business that was firmly locked down by the ancestors of West African slaves.

The young Maragh started his journey from deep in the bowels of the rough Kingston neighborhood known as Cockburn Pen, where a small group of East Indians coexisted and blended into the Negro majority.

The DJ adapted well to his surroundings and was known as a rude boy, engaging in petty criminality – hence the *Wild Apache* moniker that would stick with him throughout his career. This would benefit him in one way, as the music scene in Jamaica was not for cowards or momma boys.

Fortunately, his passion for music was stronger than his criminal inclinations, and as a teenager he hung around sound systems like **Soul Imperial**. After linking up with another Cockburn Pen artist by the name of Early B, Maragh went on to make a name on titan sounds like **Kilimanjaro**. After serving a decade long apprenticeship by toasting on various sounds systems, his first single *Mr. Walker* was released by producer Winston Riley in 1981.

His big breakthrough came three years later with 1984s *Boops* (**Techniques**), a song that stayed at number one for weeks and set off a throve of reply *"Boopsie"* records by almost every artist at the time. Another single *Wild Apache* was groundbreaking. The song was a one liner coupled with Yankee style scratching that set the clubs ablaze both in Jamaica and the US.

Super Cat wasted little time, being prolific throughout the rest of the 80s. The parade of hits on all the hottest riddims for producers like Steelie and Cleevie, Winston Riley, George Phang and Tony Kelly put him in an elite class of dancehall DJs who ruled the airwaves. Smashes like *Nuff Man A Dead, Mud Up, Animal Party, Old Veteran, Come Down* and *Under Pressure* showed off his vocal dexterity, versatility and a knack for scoring with almost any topic from his lyrical arsenal. His unique voice delivered compositions with catchy intros that grabbed the listener's attention immediately.

1981 saw a US-friendly government coming into power on the island. This' throughout the decade, made possible increased emigration by Jamaicans mainly to the east coast of the United States. Big cities especially New York City was flushed with Jamaican immigrants hungry for their native music. This enabled, Super Cat amongst other top stars at the time like Shabba Ranks, Ninja Man, and Cutty Ranks, to be in demand for live performances and to start to expand their fan base beyond Jamaica.

Cat made the most of this demand by spending most of his time in New York. While there he entered into a managerial relationship with Jamaican impresario Robert Livingston, who later went on to greater achievements with Shaggy.

Livingston's connections allowed Cat to make progress in the US market. A major result was him signing with **Columbia Records** in 1992. For **Columbia** came the albums *Don Dada, The Good The Bad The Ugly and The Crazy* (featuring his friends Nicodemus and Junior Demus and Cat's younger brother Junior Cat) (94) and *The Struggle Continues* (95). Singles off these discs: *Girlstown, Dem Nuh Worry We* and *Ghetto Red Hot* were hugely popular in the underground, but failed to crack the mainstream.

The poor sales of his albums were

disappointing and there was plenty of blame being thrown around. This state of affairs ended up in arguments between himself and his manager. The rupturing of this important relationship led to an early implosion in a promising international career.

Super Cats lack of international appeal, it could be argued also stems mainly from his freestyle approach to recording that came across like a sound system performance. This along with a perennial thug disposition and his heavy use of dialect not easily understood by non-Jamaicans was of no help either. His street upbringing manifested by confrontational behavior, made Maragh come across as being overly antisocial.

Cat a colorful character, added to his woes with a fair amount of near career killing controversies. Incidents like threatening to shoot into the audience at a Sting 1991 concert while clashing with Ninja Man, being implicated in the homicide case of dancehall singer Nitty Gritty and a scuffle with New York City police officers at an off track betting establishment, have contributed to his tainted image.

Super Cats most enduring legacy to Jamaican music history is that apart from staking out his own territory as one of the "baddest" DJs to ever come out of the island, he has influenced a specific set of aspiring artists. These are children of privilege, who found in him a sound that they could use as a ladder to chart their own ascent. Artists from the Jamaican middle class such as Sean Paul, Junior Gong, and Don Yute. Also several foreign artists the likes of Bermuda's Collie Budz and Britain's Apache Indian have appropriated his sound as their own.

Super Cat would have probably become much bigger by being more malleable in the hands of his handlers and with a toning down on the gangster lifestyle, but he is what he is and still remains "The Wild Apache".

29. Grace Jones

Christened: Grace Jones
Born: May 19, 1948

The Maverick

Jones established herself as a pop icon by being a trailblazer and a maverick.

Tall, jet black and rail thin, she parlayed what would seem to be physically disadvantageous features into her greatest assets. Somewhere in her stream of consciousness she must have come to the conclusion that, *I look different so why not celebrate it.* Essentially, she did just that by championing the outrageous, both in dress and mannerism.

Make no mistake though, behind the fanfare is someone with real God-given talents, possessing a two-octave range voice, naturally photogenic and innate acting skills. She is a pop star, model and actress whose work has stood the test of time.

Born in Jamaica, one half of twins with a brother Noel, she hails from the old capital of Spanish Town. Their hometown was one of the roughest; most violent places save for Kingston itself.

Her father, a minister of religion migrated to New York City taking his wife with him but left Grace in the care of her grandparents. At the age of thirteen, Grace joined them and was enrolled in middle school. In later years she completed her education at Syracuse University.

Longing to escape the confines of her religious upbringing, she then embraced the wild side with gusto. She moved to Philadelphia and got a job as a waitress but after a short stay, went back to The Big Apple. Back in New York City she began to immerse herself into the city's nightlife.

She made a lot of friends while nightclubbing some of which encouraged her to take up modeling. This she did landing her first job with the Wilhelmina Agency. Soon thereafter she joined her brother, at the time living in France, in the more open atmosphere of Paris, where her modeling career really took off. In Europe her unique look was appreciated more and her energetic approach and exotic image earned her coveted spots on the covers of the leading rags the likes of Essence, Elle, Vogue and Der Stern.

As her confidence grew, her attention turned to one of her other talents: singing, making her first records around 1974 in France. In 1975 she became a label mate of Third World superstar Bob Marley, signing to **Island Records**. The label however, did not have reggae on its mind when it came to Grace, but instead pushed her into the thriving disco market.

The 1977 album *Portfolio* was well received. Grace now back in America, became increasingly popular in this era. Her singles were hitting the charts and she became a celebrity and regular scene-stealer at the iconic nightclub, *Studio 54*. In 1979, *Jet Magazine* ran a piece touting her as a contender for the *Queen of Disco*, pitting her against Donna Summer and Gloria Gaynor.

The albums *Fame* (78) and *Muse* (79) continued in the disco mold, but *Warm Leatherette* (80) and *Nightclubbing* (81) started to exploit her Caribbean background in more obvious ways.

These album products of the infamous *Compass Point Sessions* took place at **Island's** founder Chris Blackwell's studio in the Bahamas and went in another direction, seeking a more indigenous feel. The bringing together of producer Alex Sadkin and the brilliant Jamaican drum and bass duo, Sly Dunbar and Robbie Shakespeare set the template for a kind of space age island groove that would become part of an emerging scene that the rock press called *New Wave*. Successful groups who adopted the sound ruled the 80s chief among them Blondie and Britain's Culture Club.

The reggae influence of Grace's native country was just the ingredient that was missing. The result of this change in direction was *Pull Up To The Bumper* the major hit that finally took her into the mainstream.

Grace was an artist with a dramatic flair. Her songs contained short skits and on a lot of them instead of conventional song arrangements in their place were mainly dub poetry. She also exploited her bilingual skills recording some of her material in French.

Image-wise her album covers had her displaying an androgynous look copied a little later by Annie Lennox of the *Eurythmics* who exploded on to the scene in 1983 with the mega hit *Sweet Dreams*. In the competitive world of entertainment where pretty sells, Grace topped everyone by employing shock tactics in the way she sang and in her style of dress.

Then there is her other career as an actress.

After studying theater in college, Grace acted in a few obscure films then came to the fore in major films like *Conan The Destroyer*, *Boomerang* and the Bond flick *A View To Kill*.

Her main forte though was as a musical artist. After the release of *Living My Life*, the last album due under her contract with **Island**, she worked on the highly ambitious *Slave to the Rhythm*, with producer Trevor Horn. *Slave* was a concept album that was more performance art-spoken word, rather than one filled with conventional pop songs.

A large part of her legacy has been her bold fashion sense and theatric, even risqué stage presentations. Later to be imitated and parlayed with far more success by white pop stars like another living legend, Madonna and recently Lady Gaga.

An irony of her survival is that a woman, who is a native of Jamaica, allegedly of one of the most homophobic countries on earth, has mainly stayed relevant through a devoted gay fan base.

Still active now in her sixties, releasing new music and touring, Grace Jones is in an elite company of Jamaicans who are genuinely regarded as international icons.

28. Garnett Silk

Christened: Garnett Smith
Born: April 2, 1966
Deceased: December 9, 1994.

Gone too soon

Garnett Silk is one of the iconic figures in the history of Jamaican music, remarkably so because of his mercurial rise and untimely death.

Jamaica woke up on the morning of December 10, 1994 to the incredulous news that the number one singer at the time died in, what could be considered as, the most bizarre of accidents. The 28 year old Smith had only been on top for close to three years. The nation was blind-sided by his sudden departure.

At the beginning of the 90s, Silk along with other artists from central Jamaica such as Tony Rebel, Yasus Afari and Uton Green, spearheaded a revival in roots music

Born in the parish of Manchester, he was part of a group of aspiring artists that relocated to Kingston in the late eighties, in an effort to *buss* (make it big). He made the rounds of most of the recording studios in Kingston, firstly presenting himself as a DJ under the moniker Bimbo, but to no avail. He abandoned that initial idea switching to singing and was renamed Garnett Silk by producer Wycliffe "Steelie" Bennett.

In the early years he recorded for a lot of producers, receiving no promotion whatsoever. This changed when he worked out of an Ocho Rios based outfit **Roof International**, owned by producer Courtney Cole. The single *I Can See Clearly Now*, a Johnny Nash cover (featuring dub poet and close friend Yasus Afari), released by **Roof** was the first chart hit for the singer. The resulting exposure triggered a melee of releases from producers sitting on previously recorded material.

The single *Mama Africa* (**Star Trail**) propelled him to the top. Garnett Silk with this single became the top singer while his friend Tony Rebel was enjoying his own success as a dj. Their arrival started one of those cyclical waves that came whenever the music seemed to be heading hopelessly downhill. Garnett's voice truly offered an original sound; this along with song content that was poetic and scriptural in the tradition of Bob Marley was a welcome change indeed.

Many of his earliest critics held to the opinion that he was not much of a singer but what his voice lacked in technical ability was more than compensated for by an earnest delivery and the power of emotion. The songs he was doing also scored high points for the quality of the writing. This we learnt was due to a writing partnership with childhood friend Anthony Rochester.

Silk's and Rochester's compositions were replete with Biblical verses and were an ordinary man's tonic; moreover, a sort of musical prayer, appealing for divine help against injustice and a mantra for coping with tough circumstances.

Numbers like *Bless Me, Taking Advantage*, and *Love Is the Answer* appealed to the better nature of people and elevated him beyond the status of just a reggae singer. Indeed Garnett Silk was been hailed as a new prophet.

The 1992 album *Its Growing* (**Digital B/VP**) provided a mixture of roots and culture, coupled with tender love tunes. This album is now amongst others considered a classic. *It's Growing* yielded at least five hit singles and its dominance in the period completed Garnett's ascent to the top.

The only weakness in his brief career was the fact that these brilliant songs were confined to instrumental tracks that were many times recycled and made him a local star but stifled his international potential. This however never stopped the hits and Silk only slowed down in mid-93 to rest, which stirred up many rumors in local circles, about his mental state and physical condition. One of these rumors hinted at abuse of hard drugs, though never substantiated.

The year 1994 was a pivotal one. In it the artist unleashed the hits *Love Is the Answer, Fight Back* (featuring Richie Stephens) and *Splashing Dashing*. Silk gave the best performance of his career at that years staging of Jamaica's biggest festival, Reggae Sumfest and also inked a major label deal with **Big Beat/Atlantic**. The signing was the move that should have taken him on towards international success. Tragically 1994 would also be the last year of his life

Success had made the artist very cagey and he had been exhibiting all the signs of paranoia. For some reason or the other, he believed that members of his community were plotting to rob and hurt him. So he acquired guns. On December 9th at his house, while fidgeting with one of the firearms, a bullet accidentally dislodged and struck a gas cylinder, causing it to explode.

His mom and his brothers were in another room when the house burst into flames. They all ran from the house, save for his mother who remained, trapped behind burning walls. Garnett rushed back into the house in a heroic attempt to save her. Inside as the building became overwhelmed by the inferno the artist and his mother perished.

As the news spread, a stunned nation was left to mourn.

Wondering.

Why?

27. Hortense Ellis

Christened: Hortense Ellis
Born: April 18, 1941
Deceased: October 19, 2000

Songbird

Hortense Ellis's body of work is a reminder of a bygone golden era in Jamaican music. She was an exceptional talent, in stark contrast to where the fortunes of the music have fallen today, especially as it relates to our women.

With Marcia Griffiths and say Etana being exceptions, presently there are no other female artists of prominence outside of the dancehall genre. Where are the women singers that have kept faith with the stellar sacrifices of Hortense? *(In the interest of being fair, during the 80s and 90s, there were a number of notable female singers namely Nadine Sutherland, Barbara Jones, Carlene Davis, JC Lodge, Diana King, Chevelle Franklyn and a songbird called Cynthia Schloss, though none that defined an era quite like Hortense).*

Hortense Ellis is aptly dubbed as "Jamaica's First Lady of Songs". She towered over lesser lights like Phyllis Dillion, Norma Frazer, and Merlene Webber. Ellis exhibited sheer force of talent and in the chauvinistic atmosphere of a male dominated music business, still managed to deliver memorable classics. Because of her, we now listen to those songs with pain in our hearts, yearning with nostalgia for the musical purity that has been lost over the passage of time.

Born in Trench Town, she was the daughter of a railroad worker father and a fruit vendor mother. The slightly-built Hortense started out at the age of 18 on talent shows like the *Vere Johns Opportunity Hour*, where she distinguished herself out-classing the competition. With an expansive vocal range matched by an unusual maturity she had a gift interpreting classic songs.

Hortense the sister of another Jamaican legend Alton Ellis, scored in 1961 on Coxsone's, **Studio One** label with her version of the American song *Eddie My Love*. In the following year came another smash *Midnight*, this one produced by Coxsone's rival Duke Reid.

She ruled the sixties and, in 1964, won the prestigious Silver Cup, a national award, recognizing her for being the *"Best Female Vocalist"*. For most of that decade she toured with premier outfit Byron Lee and The Dragonaires, but loved being in the studio.

Her prolific ways yielded a bounty of recordings for many producers. Being versatile allowed her to score with both original and cover material. She was able to tackle and have success with songs made popular by vocal titans like her brother Alton with: *Willow Tree, I'm Still In Love*, and *I'm Just a Girl*, as well as, *People Make The World Go Round* (Stylistics), *Wooden Heart, Suspicious Minds* (Elvis Presley), and *The First Cut is The Deepest* (Cat Stevens).

Her voice caressed each song and her emotional commitment made them hers. She had a special way with love tunes or compositions that mainly dealt with relationship type situations, maybe because they mirrored what was happening in her own life. The consistency of pain through heartache may have not been so convincing through pretense.

On the personal side she bore nine children. Five in rapid succession with Michael Junior Saunders, the man she married in 1971. This slowed her down considerably, especially in the area of live appearances. But she loved the recording process and still found time to do a lot of studio work. As a recording artist she was a sometime duo with her brother Alton; and at other times sang under aliases such as Mahailia Saunders and Queen Tiney.

Her biggest hit, *Unexpected Places*, came in 1979 for the brash musical entrepreneur Augustus "Gussie" Clark.

There are no public records indicating any firm managerial relationships and sadly, for all of her hard work, Hortense was neither overwhelmingly famous nor rich. People close to the singer suggested that she would have had much more success if it were not for her *"difficult"* personality. Musicians and producers who worked with her remember an unpleasant demeanor and her penchant for complaining about the most trivial of things.

After her divorce from Saunders she fell off the radar, spending most of the 80s living in the United States. Signs of serious health problems started to surface around 1989 and continued intermittently up until her death in a Kingston hospital in 2000.

Even still, Hortense Ellis remains one of the seminal female performers to lead the way, showing that it was possible for a female singer to match the success of male peers. This she did, albeit briefly, but memorably.

26. John Holt

Christened: John Holt
Born: July 11, 1947
Deceased: October 19, 2014

True romantic

John Holt occupies a special place in the hearts of Jamaicans and reggae lovers at large. Though his body aged, his voice did not take its orders.

The late singer, nicknamed *1000 Volts*, was without question one of the finest vocal talents to have ever graced the arena in the history of Jamaican music. He was an elder statesman and a father figure to a whole new generation of singers who can emulate his greatness, but never imitate his unique sound.

Holt was a pure crooner in the tradition of great American singers like Nat King Cole and Sam Cooke. Moreover, must have been influenced by the patriarch of rock steady Alton Ellis. Holt's style was unforced and silky smooth. The production on some of his releases that featured string arrangements further complimented his style and staple as a true reggae romantic.

His career began in 1963, at the age of 16, with the single "I Cried a Tear", for producer Leslie Kong. A year later he joined a vocal group called The Paragons, replacing departed member Leroy Stamp. They enjoyed a string of hits while recording on Duke Reid's **Treasure Isle** label: *Tonight, I See Your Face, Ali Baba* and *The Tide Is High*.

In a move that must have ruffled the feathers of his fellow group members he also carried on a parallel solo career with recordings for Reid's competitor, **Studio One** boss, Coxsone Dodd and scoring with *Fancy Make Up*, *A Love I Can Feel* and *Ok Fred*. Shortly after the group's debut single, they lost another founding member, Bob Andy. And if one talent can make a difference, it certainly did with Holt carrying the main workload, writing original material and handling most of the lead vocals.

After the breakup of The Paragons in 1970, Holt went solo and quickly established himself amongst the cream of the crop. With the release of *Stick By Me*, in 1972 for producer Bunny Lee, Holt catapulted to the top.

The UK label **Trojan** saw an opportunity in taking on Jamaica's hottest artist. The result was the album *1000 Volts of Holt*. The set intended to replicate the strategy used on an earlier album, *Time Is The Master*. *Time* was one of the first reggae albums with a Phil Specter like *"wall of sound"* kind of arrangement, featuring string overdubs skillfully done by Pop producer Tony Ashfield, who recorded it in London.

Holt's popularity outside of Jamaica was given a shot in the arm when his cover of the Kris Kristofferson composition *Help Me Make It Through The Night* (**Trojan**) made the UK top ten, peaking at number 6. The song is symbolic of what reggae music truly is: an interpretation of the world's music. Holt could have easily been mistaken for a country singer on a Jamaican beat.

If the success of the single had him up in the clouds, he would soon be brought back to earth upon realizing that the British market was a totally different world. Consequently, the competition from white artists only permitted him one hit.

When he turned his attention back to the local scene, the social and political upheaval in Jamaica was not the ideal setting for Holt's love songs. He quickly adjusted and scored in 1976 with *Up Park Camp*. This piece echoed the fear of the average Jamaican youth who dreaded the detention camps that were set up under the State of Emergency, by the ruling socialist government.

At heart, John Holt was a balladeer, never really establishing himself as a genuine roots artist. But in the 80s when the government changed, the militancy of the preceding decade was replaced by more western values of capitalism, and a rush to have fun and make money.

When the pro-American government of

Edward Seaga brought in US marines to incinerate the islands ganja crop, it afforded Holt a chance to win over a reluctant dancehall with the Junjo Lawes produced protest *Police In Helicopter*. The song touts the famous lines: *"If you continue to burn up the herbs, we gonna burn down the cane fields"*. Other 80s hits: *Carpenter, Fat She Fat, Sweetie Come Brush Me* and his last major hit, *Wildfire* (a duet with Dennis Brown), kept his popularity afloat.

The singer was a late-bloomer Rastafarian, boycotting the barber's chair from 1983 but still holding to his classical strain in song and appearance. The dapper look with Holt dressed in a black and white tuxedo suit is in full force on the *Wildfire* album cover standing alongside Dennis Brown.

Also not to be overlooked is John Holt's skills as a songwriter, most notably as it relates to one of his compositions *"The Tide Is High"*. The song is a perennial classic which have been covered by several international acts, the most famous of them being punk pioneers Blondie and UK pop sensations Atomic Kitten. Both took it to number one on both sides of the Atlantic.

Another point of historical significance is his composition for The Paragons, *Wear You To The Ball* which the father of Jamaican DJs, Daddy U-Roy, toasted over, giving birth to a new genre of Jamaican music.

As the nineties dawned Holt apparently lost his appetite for the business though continuing to perform and record intermittently. A notable highlight in the early 2000s was a series of concerts that he performed with the London Philharmonic Orchestra, co-headlined by another veteran, Freddie McGregor.

The evergreen vocalist stayed active throughout but, after a sudden illness in the summer of 2014, he succumbed that same fall in a London hospital at the age of 69.

Suffice to say, John Holt may not have been one of reggae's international superstars; nonetheless, his contributions are historically significant.

25. Big Youth

Christened: Manley Buchanan
Born: April 19, 1949

Roots DJ

While many point to Tony Rebel as the first cultural DJ, they are gravely mistaken as this distinction belongs to none other than Big Youth.

U-Roy was indeed the father of the DJ movement, but it was Big Youth who gave it an overtly Rastafarian identity.

In the mid-70s he would storm onto the scene eclipsing the popularity of U-Roy, dominating the charts and in the process, constructing his own era in the annals of Jamaican music.

Big Youth was born in Trench Town, influenced by U-Roy and was hooked on the new style of music popularized by the pioneer. When U-Roy revolutionized Jamaican music with the new DJ genre around 1971, Buchanan, a former mechanic, was already *nicing* up parties all over Kingston.

The former employee of The Sheraton Hotel began his ascent from the late 60s, interning on Tippertone Hi Fi, though he didn't wax his first vocals until about 1972.

Buchanan tall and lanky, hence the name Big Youth released a spate of unsuccessful singles for a number of producers. He finally scored for a young upstart eager to make a name for himself by the name of Augustus "Gussie" Clarke with *The Killer* and *Tippertone Rocking*. This pair of releases opened the gate for the song that would eventually put Youth at the very top, *S90Skank.*

S90Skank was recorded for producer Keith Hudson. The song was most noted for its sound effects that featured the actual sound of a motorbike that was brought into the studio for this purpose. Also in the intro of the song are the iconic lines where Big Youth exclaims, "*you ride like lightning you crash like thunder*" and a phrase that Jamaican radio stations would later use as a promo for years to come, "*right now riddim hold I riddim wild*". But apart from this, on the song Youth was mainly mimicking his hero U-Roy, with whelps, screams and unintelligible lyrics. Nevertheless, *S90Skank* was still a huge hit.

Thereafter the toaster evolved as more of a chanter, and in high demand. Youth far from being lazy, recorded prolifically creating new hits like *Can You Keep A Secret*, *Opportunity Rocks*, *Cain and Abel* and *Chi Chi Run.*

In 1973, Big Youth overtook all others with the arrival of the hits laden debut album, *Screaming Target.* That year he accomplished the remarkable feat of having four singles that would stay in the Jamaican Top Twenty Charts for more than a year.

This was the point at which his songs took on a more political tone. He ultimately established himself as a Rasta agitator and social commentator, operating like a musical gazette, latching onto popular topics and events, borne out by the singles *Chucky No Lucky*, about gangster life in Kingston and a sports event *"Foreman Vs Frazer"*.

His style also changed elevating him above the role of an imitator to originator. This he achieved by slowing down his delivery. The adjustment gave Big Youth's songs a more conversational feel and his increasing attention to social issues made him the first cultural DJ of prominence.

Big Youth undoubtedly became the blueprint for cultural artists that began their rise in the 90s such as Tony Rebel, Sizzla, Capleton and Anthony B. He set the trend in this respect, both musically and stylistically, even down to his sense of fashion that would also be imitated by the young lions of the ensuing generation.

In 1974 he launched his own Negusa Negast imprint and kept busy working for other producers along with his own self-produced material. The 1975 album *Dreadlock Dread* for Tony Robinson expanded his fan base upon its release in the UK. This allowed him in 76 to embark on his first British tour.

Two years later, this new focus on the overseas market would eventually lead to a contract with **Frontline**, a **Virgin** subsidiary. In the interim he recorded two brilliant self-produced albums, *Natty Cultural Dread* and *Hit The Road Jack*. They contained the hits *Every Nigger Is A Star*, *Ten To One*, *Wolf In Sheep's Clothing* and *Four Sevens Clash*.

In 1978 **Frontline** put out the album *Isaiah First Profit of Old* as the first of a three-album deal. The other two never saw the light of day. With Jamaica edging towards a politically motivated civil war, Big Youth's radical posture was deemed not commercially viable by the label. Youth aptly proved this with the anti-government *Green Bay Killing*, chastising the Jamaican army for a massacre in downtown Kingston by singing "*Green Bay Killing a murder*".

By the end of the 70s, Big Youth had peaked and the winds of change were blowing over the Jamaican musical scene. In 1980 the socialist government, with the aid of the United States, and at the cost of many innocent lives, was chased out of office and replaced by the capitalist Jamaica Labour Party under Edward Seaga. The following year, the death of Bob Marley marked a significant shift in the direction of reggae music. Culture would be by and large usurped by DJs that would now glorify materialistic values and sex and Big Youth wanted no part of it. He however, made several appearances during the decade on Reggae Sunsplash and was always an electrifying performer. He never disappointed the mixed audience of locals and foreigners.

Youth would hereafter focus his attention on touring, while recording sparingly in between shows.

In the 90s came a few more singles, including *Chanting for Niney Holness* and *Free South Africa*. A few more albums were also released, mostly best of collections: *Some Great Big Youth* (**Heartbeat**), *Natty Universal Dread 73-79* (**Blood & Fire**) and *Everyday Skank-Best Of Big Youth* (**Trojan**). In 1995 he was honored by one of his musical offspring, Capleton, through a feature on a track from Capleton's *I Testament* album, released by **Def Jam**.

In an interview some years ago Big Youth declared, "*I come into the business as a Rasta and the first to do so*". So who is the father of all the roots DJs? The evidence is overwhelming and the question seems rhetorical.

24. Sugar Minott

Christened: Lincoln Minott
Born: May 25, 1956
Deceased: July 10, 2010

Godfather of Dancehall

The branch of reggae known as dancehall took off in a big-way during the 80's. Its proliferation came about largely through the labors of Lincoln "Sugar" Minott.

His input to the culture went above and beyond just a musical career. He offered up himself as a mentor and provided a nursery for up and coming talent. His mission was to give aspiring artists an outlet for recognition.

His **Youthman Promotion Company**, an extension of his **Black Roots** label that was located at Robert Crescent, was a stone's throw from the infamous Black Roses corner in Kingston 13. Black Roses corner was the haunt for notorious gangster Willie Haggart and celebrity dancehall dancer Bogle. Minott achieved legendary status as the patriarch who created this starting point for a sizable number of stars that came of age in the dancehall era.

The compound housed a record label, distribution center, rehearsal facilities, sound system, and a literal "dancehall". In its heyday, there was always a buzz of activity and an electrifying atmosphere where the stars of the day fraternized with young hopefuls, admirers and onlookers. At the center of it all was the fatherly presence of the man himself.

Dubbed in the Jamaican press as the "Godfather of Dancehall", he got his start like most at the venerable **Studio One** label, at least as a solo artist. Several years prior to falling into Coxsone's orbit, he was part of a vocal trio called the African Brothers. The group came together in 1969, consisting of Minott, Tony Tuff and Derrick

Howard. They lasted five years after releasing a few unnoticeable singles on the **Micron** label as well as on their own **Ital Records**.

Minott's solo work began in 1974 while recording for Coxsone, as well as supplementing his career by being a drummer and guitar player at the label. He scored with a number of singles: "*Hang On Natty*", "*Vanity*", "*Jah Jah Children*" and the classic "*Mr. DC*". By 1979 he had two albums, *Live Loving* and *Showcase*.

Going from strength to strength, he established himself as an artist, straddling multiple styles within reggae but never engaging in material that was frivolous in nature. His catalog – containing lover rock, dub, deep roots and dancehall – is a kaleidoscope of Jamaica's musical history. It boasts songs that expose his versatility as a vocalist, while also validating him as a serious songwriter.

The next chapter of his storied career saw him migrating to Britain, the colonial motherland. His "*Hard Time Pressure*" single won him many fans in the black community – natives as well as immigrants. The top five single, a cover of the Jackson 5's "*Good Thing Going*" only helped to raise his profile in the UK, opening him up to white audiences. The success of *Good Thing* is also evidence of Jamaican music's kinship with the best pop music from Europe and North America.

This period was also marked with a brief stint on the **RCA** label and on the strength of *Good Thing Going* released an album of the same name in 1981. His extended stay in Britain made him a central figure and major influence in the development of the UK reggae scene. There he recorded prolifically and turned out an impressive list of songs specifically for that market. One surprise hit was *Make It* featuring singer Carol Thompson. After leaving **RCA**, he released albums on his own **Black Roots** label, while using **Island** and **Trojan** for distribution.

As a bird never strays far from its nest, Sugar returned to Jamaica in the mid-80s to reconnect with his native audience. He embarked on a mission to give back to the business that he owed so much of his success. This led to the formation of the **Youthman Promotion** enterprise.

In a business renowned for people dedicated only to self, often times manifested by egotistical behavior and ingratitude, Sugar became a leader. He was not afraid to drag others up from an all too familiar place, one of obscurity and poverty. He became a leader of men and, in the process, helped many along the path to success. The illustrious but not exhaustive list of artists he aided includes Junior Reid, Garnett Silk, Tony Rebel, Ranking Joe, Johnny Osbourne, Tenor Saw, Yami Bolo, Color Man, Daddy Freddy, Nitty Gritty, Barry Brown, Little John, Michael Palmer and Tony Tuff.

The main avenue of exposure was his **Youthman Promotion Sound System** that featured the young talents of the day. He also made selectors popular, as they labored behind the turntables. This afforded many of them a respectable livelihood; with some even becoming more famous than the recording artists whose records they played. A conversation with many aspirants to stardom who walked the streets of Kingston could not end without them mentioning that they made a stop at *Sugars House* at some time or the other.

It was this pioneering move that gave rise to dancehall as a force of the new wave of Jamaican music. And while the 80s have been cited as a period of wanton mediocrity, it would be unfair to lay the blame at the feet of Minott.

Along with his musical philanthropy was also a career that never abated, for the hits kept coming. His demand kept growing and during the 80s, all the top producers sought after him. Names like Sly & Robbie, George Phang, Prince Jammy, Niney Holness, Striker Lee and Donovan Germaine came knocking. The biggest of his releases being *No Vacancy*, *Herbman Hustling*, *Devil Pickney*, *Rydim Rydim* and *Buy Off De Bar*.

Another accolade is the major achievement of being one of the few Jamaican entertainers who broke into the Japanese market. Japan, with its voracious appetite for reggae, was ripe for exploitation. In 1984 he toured Japan for the first time, and eventually did so more frequently than others. Later on, due to a high demand for him in the region, he recorded and had several releases in that market. His presence there also had an influence on Japanese homegrown reggae talent, Nahki – who scored big collaborating with Yami Bolo, one of Sugar's protégées. This flung the market wide open and would benefit other stars of the nineties like Shabba Ranks and Diana King.

In the 90's as the music took on a harder sound with the audiences, turning to the DJs and emerging singers who mainly did cover versions, Sugar's local popularity tapered off. But he kept recording and dedicated most of his time to touring and maintaining his Robert Crescent headquarters, where several of his children, out of fourteen, worked in the organization.

His wife Maxine Stowe, a former **Columbia Records** executive at the time of Sugar's sudden passing, said that he'd had a heart condition for several years. Sugar's inner circle can attest to the fact that this giant of a man worked hard and played hard. It was no secret that Minott indulged heavily, smoking marijuana and drinking alcohol.

When he checked into a Kingston hospital on July 10th 2010 with chest pains, the godfather of dancehall did not suffer, but went quickly. However, his name cannot be forgotten in the annals of Jamaican music. Never has a man done so much with so little.

23. Freddie McGregor

Christened: Freddie McGregor
Born: June 27, 1956

Marathon Man

Freddie McGregor has perfected the art of musical survival. Through self-reinvention he accomplished longevity, a rare feat in a business known for fleeting success. He is one of the few living reggae artists who started out as a child and is still active today.

At age seven, and being called "Little Freddie", he lived at the house of Sir Coxsone Dodd and recorded his first song at that early age. As the story goes, he was taken from his home parish of Clarendon to Kingston, to meet the legendary producer, who was impressed upon hearing him. At that time, the young McGregor had to be placed on several beer crates so he could reach the microphone.

The fires of ambition were stoked from just being at **Studio One**, which was Jamaica's version of **Motown**. There the impressionable youth was able to meet future legends like Bob Marley and Alton Ellis. McGregor had a front seat view of reggae history; a history that he would also become a part of.

Contrary to popular belief, McGregor was not a part of The Clarendonians group, but only assisted with backing vocals on some of their tracks. However, in 1963 after the group became defunct, he teamed up with former member Earnest Wilson to create the duo Fitzroy and Freddie, and cut several singles including: *Why Did You Do It* and *Do Good and It Will Follow You*.

The indefatigable McGregor served his apprenticeship through much of the 70s staying, close to Dodd and building his confidence with session work, as both background singer and drummer. Trying hard to make his way, he also recorded outside of the duo, in an effort to break out as a solo act. Afterwards he became friends with a songwriter/guitarist named Sangie Davis. It was at Davis's house in Hermitage, that he met members of a band called *The Generation Gap* and became their lead vocalist, albeit for a short time.

In the mid-70s the rise of nationalism, ushered in by Jamaica's left leaning Prime Minister Michael Manley and the growing disaffection amongst Jamaica's poor, was fertile ground for the islands own "hippie" like explosion called Rastafarianism. McGregor was swept up in this tide and started to grow his locks.

Being around Rasta musicians like guitarist Earl Chinna Smith he cut the sides: *I'm a Rasta* and *Rastaman Camp*, which were released on Smith's own **High Times** label. McGregor ran with the anti-establishment crowd and belted out songs representing their views, *Mark of the Beast*, *Sergeant Brown*, *Natural Collie*, *Walls of Jericho*, *Africa Here I Come* and, the hugely popular title track off his 1980 album, *Bobby Babylon*.

In 1981 came his signature hit, *Big Ship* the one signaling his arrival as a major artist. This newly earned status placed him on the post-

Marley relay team, entrusted to carry the music forward. In this group were other top singing stars Dennis Brown, Gregory Issacs and John Holt; considered as the new class of icons. An album of the same name came in 1982, and was followed by *Come On Over* ('83) on US based **Ras Records**.

The 1984 hit *Guantanamera* came off of the *Across The Border* album. With this release, McGregor changed direction in an effort to embrace a different audience beyond his hardcore fan base. He moved past his roots reggae phase and was briefly vindicated with *Push Comes To Shove* which was a massive hit in 1986. The new "sex symbol with locks image" was now in full swing.

As his popularity continued to soar, he received and subsequently accepted an offer from UK major **Polydor**, seeking to capitalize on McGregor's recent chart successes. His international breakthrough became reality by way of two cover songs *That Girl* and *Just Don't Wanna Be Lonely*, both topping the UK charts. The album *All In The Same Boat*, which contained the hits also sold well. This was a very lucrative period for McGregor and afforded him the luxury of building his own studio, which he called *Big*

Ship.

This newfound fortune however, proved to be a financial watershed but a creative waterloo. McGregor it seemed had achieved his main goal of commercial success and was driven by little else. His career from then onwards mainly devolved into that of a cover artist.

In the early 90s he managed to score a few more hits with *Winner* and a cover of Little Roy's, *Prophecy*, but overall his direction appeared unfocused. The hits dried up and he became the proverbial rolling stone that gathered no moss.

While Dennis Brown and Gregory Isaacs amassed a body of critically acclaimed work and increased in the public's affections, Freddie's musical hop scotch, careening from style to style, more or less robbed him of a loyal fan base. With the 1992 surge of another veteran singer by the name of Beres Hammond, who became a literal hit machine, McGregor was pushed further out and unable to come up with a hit when needed.

One certain thing is that Freddie did well for himself. And when all is said and done he is still a formidable live performer and a tireless worker with business acumen to boot.

For the better part of the last two decades, he made a second home in the South Florida area of the US, where he is a celebrity. He is one of the few Jamaican artists to be honored by receiving the keys to the City of Miami. There he organized and ran a major concert, for several years and also keeps the income stream flowing with festival appearances, regular touring and seasonal cruise ship work.

With a career spanning forty years that includes the winning of many awards and a Grammy nomination, McGregor's work and the weight of his contributions to the growth of reggae music need no interrogation.

His legacy continues through his bloodline with his sons Stephen "Di Genius" McGregor and Collin "Chino" McGregor coming to the fore as a new generation of artists and producers that have emerged.

Freddie is a marathon runner. He is still a crowd pleaser and continues to enjoy the respect and admiration of the Jamaican people.

22. Buju Banton

Christened: Mark Myrie
Born: July 15, 1973

The Rise and Fall

It came as a surprise when, in December of 2009, the man who was reggae's last great hope was arrested in Florida on charges of conspiracy to distribute cocaine. The news reverberated through the reggae fraternity like a shock wave as Buju Banton had just successfully concluded a world tour to promote his album *Rasta Got Soul*.

Amongst ordinary folks the emotions ranged from disbelief, to feelings of trepidation and a sting of betrayal. One thing for certain, the sentiment across the board was that the beloved artist whatever the truth was, had let everyone down.

The long, strange journey leading up to this unlikely event started at Salt Lane in downtown Kingston where Myrie was born as the last of fifteen siblings. The death of a brother left him as the lone male child encircled by thirteen sisters.

His fascination with his future profession began with hero worship of the DJs who ruled the dancehall. As a teen he hung around the stage for hours sucking up the performances of his heroes, especially Burru Banton. At the expense of being flogged by his father, he stole away from home just to be in the dances.

By age twelve he began his journey, toasting on two sounds *Sweet Love Disco* and *Rambo Mango*. At age fourteen he recorded his first single called *The Ruler*, for singer/producer Robert French. Afterwards, the unusually tall, skinny teenager would start to spread around his talent by recording for multiple producers.

After he was taken to producer and future manager Donovan Germaine, owner of the

Penthouse Label, by his childhood friend Von Wayne Charles (a singer popularly known as Wayne Wonder) things moved exceptionally fast.

At the age of 18 he scored his first major hit on **Penthouse** called *Love Mi Browning*. From that point on, the young DJ proved to be somewhat of an overachiever as the hits came at a historically furious pace. *Browning* was followed by its response *Black Woman*, then *Batty Rider*, *Woman Nuh Fret* and *Bogle*, which were only a few among many other smashes.

This was the herald of a major new talent at a time when the man he would be mostly compared to, Shabba Ranks, was at the zenith of his career. While Shabba was making serious gains in the US market, recording with the likes of Johnny Gill and Queen Latifah, Buju was fast becoming the new local champion. The intertwining of the two stars would, in a few short years, have an effect on both of their careers that can only be described as bizarre.

In 1991 and 1992, Buju scored the most number one hits in the history of the dancehall, sweeping away the entire old guard of artists that preceded him. The musical firestorm he caused would revolutionize the sound of dancehall DJs.

Furthermore, after his arrival, it would be mostly those imitating his style that were able to break through. A slew of sound alike DJs such as Terror Fabulous, Jigsy King, Galaxy P and Mega Banton came to prominence. But it was Buju who achieved the fastest international signing of a local artist ever.

In 1992 two albums, *Stamina Daddy* and *Mr. Mention*, were rushed out to capitalize on the enormous popularity of the new star. By the end of that same year, the artist would be snatched up by **Mercury/Polygram**. Lisa Cortes, the A&R responsible for the signing, immediately put to work Jamaica's top producers: Sly & Robbie, Donovan Germaine and brothers Dave and Tony Kelly. The result was the *Voice of Jamaica* album. It contained local hits like *Operation Ardent*, *Willy (Don't Be Silly)* and the cultural landmark, a monster single called *Deportees (Things Change)*.

The *Deportees* song warned Jamaicans who were non-citizens of their host countries, to not become complacent but to take care of their relatives and to acquire assets back home, in the event of deportation. After the massive hit and the social stigma it tagged on neglectful emigrants, the remittance industry in Jamaica boomed almost overnight. Foreign remittances became so huge that it lifted the economy out of negative growth. An argument can be made that it helped the ruling Peoples National Party to stay in power for more than a decade and a half. The song crystallized Buju's image as an artist of significance. He had, at last, started to escape his previous image of plugging sex and partying. The coming controversy however, would only add to his growing legend.

The song *Boom Bye Bye* that called for homosexuals to be killed was first recorded and released in 1988, when the not yet famous Banton was only 15. In 1992 it was re-recorded for Clifton "Specialist" Dillon on the same track that contained *Flex*, the monster single for Dillon's artist Mad Cobra. At this time Dillon headed the powerful **Specs/Shang** record label that was being distributed by **Sony/Epic**. His empire saw him managing the biggest reggae star since Bob Marley, the two-time Grammy winner Shabba Ranks. **Specs/Shang** which was also a partnership with politician Olivia "Babsy" Grange also had on its roster red-hot artists Bounty Killer, Ghost, Lady Patra (signed to Epic), Mad Cobra (signed to Capitol) and Richie Stephens (signed to Motown).

The rumor is that the release of the *Boom Bye Bye* single was not sanctioned by Buju's management. It was said to be a ploy by Dillon to neutralize Banton, knowing very well the backlash that was sure to follow the release of such an incendiary record. The reason for this according to many sources was that Buju was eclipsing the popularity of Shabba, Dillon's top money maker.

No one knows for sure how the anti-Buju campaign that was being led by gay rights organizations was drummed up, but it quickly started to derail Buju's prospects of becoming a major international star. In its wake, his label unceremoniously dumped him.

But In an irony of bad karma, the uproar slowed down Buju but subsequently entangled Shabba and brought his career to a complete halt.

In 1993, the host of a popular British TV show *The Word* asked one of the guests, none other than , *surprise*, Shabba, if he supported the views that were expressed by Buju in *Boom Bye Bye*. Shabba incredulously told the show's host that he held the very same views and that, gays deserved to be, in his own words, "*crucified*".

The response by the media was swift and a vehement retaliation by the gay community buried

Shabba in an avalanche of show cancellations and bad press. Dillon's alleged plan, if he was guilty of one had backfired. Shabba, instead of Buju, was irreparably damaged by the whole affair. Buju would live to fight another day.

Developing a reputation for controversy, Buju could not foresee his coming troubles. But in the interim things would improve dramatically.

Wherever the inspiration came from, it was to Buju's advantage that he converted to Rastafarianism and started to sprout locks. In a remarkable feat, he reentered the musical fray as a love child, denouncing the hatred of *Boom Bye Bye* with a new album regarded as an instant classic. The album, *Til Shiloh*, was released on **Loose Cannon/Island**. It outsold **Mercury's** and was such a masterpiece that it catapulted Buju into the elite class of reggae artists.

It was a spiritual transformation from his previous efforts, artistically putting the artist at a peak that he would never surpass. Singles like *Till I'm Laid To Rest, I Wanna Be Loved, It's Not An Easy Road, Murderer,* and *Untold Stories* went straight to the top of every reggae survey. The album started to show the artist in a different muse, by showcasing him more as a singer instead of the straight toasting he was known for. After the storm, Buju was clearly back on top. The follow up, *Inner Heights* (**VP**), continued in the same vein and was also an independent success. Banton was vaulted into the ranks of super-rich artists; with money pouring in from live shows, dub plates and royalties.

But he would not be consistent on this path that gave rise to questions of his sincerity in this new reality. In interviews around this period he appeared to be a wise sage, espousing spiritual themes. But sometimes he came off in a superficial manner, using overblown superlatives and exaggerating his own importance. It was obvious to some that his success was outrunning his level of maturity.

The albums that followed, *Unchained Melody* (**ANTI/Epitaph**) and *Friends* (**VP/Atlantic**) were pitiful and not without reason. In the wake of the overwhelming success of *Til Shiloh*, and with his newfound riches, the artist started two labels in succession. The first of them was **Cell Block**, a partnership with producer Sylvester Gordon, with whom he later parted ways in order to start the sole proprietorship called **Gargamel**. In an apparent case of ego-tripping, or potentially through greed, the artist mistakenly fancied himself as his own producer and did the projects at his own studio. Then negotiated his distribution deals. The songs from these sessions were of inferior quality to say the least.

Then there was another side to the artist that was coming into full view. One that smacked of arrogance, in direct contrast to the picture of humility he portrayed to the public.

The years following the remarkable success of *Til Shiloh* were ones where his image of righteous Rasta man became tainted. Incidents like being taken into custody as a person of interest in a case of homicide that occurred in his community of Red Hills Road, an arrest for growing marijuana openly at his Carlyle Avenue business compound and shooting his manager's dog because of a so-called money dispute. It seemed that the artist was on a collision course, but lacked the wisdom to apply the brakes. Way into his supernova phase, he was a luminous star collapsing from the inside.

Musically however, he would regain his footing in 2006 when the single *Driver*, done on Sly & Robbie's, rehashed Taxi Riddim returned him to the top of the charts. The album *Too Bad* containing the hit was also brought to market.

With mediocre artists all around, it seemed as if Buju was now the only act with enough credibility to be the standard bearer of an ailing genre. With the release of the *Rasta Got Soul* album, the artist embarked on a world tour. The tour showcased an artist that had come of age. After being in the limelight for 18 years he had mellowed into a seasoned veteran and, on this tour, he was in rare form.

On the surface everything seemed to be going Bujus's way but for what was just around the corner. *Driver*, the song that spearheaded his comeback, proved to be a harbinger of troubles to come. In the song, in quite surreal fashion, the artist lays out a drug deal in extraordinary detail. One can only speculate if it was the song, his long running feud with the gay community or other reasons that caused US law enforcement to target him. But as subsequent events would prove, he was indeed under the microscope. Banton, who owns a house in Florida on his way home on a flight from Spain, was conveniently seated in the same row with a passenger who would cause his world to literally crumble.

On this fateful flight, the man beside Banton was Alexander Johnson a confidential informant working for US drug enforcement. Johnson wormed his way into a tight conversation with Buju. The talk, which began innocently, would eventually evolve into a seductive back and forth about opportunities for making money. The man told Banton he was a major player in the drug game and if the reggae star was interested in making "big" money they should stay in touch. This they did, and subsequently met on at least two occasions to discuss the finer points of a deal.

The informant, later discovered to be a Columbian with an impressive rap sheet of his own, was paid US $50,000 by the DEA. He also recorded their conversations and coordinated with the police to get Banton on tape. He successfully videotaped the artist in a secured warehouse in Sarasota Florida, testing the cocaine, which he was supposed to be purchasing.

The whole saga reeked of classic entrapment, but with enough damming evidence the singer was taken into custody after, James Mack and Ian Thomas, his alleged accomplices were nabbed in the act of paying for the stuff.

In the wake of Banton's arrest, gay rights groups were ecstatic and their contempt for the artist was poured out on numerous websites and blogs.

The case went to trial and, in September of 2010, was declared a mistrial. Undaunted federal prosecutors reopened the case in February 2011 and this time around were victorious. The artist was given a ten year prison sentence which according to observers could have been avoided if Banton had entered into a plea agreement instead of the feeble defense he was able to muster in a trial.

Buju Banton's rise and fall is the stuff that Hollywood dramas are made of. In the aftermath, the artist languishing in federal prison has mounted several appeals but to no avail.

This was another blow to the image of reggae music and its practitioners, and plays out more like life imitating art instead of the other way around.

21. Sean Paul

Christened: Sean Henriques
Born: January 9, 1973

Sweet Revenge

The dancehall fraternity did not welcome Sean Paul's arrival. After all, dancehall music belonged to the ghetto and all its major stars have emerged from the lower end of the class divide. Paul, a product of "upper" St Andrew where middle class and wealthy Jamaicans live, was seen as *one of them* instead of *one of us*.

He was born to Garth and Frances Henriques, of Portuguese-Jewish heritage on his father's side and Caucasian-Chinese on his moms end. The youngster attended Wolmers Boys and Hillel Academy, and was an athlete who represented his school and, later on, Jamaica on the water polo team.

His interest in music started to surface during his teen years and, in the early 90s, he made some valuable connections through members of legendary reggae fusion outfit Third World. He also felt encouraged by the inroads that were been made by another DJ from a middleclass background like himself, Don Yute.

Another early connection was made with Robert Livingston, at that time the manager of reggae superstar Shaggy, who released one of Paul's early singles.

But all the stars started to align after he met producer and future manager Jeremy Harding, who had recently returned to Jamaica from Canada, after majoring in Music Business at Toronto's Trebas Institute. Harding was also a child of privilege and the son of Oswald Harding, a former Minister Of Justice.

Mimicking the vocal style of another artist who was an ethnic anomaly in Jamaican music the East Indian, veteran Super Cat, Paul began to build up a string of popular tunes: *Infiltrate, Nah Get Nu Bly, Deport Dem* and *Hackle Mi* among others.

The success he was enjoying did not sit well with his musical peers. On his songs, his vocal delivery was not aggressive and the accent was unmistakably "uptown", veering in the direction of proper English speech instead of the straight patois (Jamaican dialect). Jeremy Harding tried to diffuse the tension by surrounding Paul with some ghetto youths in a clique known as the *Dutty Cup Krew*. But the distrust by downtowners of those from the middle and upper class was entrenched. The indifference towards Sean Paul persisted.

For a brief period his detractors even had something to cheer about, as his career went into a slump. This invited ridicule from fellow artists who apparently took pleasure in his time of crisis. His fraternal colleagues were even dissing him on their records and Paul was finding it difficult to secure show bookings.

However, the artist would muddle through this difficult time, hoping for a turn around. And things certainly did turn around. He would get revenge, and he did in a very big way.

Under the guidance of his manager, Paul took the more structured approach to his career by signing with reggae giant VP Records, where he could concentrate on making albums. While his manager worked closely with his record label, a proper marketing plan was executed on the artist's behalf. His first opening to the international market came by way of a pair of collaboration with dancehall DJ Mr. Vegas. The singles: *Hot Gal* and *Here Comes The Boom* (with American rapper DMX) appeared on the soundtrack of the motion picture *Belly*, a hip-hop drama.

In 2001 his association with **VP Records**, with whom he previously impressed with the numbers they did on his debut album *Stage One*, began to bear fruit. In Murray Elias an A&R executive for the company Paul and his manager found someone who was gung ho about the artist's career. In the single *Gimme Di Light*, they found a potential hit. Previously released with not much success the song when resurrected and placed on American radio began to show signs of life. When the video dropped *Gimme The Light* became a runaway success.

The song's popularity, in no small way, owes everything to the video that showed Paul exhibiting some neat moves. In it was a group of dancers, from the Caribbean, who sold the video to a new audience. The dancers showed off, for the first time to the BET demographic, all the latest moves coming out of Jamaica with such dramatic style and flair that hooked viewers.

The song's content, calling for one to "*gimmi di light and pass the draw*", obviously referred to marijuana smokers lighting up and also appealed to the pot culture endemic of both urban and suburban American youngsters. These factors, coupled with the newness of the song's sound and the fresh-faced attractiveness of the artist, pushed it all the way to number two on the Billboard Hot 100. Thus the success of *Gimmi Di Light* became the foundation on which Sean Pual's pop stardom would be constructed.

The follow up single *Get Busy*, on Jamaican producer Lenky's Diwali riddim, did even better by reaching the pole position. The third single *I'm Still In Love*, a duet with a little known female singer Sasha, was a multinational smash that displayed a more mellow side of the artist. **VP** hastily rounded up the hit singles with some other songs and rushed out an album *Dutty Rock*. **VP** an independent label wisely partnered with major label **Atlantic** to distribute the album. As a result three million copies flew through the pipeline. At the end of this wild ride Sean Paul was an international star.

His reluctant colleagues, not wanting to appear to be envious of his success finally embraced him as a fraternal brother. Paul, who was once slighted, became the darling of the Jamaican media and became the pride of his countrymen in a sort of selfish overture.

The momentum carried over to his next album *Trinity*, a double-platinum seller. It contained more smash hits *Give It Up* (featuring R&B songstress Keisha Cole) and the summer anthem "*Temperature*" produced by Rohan "Snowcone" Fuller.

If nothing else was indicative of genuine international success, it was teaming up with the biggest female artist in the world, pop princess Beyoncé, on another number one record *Baby Boy*. It seemed that envy of Sean Paul was not confined to his fellow Jamaicans as Beyoncé's husband, rap kingpin Jay Z, was keen not to allow him to perform the song with her at the American Music Awards, even though Paul was present at the ceremony. The artist, as part of the audience, watched Beyoncé's performance wearing a stiff mask, while his parts were reproduced on tracks.

Sean Paul also won all the major industry awards: *American Music Award, Reggae Grammy, Britain's MOBO, Billboard,* and *ASCAP*. Sean Paul had arrived.

But as hard as it is to attain international stardom it is even harder to maintain. With his fourth album *Imperial Blaze*, this reality began to sink in, as it did not live up to either artistic or commercial expectations. The first single *So Fine* sounded like a bad marriage between his melody and the Stephen McGregor track. Also in this period, Jamaican-American rapper, the corpulent teen sensation Sean Kingston, with an even more syrupy sound that was hard to resist by the fickle audience was stealing a lot of Paul's thunder. Other shortcomings of the star that became apparent were an absence of natural charisma and his persistent problems of being a weak live performer.

In 2011 he elected to part ways with long time manager Jeremy Harding and, under new management, released another disc *Tomahawk Technique*. In the US it tanked but had better results in Europe, where a number of singles – *She Doesn't Mind* and *How Deep Is Your Love* (feat. Kelly Rowland) charted.

To his credit, Paul continues to maintain a high profile on the European continent where he is a bigger star than in the US, with a slew of features on hit records by other emerging artists. His new strategy is to increase his standing in the Latin community making a good start in 2014 by guesting on Enrique Iglesias's transcontinental hit *Bailando*.

The vicissitudes of his career aside, his past hits continue to enjoy steady rotation on American and European radio; while, his global look has taken him into markets not even fully conquered by many hip hop stars and unheard of for most reggae artists. Along with the far more successful Shaggy, Paul has scaled heights that most of his contemporaries can only dream about.

20. Ziggy Marley

Christened: David Marley
Born: October 17, 1968

His own man

Amongst sons of other musical legends, Ziggy Marley's career has been much more rock solid and enduring.

Compared to Bob Dylan's son Jakob in his

role of lead singer for the 90s flash in the pan group The Wallflowers, and John Lennon's sons Sean and Julian, Ziggy the eldest son of reggae superstar Bob Marley has held his own more substantially. He heads the most prolific of all musical dynasties with different solo careers, followed by his brothers Kymani, Damian, Stephen and Julian.

While he may never be able to emerge from the shadow of his father, through no fault of his, he has nonetheless matured into his own man. He is one of the most respected Jamaican artists, with a body of work that can stand on its own merit.

Born in poverty-stricken years, when his father was not yet a superstar, Ziggy tasted enough of the hard life to not take what he has for granted. Two years before Bob Marley's death, the group that Ziggy would lead was conceived as the Melody Makers consisting of himself, sisters Sharon and Cedella, and his six-year old brother Stephen. Their first recording was *Children Playing In The Street*, written and produced by their famous father.

By the time they signed to **EMI America**, the group was repackaged as Ziggy Marley & The Melody Makers. The first single proved at once the thickness of the bloodline, as the eleven-year-old Ziggy's lead vocals sounded as if his father was the one singing. The single in question was the lead track on their 1985 debut album *Play The Game Right* (**EMI**) produced by their mother Rita Marley. The title track, as well as another cut *What A Plot*, became favorites and received steady airplay on Jamaican radio. The follow up, *Hey World*, also yielded two popular singles *Lord We A Come* and *Give A Little Love*.

It was obvious though that their record label was trying too hard to market them in a very syrupy clichéd-type of way, in an effort to capitalize on their father's hard won popularity, instead of allowing a more organic development.

However, Ziggy's strength as a live performer was in evidence as early as 1983 when The Melody Makers had a stunning debut on the legendary Reggae Sunsplash concert, with the group, not yet having their own set of musicians, being backed by The Fabulous Five band.

The Melody Makers hit pay dirt with 1988's *Conscious Party*, under a new contract with Richard Bronson's **Virgin Records**. Produced by Chris Frantz and Tina Weymouth, former members of avant-garde band *The Talking Heads* and buoyed on by the hit single *Tomorrow People*, the album went on to platinum sales across the globe and won the group's first Reggae Grammy. *One Bright Day* followed, faring equally well with the number one smash on the US R&B charts, *Tumblin Down*. Ziggy Marley & The Melody Makers was now a major group in its own right and many sold out concerts followed.

Six other group albums came rapidly, but none lived up to the commercial successes of *Conscious Party* and *One Bright Day*. Starting with 1995's *Free Like U Want To Be*, Ziggy and company switched to **Elektra** up until the time he embarked on a solo career. The last album on which he served as front man for the group was 1999's *Spirit Of Music*.

His solo albums: *Dragonfly, Love Is My Religion Family Time* and *Wild and Free* haven't yielded any hits, but all have been warmly received by fans and critics alike.

A major flaw evident in Ziggy's solo career is the absence of a defining song. This is mainly because Ziggy writes and produces most of his material. It is safe to say that continued work with outside producers and songwriters, as in the early years with the Melody Makers, may have produced quite different results.

What can be said about Ziggy Marley though is that while his brothers like Damian and Kymani have found success through commingling with dancehall and hip hop, he has resisted these temptations. His integrity has not been traded in a pursuit for acceptance or hits. Consequently, he is seen as an artist of substance.

Also, not to be overlooked is his commitment to family life, and an involvement in public service and humanitarian endeavors, which is uncommon amongst many musicians. On top of all this, he is still the most fitting envoy for his dad's legacy. He has taken Bob Marley's music, by performing songs from his father's vast catalog, to places such as China and other countries where his father never went due to an untimely death.

Ziggy regardless of what many may think about him, is still one of the few reggae artists with a strong pulling power. He works regularly especially on the circuit outside of traditional reggae circles.

Starting out as a child in the business and being the son of the most famous Jamaican he has been able to keep his wits about him and to go about his career in a workmanlike fashion. Escaping the pitfalls of other children of celebrity, who have fallen prey to drugs etc. Because of his consistency he has been able to on his own become a two time Grammy winner and command the respect of his peers as well as the public at large.

19. Lee Scratch Perry

Christened: Rainford Hugh Perry
Born: March 20, 1936

Mad Genius

In 2003 it was a surprise when Lee Scratch Perry won the reggae Grammy for his album *Jamaican ET*. I mean there is a whole generation or two of Jamaicans who don't know him. He is virtually unknown to many, except for those who are serious scholars versed in the history of Jamaican music.

Outside of Jamaica, his reputation precedes him as one of the founding fathers of reggae. Alongside King Tubby and Augustus Pablo, Perry is known for experimenting with reggae instrumentals that eventually gave birth to dub. It is a matter of historical fact that his hands are dirty in the construction of modern Jamaican music.

Perry started out in the 1950s peddling 45rpms for Clement Coxsone Dodd. He was also an assistant producer to the legendary record man and, more than likely, contributed to the making of records, without receiving his share of the credit. Working with Coxsone was not easy, as the two could not see eye to eye. They clashed often as two more contrasting characters you could never find. Coxsone liked order, while Perry was the opposite.

After splitting from Coxsone, Perry took a job with producer Joe Gibbs, with whom he would also have a falling out. Perry's bones of contention were always the same wherever he went: financial disputes and creative differences.

In 1968, the man known in his early years as Little Perry, standing at a mere 4ft 11inches, (*keeping in mind that short men are known for their big egos*) started his own outfit **Upsetter Records**. His first release as an artist, a jab at his former employer, Joe Gibbs, *People Funny Bwoy* sold over 50,000 copies. This was the equivalent of a platinum record by US standards. He then assembled the *Upsetters Band* that included the drums and bass of future Wailers, the siblings Aston and Carlton Barrett.

He then stepped out of his mentors shadow producing some of the first progressive sounding Jamaican records. These records were different and the kind that could be exported to please white listeners in Europe. Around the same time that Davie Bowie started to push the envelope with songs like *Space Oddity*, Perry was exploding the conventions of a market familiar with the assembly line homogeneity established by **Studio One**. The scene was now ripe for change.

When The Wailers, consisting of Bob Marley, Peter Tosh and Bunny Wailer, grew tired of the commercial sound of **Studio One**, they sought

Perry out. The sessions that followed were nothing short of epoch making and the results were the first set of songs that would bring the legendary group international recognition. Through Perry's capacity as producer, the Wailers delivered classic songs: *Small Axe*, *Duppy Conqueror*, *African Herbsman*, *Kaya*, *Sun Is Shining* and *Four Hundred Years*. Recorded between 1970 and 1971 the new material steered The Wailers away from their previously ska inflected sound, putting them in the forefront of a new movement known as *rockers*. This collection of Perry produced songs made up the *Soul Rebel* album that Perry then licensed to **Trojan**.

According to sources, Perry greedily took the entire advance from the company and kept all of it. The silver lining behind this dark cloud however was that this turn of events is what brought the Wailers to the attention of Chris Blackwell, a shareholder in **Trojan** and the owner of **Island Records**. In 1973 Blackwell signed the Wailers to **Island** and, as the saying goes the rest is history. Perry, for better or worse, had a pivotal role in all of this.

Perry thrived as a producer and artist, though not in the traditional sense. After building his own studio, by the name of *Black Ark*, in the Kingston community of Washington Gardens, his penchant for innovation soared to new heights. It seems that the luxury of his own recording facilities allowed him to indulge in his wildest creative fantasies. Using kitchen utensils and random objects in recordings to sound like instruments or for sound effects was the norm. His recording sessions would be part music production, part séance and part theater. One such case in point was while he recorded one of his songs, *I Am the Ganja Man*. Here he undertook a bizarre ritual before voicing this particular song where he laid stalks of marijuana inside of a Bible then placing everything in front of the microphone.

His behavior grew increasingly erratic and he would act and speak like someone possessed by outside forces. His habits became inconsistent and less like a man in control of his faculties. His own songs were peppered with megalomaniac ranting, religious jargon and pure outright nonsense. But in his role as producer he was still able to turn out an impressive amount of hits working with artists such as Max Romeo: *War In Babylon* and *Chase The Devil;* Junior Byles: *Curly Locks* and *Beat Down Babylon*; I Threes: *Many Are Called*; and Junior Murvin: *Police and Thieves*

(Police and Thieves was released in 1976 and charted in the UK in 1980). Perry ultimately

reached the zenith of his creative powers in the 70s.

Later on Perry descended into a drug-assisted state of insanity. He claimed that his studio *The Black Ark* had become a haven for Satan so he burnt it to the ground. The curse of *The Black Ark* then claimed one of Perry's biggest stars Junior Byles, who lost his own house to a fire and was also driven to insanity, effectively ending his musical career. But Perry the "people funny boy" from Kendal in spite of all this would end up having the last laugh.

Even with his alleged mental instability he has survived and sustained a career mainly as an artist doing a decent amount of shows on an annual basis. Working with those he has inspired, such as European producers Adrian Sherwood and Neil Mad Professor Fraser, he is revered for all he's done for reggae in an historical sense.

Another triumph is his lofty position as a father of electronica (an offshoot of dub). At the same time, he is widely respected and admired by musicians from various genres – rock, punk and techno. Homage is paid to him many times over, with his work being sampled by the likes of The

Beastie Boys and Jay Z and his compositions covered by punk legends, The Clash.

Perry, now in his seventies, still puts out new material and tours the world. His catalog holds material that he produced for others over his long and storied career. One of his most famous quotes is "you should realize that everything starts from scratch".

18. Beres Hammond

Christened: Hugh Hammond
Born: August 28, 1955

The Survivor

Beres Hammond's talents go deep. He's been good for a very, very long time. And though the recognition wasn't initially there, it eventually materialized.

Hammond was born in the rural town of Annotto Bay in the Parish of St Mary on Jamaica's northern coast. He grew up listening to jazz and R&B, which was preferred by his father. He had his beginnings in the church, where he was often times asked to do solos of the popular hymns. He then branched out to performing at school concerts and was encouraged early on by the favorable responses he got, especially from the opposite sex.

Later on, in an effort to be situated at the center of the music scene, he began making frequent trips to Kingston. These initial steps saw him entering talent competitions, at which he usually distinguished himself as a promising new talent. One of these talent contests was organized by Winston Blake of Merritone fame. There, he had to do battle with singers who would later make names for themselves such as Ruddy Thomas, Jacob Miller, and Cynthia Schloss. This venturing out put him in touch with various operators within the industry and helped him to forge friendships that would serve him well in subsequent years.

Beginning his professional journey from the early seventies, he composed ballads in an effort to get on the map. But it would be the big hits from the 90s onwards closer to an indigenous format that would blow him up.

The trajectory of his long career plays out back

to front instead of the natural way. Hammond, in what must be the greatest tell-tale sign of the music's decline, had to actually "lower" his standards in order to gain the acclaim and fortune that he should have attained, back when he was really, really good. In his story is also a lesson of long-suffering and patience for up and coming artists believing that the road to stardom should be quick and easy. Hammond, for a time, became a casualty of a cultural reality that did not allow for one to operate outside of its parameters.

Hammond, in his neophyte stages, aspired to be a soul singer in the tradition of Sam Cooke or Marvin Gaye. This was quite naïve on his part. Soul singer? *In Jamaica?* This just was not realistic. Many Jamaican artists came to national attention by scoring hits in this format. But none had been able to viably sustain a career by continuing along that path. For a while however, the early chart success of Hammond's soul hits led him to believe that it could be done.

His first studio experience resulted in the Alton Ellis cover, *The Wanderer*. Then in 1975 a group of musicians asked him to front their roots band which they called *Zap Pow* which he did for three years. *Zap Pow* played a progressive strain of reggae and scored with the Third World inspired, *The System*. At the same time Hammond explored the possibilities of becoming a solo artist, but not in the traditional sense.

His first solo hit *One Step Ahead* (**Water Lilly/Aquarius**) in 1976 was not reggae but soul. Sounding like Marvin Gaye and arranged like the best of the **Motown** classics, the song caught the audience off guard. The song was irresistibly appealing due to its superior lyrical quality, fine musical accompaniment and pure talent that oozed from the vocal chords of Hammond. The single was from an excellent debut album titled *Soul Reggae* produced by his close friend Willie Lindo. It seemed Hammond's ambition was to create a new, or even more presumptuously his own, brand of reggae.

With a voice that was uniquely sexy, he was different and doing a pretty good job standing out. Known, even from these early days for his stubbornness, the singer wanted to stay above the fray of the typical dancehall scene. Even though he looked up to stars like Dennis Brown and Alton Ellis he was fonder of American R&B and its practitioners. In his heart he told himself, *this is the music I want to sing and this is the type of artist I want to be*. Hence he followed up with the equally pleasing *Got To Get Away*, which was also produced by Lindo and *I'm In Love*, for Joe Gibbs.

The records enjoyed heavy rotation on radio and consequently made the charts. But the average man on the street believed them to be foreign imports, not realizing that the sweet sounds came from one of their own. Hammond's insistence on being different was paying off, but only in the form of critical acclaim.

Top singers in this era (Brown, Issacs, McGregor and Holt) were simply giving the people what they wanted: roots reggae and dancehall lover's rock. Hammond in this scenario became the odd man out. His foreign sounding songs were nice for parties but did not enjoy the kind of mass support that could make him into a top draw for live performances. Therefore, he was not able to make a decent living.

This reality grated at his insides, confusing him about his future and shaking the convictions he held about his preferred style of music. But even in his dilemma, he possessed two gifts that would later take him over the hurdles – he was an excellent songwriter and a vocalist of the highest order. There is also the factor of having his own style and sound, which is critical to any artist to build a following. In the meantime however, he had to face his current situation of being somewhat famous but broke.

Herman Chin Loy, one of Hammond's earliest backers and the owner of **Aquarius Records,** with the interest generated by these "soul" hits was said to have received an offer from **Warner Bros** to sign Beres. But Hammond was overwhelmed with stress and, rather than play ball, chose to retreat to the country.

Whenever he reemerged from his self-imposed exile, he was really more interested in doing his own little thing with Lindo. So, from 1978 into the early 80s, they turned out other popular soul type singles: *If Only I Knew, I Miss You* and *Love Delight.*

Still, the lean years persisted. While other popular singers of the period could at least afford to ride a motorbike (*in those days a visible sign of upward mobility*), Hammond had to make do with public transportation or walk. No man of intelligence would keep beating his head against a wall and Hammond had to wake up. He was now forced by his state of poverty, to see the music business not as he wanted it to be, but as it really was.

The turnaround came in 1980 with a minor hit called *Groovy Little Thing*. Then with a hand from Sly Dunbar, who was just getting into the new drum machine technology, came the song that would officially begin a new phase of the singer's career in the mid-80s. The humorous *One Dance* was released on his newly minted, self-owned **Harmony House** label. The tune depicted a man losing his girl to a smooth operator who stole her after only one dance. It caught on instantly. The momentum was maintained with *She Loves Me Now* (a kind of serial to *One Dance*) and another single *Settling Down*. He was at last getting a firm footing then out of nowhere came trouble.

In 1987 Kingston was caught up in a deadly wave of crime with too much guns being in too many hands. Hammond fell victim to thugs who broke into his house. Once the thieves were inside Hammond was tied up while they ransacked the house before making off with all of his worldly valuables. The experience unnerved Hammond so much that he left Jamaica in anger bound for New York City.

Unfortunately, a career that was just taking off had to be ushered back to port by the unexpected turn of events. In the *Big Apple*, he went back to work recording and releasing the album *Have A Nice Weekend*. In New York City he was delighted to be able to collaborate with, British reggae star Maxi Priest, with whom he recorded an excellent single *How Can We Ease The Pain*.

But singers of Hammond's caliber don't grow on trees. Producers back in Jamaica were eager to get him in the studio and were constantly hounding him to return home. Hammond sensing that the dream was slipping away complied, reentering the fray singing like a man reborn. Producer Donovan Germaine pounced on Hammond by recording the singer on his new riddim, alongside new stars Tony Rebel and Buju Banton. This allowed Hammond to score with *Tempted To Touch*, the first of what would become a parade of hits in the 90s.

This move announced that Beres was back, and this time thankfully, to stay. The year 1992 became his, with his only competition coming from a young upstart called Garnett Silk. That year he broke the bank with the biggest single, yet in his now sixteen-year career, the Tappa Kukie produced *Putting Up Resistance*. The song was his hardest hitting piece of social commentary, becoming an anthem for the working class. After this, Hammond was unstoppable.

Now recast as a reggae-lovers rock artist, there would be no more musical gyrations or further shying away from the spotlight. Through the difficult periods, he recognized that his native people wanted indigenous music. Change he would but did not abandon his original ethos of quality as a songwriter and vocalist. Most importantly, this resurgence gave him the financial security that had previously eluded him for too many years.

From then onwards the hits started piling up: *Can You Play Some More*, *Double Trouble*, *Full Attention*, *Show It Off*, *Queen and Lady*, *Rockaway*, *They Gonna Talk* and *I Feel Good* being just a few.

Then **Elektra Records** came calling for Hammond now a hot commodity. The artist quickly struck a deal. This resulted in 1994's *In Control* album, featuring the single *No Disturb Sign*. This completed a total financial turnaround for Hammond and with his earnings now way up, built a mansion in the upscale St. Andrew neighborhood of Stony Hills.

After his relationship with **Elektra** ended, he entered into a successful partnership with **VP Records** and became their marquee artist. In his deal with the label, he produces the material for his own **Harmony House** imprint, while VP handles manufacturing, marketing and distribution.

Hammond is the most consistent of any artist remaining in the reggae genre. He is one of the few headliners that are left and not many Jamaicans can play Madison Square Gardens and do so profitably; Hammond can.

In early 2011 the living legend was paid the highest compliment with the release of a tribute album: *Our Favorite Beres Hammond Songs* (**Penthouse**). The album is a collection of the artist's biggest hits covered by both established and newer artists.

In October of 2013, Hammond received one of Jamaica's highest medals from the government, *The Order Of Jamaica*, for his contributions to the nation's arts and culture. He is now officially Beres Hammond O.J.

Hammond's story is still unfolding even as we speak, and proves that if you are able to hold on long enough you will receive the rewards that are just around the corner.

17. Barrington Levy

Christened: Barrington Levy
Born: April 30, 1964

True Original

Barrington Levy, through old fashion hard work and dogged persistence, has outlasted most. He proudly owns a hall of fame length career that spans over thirty years, and with it are hits in almost every decade since he burst onto the scene.

Levy was born in Kingston, but spent his early years in the central parish of Clarendon. He was only fifteen when he started to rack up an impressive amount of popular singles.

Beginning his career as a member of the short-lived group, The Mighty Multitude, with a cousin Everton Dacres, the single *My Black Girl* was Levy's first vocal feature.

The restless teenager when first striking out moved from dance to dance, singing on many of the popular sound systems. On one such occasion a street wise hustler called Henry "Junjo" Lawes, a former singer turned producer, discovered Levy. Lawes knew talent and was not about to let this kid slips through his fingers.

Lawes quickly summoned seminal backing group Roots Radics to the legendary Channel One studio on Maxfield Avenue to cut a few sides with his new find. Roots Radics, which consisted of Eric "Bingy Bunny" Lamont (guitar), Errol "Flabba" Holt (bass) Wycliffe "Steely" Johnson (keyboards) and Lincoln "Style" Scott (drums), recycled some of the popular riddims from the Studio One period.

The artist, over the course of the coming weeks, was kept busy in the studio.

Lawes method in those days had him recording the instrumentals at Channel One then hopping across town to Waterhouse to see Osbourne "King Tubby" Ruddock, to lay vocals and mix. King Tubby's unique sound was made partially in the hands of a brilliant understudy. An engineer called Scientist, who provided the clean vocal mixes that would be heard on Levy's first hits starting in 1979: *A Yah Wi Deh*, *Shine Eye Girl*, *Looking My Love* and, the song that put him on the map, *Collie Weed*.

These songs heralded the coming of a fresh face, with a voice that was easy to love. Levy's vocals had traces of his musical idol Dennis Brown, though more in style than sound.

His eagerness to work hard and big ambitions cleared a path for him to quickly race to the top of the business. By 1980, he could already boast of four albums *Shine Eye Gal* (**Jah Life**), *Bounty Hunter* (**Burning Sounds**), *Englishman* and *Robin Hood* (**Greensleeves**), on the market. This was a remarkable achievement for such a young singer.

His direct approach to songwriting and simplicity with words appealed to the everyman and his unusual use of melody became his signature. His singing style also employed a lot of adlibs, a kind of scat like singing more popular with jazz vocalists than with reggae artists.

Most of his tunes sounded like an intimate conversation with the listener. It's as if you were privy to some very personal details. In *My Woman* he starts with *"my woman my woman she is a problem"* and in *Looking My Love* he moans, *"looking my love it's not easy"*. In *Shine Eye Gal* he also gives his male audience a salient piece of relationship advice, a warning to watch out for a woman's greed singing: *"a shine eye girl is a trouble to a man"*. Levy has a special way with melodies that is distinct and, in spite of not being a lyricist of high order, made unforgettable songs.

In the eighties Barrington was huge scoring one chart topper after the other. The biggest of them being: *My Woman, Under Mi Sensi, Black Roses, Money Move, Mary Long Tongue, She's Mine, Dances Are Changing* and *21 Girls Salute*. Countless hits showcased him as a talent of uncommon versatility. He could out sing most singers and ride the riddims better than most DJs. Sweetly serenading on *My Woman* and *Black Roses*, he could effectively switch into sing-jay pattern with a display of tongue twisting acrobatics on *Under Mi Sensi* and *Dances Are*

Changing.

From 1980 he made the first of what would become a record thirteen appearances, second only to Dennis Brown, on reggaes preeminent live show Reggae Sunsplash. In 1984, Levy won the British Reggae Award for Best Male Vocalist.

After an ultra-successful decade, he began the 90s reinventing his style and hitting with a mellow sounding Bob Andy cover, *Too Experienced*. Although over the years he had worked with many different producers, most notably: George Phang, Joe Gibbs, Jack Scorpio and Alvin Ranglin he had a special chemistry with Henry Lawes. This *midas* partnership would now be repeated when he worked with producer Paul "Jah Screw" Love. Love was the owner of the **Time One** imprint. He was able to create a more mature sound for Levy, which served to deepen his fan base. *Too Experienced* was the first big hit out of this partnership followed by *My Time*, and the *Soul-to-Soul* like sounding Don't *Throw It All Away*.

The next natural step for the upwardly mobile Levy was to get into bed with a major label. The first, **Island** released *Divine* in 1991. With **MCA** came *Barrington* in 1993. Divine spawned a top

20 UK hit *Tribal Beats*, which sampled Levy's *Here I Come*, featuring Rebel MC and Tenor Fly. *Barrington* produced by Lee Jaffe remade some of his old classics like *Murderer* and *Dances Are Changing* and put out two singles – the bouncy *Work* and the misguided ballad *Vice Versa*.

These albums were poor sellers, and for good reasons. The songs were poorly crafted and the marketing was wrong. In hindsight, if **MCA** and **Island** had built on the chemistry Levy had with producer Paul Love, who knew what songs to choose for the artist, the results may have been different. You see, Levy wrote in a simple style in Jamaican patois, which sometimes worked for the DJs, but suicidal for a singer trying to break internationally. One review in an American daily, The St Louis Post Dispatch, panned the *Barrington* album for "commercializing" Levy's sound and called it a "drastic shift in musical direction" and "painful" to listen to.

It took Love to ultimately produce the song that returned Levy to the charts 1996's *Living Dangerously* (featuring Bounty Killer). The hit became the title track on Levy's 1998 album on **Breakaway Records**. In an effort to bridge the generation gap, he then recorded a host of singles, which were collaborations with the young dancehall DJs reigning at the time. The most notable of these being the *Murderer* remix with Beenie Man for the *Duets* album.

Levy's indefatigable march continued into the 2000s, mostly touring on his vast catalog and reintroducing himself to a new audience, young Americans. Spending most of his time in Los Angeles he attempted to expand his fan base working on the same bill with reggae influenced "alternative" groups like Sublime and Slightly Stoopid. For the urban market he paired with rappers Kardinal Official, Snoop Dogg and the incarcerated Shyne. Most of this a result of a strategy by his management **Platinum Camp** to which he was signed to at the time.

Many were indifferent to this new approach and thought Levy should concentrate on quality songs instead of pandering to the now crowd.

Yet still the veteran has a small but rabid fan base that keeps turning out for his many dates all over the world. Truth of the matter is that Levy has nothing more to prove.

Barrington Levy's longevity is living proof that in the entertainment business, where the attrition rate is extremely high, the longer you survive is the more you become an institution.

16. Yellowman

Christened: Winston Foster
Born: January 15, 1956

The Waymaker

Yellowman is not the most successful DJ to have come out of Jamaica in the commercial sense, but is certainly the one who cleared the path for others who would do better.

He is arguably, the most charismatic of his time, and the first to be elevated from being a mere DJ to superstar entertainer. Crowned as "King of the DJs" and credited for taking a heretofore parochial art form on to the world stage.

The story of Yellowman is one of the most inspiring. It is said that his parents abandoned him so he had to be placed in an orphanage. His first home was the Maxfield Park Children Home, and later the Alpha Boys Home, a Catholic School known for its music program, ran by nuns.

Foster was born an albino: which is usually a Negro person with a rare skin disorder and his condition manifested in a high yellowish complexion, usually accompanied by blemishes and legions. Back then in Jamaica, an albino was usually scorned and ostracized. Those in this category were known as a "*dundus*"; and lived lives of quiet desperation. Albinos were supposed to stay hidden from public view, as they did not fit the image of blackness nor whiteness.

For the young Foster, becoming aware of his musical talents was no instant panacea, as he was endeavoring to make it in the toughest profession of them all. With the deck stacked against him and not having anything else but his talent and love for music, he had to learn to swim with sharks in an ocean of rejection.

Reflecting on the early difficult years of trying to make it, in some interviews, he explained that many producers refused to work with him and other entertainers scorned him. Some did this to the point of not even wanting to touch the microphone. Many disdainfully use their handkerchiefs to cover the instrument in order to not handle it with their bare hands.

The name Yellowman was a nickname that was due to his condition, though not meant as a compliment. The daily taunts and the ridicule he had to endure was a cruel reality that seemed to strengthen his resolve. In what would become characteristic of his rise to prominence, he dug deep within, mustering the strength to see the day when he would turn the joke back on his detractors. Instead of being negative about the whole thing, he used it to his advantage and made it his greatest asset. His problem, he decided, would become his calling card, a badge of honor to say, *"Look I'm special"*.

At the beginning of his career performing at

dances and at talent shows, he was often times booed by the crowds, even still he never ran away in shame. He would always continue to perform until the hostility was won over. He persisted against the odds and this trial by fire was the thing that refined and turned him into one of the greatest performers of the dancehall.

He had his beginnings on sound systems in the mid-70s such as *Black South* and *Aces* alongside fellow DJ and future sidekick Fathead, but shot to national attention by winning the celebrated Tastee Talent Contest in 1979. At the contest that was held at Cross Roads, he pranced and toasted his way into the hearts of both the judges and the large audience. In delivering the winning number *"Barnabas Killing"*, a story about a "vampire slaying", he worked the crowd as if his life depended on it. In many ways it did. After gaining major publicity from his victory at the contest, many producers were finally willing to give him a fair chance.

His first hits *Mad Over Me* and *I'm Getting Married* came in 1981. Yellowman had his own recognizable sound and the public gravitated to it. His delivery was a bit slower than other emcees at the time, allowing for clear diction. His baritone register in which he toasted gave his voice and air of seduction and an irresistible quality.

In a genre known for its expression through aggression, he seemed to be caressing the listener, bringing him or her his way. He accomplished this by employing every weapon in his arsenal, such as humor, sarcasm, and of course, sex talk commonly called "slackness". His songs would incorporate everything from advertising slogans, nursery rhymes, church hymns and bits and pieces of popular as well as classic tunes. His main goal was to entertain, and he was becoming the best at it.

In the early 80s, albeit for only three short years, he conquered the dancehall by displaying bravado and shameless self-promotion. The impact he made however, would linger long after the hits stopped coming. If word of mouth is the best kind of promotion he proved it. He would mention his name several times in most of his songs turning ridicule on its head. He would say things like *"I'm yellow and I'm attractive"* or *"she have my yellow baby"*. He would tout that *"Yellowman is sexy"* and *"Yellowman is great much like a musical Ali"*. He sold his claim to greatness to such an extent that the hype became the reality. It was evident that this artist had nerve with talent to match.

On stage he gave complete performances, unlike most artists of the period whose common practice was to start then stop before running off stage. This was done in anticipation of being called back by the audience. Yellow, in contrast, much like one of his musical contemporaries Brigadier Jerry, would turn one song into a marathon affair. During one particular appearance at Reggae Sunsplash 1982, the DJ gave a legendary performance by winning over the 30,000-strong crowds with raw honesty. On this occasion he spoke about his hard childhood, but ended triumphantly with a slogan borrowed from the black power movement. He declared, "I'm proud to be yellow". It was one of his finest moments and made him into a star.

He was keener than most to recognize the power of imagery and made a conscious effort to appear more than ordinary. He posed for pictures like a model and dressed like a rock star. The pictures of him at the height of his career are now among the few, Bob Marley and Shabba Ranks included, of Jamaican artists that are regarded as collector's items.

Another factor of his success was in teaming

up with producer Henry "Junjo" Lawes, owner of the **Volcano** label who also became his manager. Lawes was one of the top producers with enough clout to have Yellowman's records on the radio all day long. From 1981 to 1984, he promoted the artist to the point of saturation.

In those days, you needed the full support of a top radio jock and fortunately in Lawe's pocket were on air impresario Barry "Barry G" Gordon of JBC Radio. In the 80s Gordon held court and wielded so much power that no artist could possibly succeed without his endorsement.

After Yellowman became wildly popular with a lot of gimmick type songs he then turned his attention to addressing issues of social concern. On later hits like *Mr. Chin* he warned some Chinese merchants about their unscrupulous behavior and on another song *Operation Radication* lambasted a special police squad for exercising brutality.

In 1983 he unleashed the monster hit unforgettable for its long title, *Zunguzungzuguzungguzeng* and crowned as "DJ of the Year", a title he held for the previous two years. It was also in 83 that the title *King Yellow* started to be bandied around entertainment circles.

After the release of another big hit, 1984's *Nobody Move* and now regarded as the undisputed King; he inked a contract with **Columbia Records** becoming the first Jamaican dancehall dj to sign with a major label. This in itself was historical. He then reached another milestone in his career by also being the first in the dj genre be nominated for a Grammy

The impact of Yellowmans signing was huge. He was the trailblazer to clear the way for many more to come. This would culminate in a similar situation for another dancehall star Shabba Ranks who after signing to Sony/Epic took dancehall music to stratospheric heights.

Yellowman's album for **CBS** *King Yellowman* was not a commercial success. Nevertheless, it was a cultural triumph that secured the artist's place in history for taking the dancehall genre into unchartered territory.

To promote the album, **CBS** put the artist on tour for an extended period of time and not being in Jamaica allowed the ascension of others like Josey Wales and Admiral Bailey to fill the vacuum created by his absence. As a result his local popularity took a severe hit. Poor sales of

King Yellowman also sealed his fate at the label, which opted not to renew his contract.

After this lull, Yellowman proved why he was a cut above the rest with a cover of Fats Domino's *Blueberry Hill*. The single, had a hand from two bright young engineers, Bobby "Digital" Dixon and Tony "CD" Kelly. Released in 1987 on the **Kangal** label, it became up until then, the fastest song to reach number one in Jamaican. On *Blueberry Hill* Yellowman was singing, a surprise move that floored even his harshest critics. He continued in the same vein with the less successful but equally pleasing *Three Nights A Week*.

His career was in good shape but his health was a different story. Complications of his albinism followed him into adulthood and at the height of his popularity he was diagnosed with skin cancer. Doctors ordered immediate surgery to remove a tumor in his mouth. The procedure was a success but necessitated the removal of his left jawbone.

With his physical appearance radically altered by the surgery, out went his sex appeal through the window. Some prominent religious ministers at the time called the episode "judgment from

God" because of what they considered to be the artist's "glamorization of slackness". But the ever-resilient Yellowman kept going, health problems and all.

Today, Yellowman remains one of the hardest working men in showbiz by constant touring, while other stars of his era have faded, due to inactivity.

Beenie Man, one of his successors, in the 2000s would crown himself "King Of The Dancehall", but it is a title that he will never be able to legitimately own. Moses Davis's defiant act seems to smack of treason. Winston Foster, on the other hand, was duly anointed as such.

15. Louise Bennett

Christened: Louise Bennett
Born: September 7, 1919
Deceased: July 26, 2006

Mother of a nation

Sister Nancy was the first female DJ to break through in the annals of Jamaican music. Lady Saw is the first genuine female superstar within the DJ genre, but the mother of the spoken word set to music is cultural legend, artist, actress, historian and poetess Louise Bennett.

Not only was she a poetess but also a gifted singer with several albums to her credit. But her single most important achievement is to have elevated the Jamaican dialect (a mixture of English with local improvisation) called Patois, to the status of being considered a language in itself. The pride that all Jamaicans have in their native speech can be attributed to her work.

She practiced the Jamaican art form in its infancy, singing folk songs. These same folk songs were later translated into mento which was the earliest form of recorded music in Jamaica. She argued at a time when it was taboo, that the Jamaican dialect being described in intellectual circles as "a corruption of the English language" was "complete nonsense". She put forward the point of view that in the same way that English was a derivative of Latin, Patois in turn is a derivative of English (*mixed with the African mother tongue*).

Louise Bennett was born on North Street in the heart of downtown Kingston. She realized her gifts at the tender age of fourteen, when she wrote her first poem *Pread Out*. The piece was inspired by the ordinary folks who in those times were consigned to the back of the tram cars running in the capital. In colonial Jamaica native blacks had to give up their seats to whites. In the poem she urged people to resist and instead of getting up they should *"Pread Out"*.

In one interview she spoke of how her seamstress mother encouraged her foray into the expression of language through poetry by saying, *"if you write as well as I sew you will be okay"*.

For formal education she attended Ebenezer and Calabar Elementary, St Simons All Age and Excelsior College. As her talent blossomed she became the only Jamaican to be accepted into The Royal Academy of Dramatic Arts in England, via a British Council Scholarship in the 1940s. After graduating she worked with a number of repertories all over London and shot to international prominence with a legendary performance on the BBCs Christmas Special in 1944. In this same decade she wrote no less than five books of Jamaican poetry.

As the 1950's rolled in, the nation was pregnant with cultural expectations, and the manifestation of Jamaican expressions through recorded music was on in earnest. This gave the pioneer an opportunity to document her love for the forerunner of all Jamaican musical stages, the original folk songs. The result was an album released in 1953 called *Louise Bennett's Jamaican Folk Songs*. She soon followed with *Jamaica Singing Games* (1953), *Miss Louse Views* (1967), *Listen To Louise* (1968) *Carifesta Ring Ding* (1976), *The Honorable Miss Lou* (1981), *Miss Lou Live In London* (1983) and finally *Yes Mi Dear* on **Island Records.**

The full-figured Miss Lou came to embody all things Jamaican and, even before independence that came in 1962, she was already being regarded as a national treasure. Her attire was always in the traditional style. The outfits she created had an afro-centric lean and came to embody a look that was indigenous to Jamaica. Her personality typified what was good about Jamaican people, known for their sharp wit and sense of humor.

In 1969 Bari Johnson, actor and pioneer, was producing a local children show for television, called *Ring Ding*. He originally offered hosting duties to one of Jamaica's leading acting talents, the slender and sexy Leonie Forbes, who declined. Miss Lou when offered the same role accepted. So from 1969 to 1980, she was welcomed into the homes of thousands. The show was aired on the Jamaica Broadcasting Company's television station and Saturdays would never be the same.

Ring Ding was a variety show where kids performed in front of an audience of their peers. It was more than entertainment. It was *edutainment*; the show raised a whole generation of Jamaican children who became stars in their own right.

In the voice of every female DJ, and many of their male counterparts, is the presence of Miss Lou. The entire genre of dub poetry later to be popularized by Mutabaruka and to a lesser extent Grace Jones owes Ms. Lou a debt of gratitude.

Many folk songs having their origins a generation or two before her birth emanating from the slave plantations were recorded and popularized by her. Due to her efforts, these same folksongs found their way into the mainstream. An example is Lady Saw being inspired by Miss Lou's *Under The Coconut Tree*, to write her hit *Under The Sycamore Tree*. There is also an uncanny similarity of Ms. Lou's *Chi Chi Bud* to parts of Eric Donaldson's Festival winner, *Land Of My Birth*.

Besides writing and singing, Miss Lou also acted in many folk stage productions called Pantomimes. These took place around Christmas time, usually at the historical Ward Theater located in the heart of downtown Kingston. Many of them were sold out affairs owing in no small part to her star power.

She then branched out into motion pictures most notably appearing in 1986s *Club Paradise* alongside Jimmy Cliff, Robin Williams and, screen legend, Peter O'Toole. On top of all this she still found time to be an educator teaching speech and drama at the University Of The West Indies.

Her husband was Eric Coverly whom she married in 1954. Many Jamaicans mistakenly thought that her spouse was her faithful acting partner Ranny Williams. This misconception was not mere innuendo as in showbiz circles and in the eyes of the public Mas Ranny and Miss Lou was inseparable.

Her status as a cultural icon and her place as Jamaica's "foremost folklorist" were solidified with the Norman Manley Award for Excellence in the field of arts (MBE), the Order of Jamaica (OJ) (1974), Jamaica's Musgrave Silver and Gold Medal awards for Arts and Culture (1983). In 1988 The University Of The West Indies bestowed her with an Honorary Doctorate. And in

2001 the Jamaican Government appointed her as Cultural Ambassador At Large.

Miss Lou is the mother of the nation who helped to define a people who desired to take their place in the world. She engraved into the minds of Jamaicans the ethos of what it meant to be independent. A cultural giant in the same league as Garvey and Marley she weaned a proud people in at least a cultural sense, off of the colonial milk. This was achieved in part with Jamaicans utilizing something from their own unique culture, manifested by the worldwide popularity of reggae music.

In later years she made Toronto, Canada a second home and continued to perform, lecture and even write songs for film. She died in 2006 in Toronto. And is gone but not forgotten, especially by Jamaica, the nation she served so well.

14. Bunny Wailer

Christened: Neville Livingston
Born: April 10, 1947

Last Man Standing

The Beatles lost key members, so did The Who and The Rolling Stones. Then there is The Wailers. Bunny Wailer is the sole surviving member of the group that emerged from tiny Jamaica to become one of the most influential of all time.

Two small body boys, Neville Livingston and

Nesta Marley, were childhood friends from back in the rural parish of St Ann. They both attended Stepny All Age in the district known as Nine Mile. The youths literally became a family when Neville's father Thadeus and Nesta's mother Cedella became intimately involved and had a child Claudette. The boys then moved to Kingston as stepbrothers with their respective parents.

In Kingston while living in the slum called Trench Town, they met Winston McIntosh, who in contrast to both was tall and darker in complexion. With all three realizing that they had the common bond of musical talent, they took up with each other.

A big plus was in finding their way to the home of Joe Higgs of the Higgs and Wilson fame. He was a neighborhood musical mentor for youths in the area. With Higgs, they started to learn the rudiments of songwriting, instrumentation and vocal harmonies.

While there, the three also met Beverly Keslo, Junior Brathwaite and Cherry Green and became a group that went through several name and lineup changes. They came to be known as The Teenagers, The Wailing Rudeboys, The Wailing Wailers and finally, The Wailers.

They ventured out from around 1963 and did their maiden recordings for the legendary record man Coxsone Dodd. With whom they scored a number of hits. The Wailers had in the group two strong personalities Bob Marley and Peter Tosh. Bunny, though possessing a voice of gold, fell in line behind the two natural leaders and mostly sang harmonies on their compositions.

But according to many sources, when it came on to sticky situations and fights Bunny was no shrinking violet and would be the first to throw a blow in spite of his diminutive stature standing around five feet. Some **Studio One** musicians of yore, session players for Coxsone, remember Livingston as one with a quick temper. When crossed he, in an instant, would hurl objects at the intended target. Another case in point is when Lee Scratch Perry allegedly sold out the rights to some of the Wailers recordings without compensating them. On running into Perry, it is said that, Bunny initiated a beating.

By 1964 The Wailers scored the hit *Simmer Down* and in 1967 Livingston was arrested for marijuana possession. According to Livingston, he was never formerly charged but still served a year and a half in prison. On his return in late

1968, the group released the single *Nice Time* on their own **Wail N Soul M** label.

As history goes, the group went from strength to strength until that fateful visit to the London office of **Island Records** founder Chris Blackwell, who signed then in 1972. Blackwell handed over four thousand pounds in exchange for delivery of the first album.

By the time of its release, the groundbreaking *Catch A Fire* album, the first by a Jamaican group to be marketed to rock audiences, trouble was already brewing amongst the musical brothers. This became evident as after the tour in support of the album in 1974 Bunny left the group while they were preparing the *Natty Dread* album. This was according to many sources, including Blackwell, because of reluctance on Bunny's part to tour. Marley was reportedly to have said in interviews that Bunny was "afraid of the cold weather". Tosh, for his own reasons, soon made his exit as well.

Bunny then took some time off from the music business and relaxed a little with walks in the hills and spending time fishing. Soon thereafter, he started his **Solomonic** label as a vehicle for his own compositions. On **Solomonic** he put out a slew of singles, some of them became successful and many just releases. It would appear that even though he walked away from the Wailers, he was still technically under contract with **Island**. So in 1976 he gave the label the *Blackheart Man* album.

The disc was critically acclaimed and considered by many musical historians as a reggae classic. With cuts such as the autobiographical *Fighting Against Conviction*, the soothing *Dreamland* and the biblical tome *Armageddon*, This was Bunny Wailer at his best.

The following year he satisfied his obligations to **Island** with the *Protest* album. However, he still refused to tour in support of these releases. This may be the reason why he is the least known and celebrated of the three Wailers, especially outside of Jamaica.

Livingston's solo career highlighted his strength as both a vocalist and songwriter. He has a distinct sound and was revealed to be a unique vocal stylist and lyricist of the highest order. Bob had his sound, Peter had his own voice and Bunny began to establish his own identity as well. His melodies were simple but catchy and his material placed emphasis on the lighter side of life such as dancing and fun. Of the three Wailers, Bunny was more of a comedian in a peculiar way, and his radical views were expressed in ways that were non- threatening.

Yet still, his political songs carried weight as with the case of *Crucial*, a single released in the election year of 1980. The song though not sanctioned by Livingston was adopted by the opposition party of the time, Jamaica Labour Party, for their campaign. The song spoke so vividly of the hardship being experienced by ordinary Jamaicans that politicians co-opted it for their own selfish purposes.

He followed the **Island** releases with a few more albums but in a twist of irony came into his own right as a major star in 1981 the year of Marley's death.

In that year came the hits laded, the brilliant *Rock N Groove* album. The disc contained at least five smash hits: *Dance Rock*, *Roots Man Skanking*, *Cool Runnings* (a movie was later named off it), *Ballroom Floor* and the title track. At this point it felt like the baton had been passed, as Bunny ascended to the individual medal podium of reggae.

His unwillingness to tour built a strong

demand for him overseas. So when he finally relented and announced that he would play Madison Square Gardens in New York City, it created a media frenzy not seen since the heyday of Marley himself. The 1986 concert was a sold out affair, and is regarded as one of those noteworthy occasions and received a lot of international press.

As the 80s came to a close, Wailer characteristically started to turn his attention to the dancehall craze that was sweeping the island. It seemed that he feared being left behind by the more popular DJ acts of the time and declared himself to be "*the original dancehall dada*"

However, this was met with more ridicule than respect by both die-hard older fans and a newer generation that hardly knew him. In an attempt to connect with hardcore dancehall fans at a 1990 Sting concert he was booed off stage.

On another front in his role as a songwriter he is one of the more established figures. The accolades are well deserved as he gave Marcia Griffiths two of her biggest hits *Dreamland* and the worldwide smash Electric *Boogie.*

A weak point in his profile, though is his

penchant for stirring up controversies. One such episode his when he was included on a panel with Chris Blackwell at the Rototom Festival in Europe. On this particular occasion he inappropriately proceeded to level numerous accusations of dishonesty against Blackwell, hardly the forum for such things and seemingly without much hard evidence.

There is also the public spat between himself and the American rap superstar Snoop Dogg. In 2012, Snoop visited Jamaica and professed to have converted to Rastafarianism and subsequently changed his name to Snoop Lion. He sought out Bunny as one of his spiritual advisors, did a song with him for his so-called "reggae album" *Reincarnated*, and shot a movie featuring Bunny. However, when time came for the release of both the film and the album Bunny, suddenly turned on the rapper labeling him as a fraud. Snoop retaliated in the press with his own barrage of put-downs. Bunny Wailer obviously seeks the spotlight just for the sake of being in it.

Bunny's legacy as an elder statesman of reggae however is secure, especially with him being a three-time Grammy winner by way of – *Time Will Tell: A Tribute To Bob Marley, Crucial Roots*

Classics and Hall Of Fame: A tribute to Bob Marley's 50th Anniversary.

These three formed the so-called Trinity of Reggae/The Jamaican Beatles. Cancer claimed Bob and Peter got murdered. Bunny, in every sense of the word, became the last man standing.

13. Desmond Dekker

Christened: Desmond Dacres
Born: July 16, 1941
Deceased: May 25, 2006

The First

The first Jamaican artist to break internationally, on both sides of the Atlantic, with an original song is not one of the more famous names that would readily come to mind. This distinction belongs to the great Desmond Dekker.

In 1964, Millie Small had a hit with cover song *My Boy Lollipop*. However, she did not go on to being the star of significance, as did Dekker. In 1969, he took his ode of poverty and struggles to number one in Britain. It even made way into the US top ten. The title is a little ditty called *Israelites*.

All artists of his genre who have had successes internationally owe him a debt of gratitude. He was the superstar of Jamaica's first popular musical art form ska, and the pioneer of the pure indigenous sound even before the impact of reggae.

Born in Kingston during the years of the second World War, the young Dacres tragically lost both his parents and was orphaned at the Roman Catholic school Alpha Boys Home. The school had the best music program on the island and he soaked up the atmosphere.

Luckily for Desmond even though losing his parents was tough; he still had a support group consisting of grandparents and several aunts who looked out for him. Making sure he was on track with his school work and taking him to church. This religious background informed a lot of his music, which turned out to be like hymns within a secular framework.

Still, the road was not straight and he was forced to fend for himself during teen years by apprenticing as a tailor and welder. Then music crept into his life and eventually took him over. He could not concentrate on anything else and at his place of work; he could be heard singing at any time of the day.

Encouraged by friends to take his talent seriously he began to audition for the producers of the day, and turned down by all. When he showed up at **Beverly Records** on Orange Street, he sang for Derrick Morgan, an artist and talent scout for the label. Morgan liked what he heard and Dacres got to record for producer and label owner Leslie Kong. Renamed as Desmond Dekker he became label mates with another Jamaican great, Jimmy Cliff. Kong also became the manager for both Dekker and Cliff.

Dekker's first release *Honor You Father and Mother* brought him instant recognition, but only after serving a two-year internship before Kong deemed him ready for the road. A slew of singles that included *Labor For Learning, Sinners Come Home* and the masterpiece *King Of Ska* soon followed.

Kong then put Dekker with brothers (Carl, Clive, Barry and Patrick Howard), known as the *Four Aces*, as his background singers. Dekker and the Four Aces proceeded to take over the local scene piling up twenty hit singles in a row. The most popular were *Ah It Mek* and *007(Shanty Town)*.

The Howard brothers, now simply called The Aces when one member departed from the group, with Dekker out front, ruled the roost. Even though they became popular with songs that were moral cautionary tales, they also patronized the rude bwoy phenomenon sweeping over Jamaica with bad boy anthems like the aforementioned *007, Tougher Than Tough, Rudie Got Soul* and *Rude Bwoy Train*.

The pairing of the Aces with Dekker produced records with an exquisite sound on which brilliant harmonies soared, taking the songs to unimaginable heights. Also, at this time, most of their hits were on tracks played by musicians that would later form the Skatalites, the standard-bearers of ska .

In 1967 Dekker shattered the proverbial glass ceiling that deemed music from the Caribbean as one that was only for its ethnic borders. International acclaim began with *007(Shantytown)* on **Trojan** charting in the UK top twenty. Within a matter of months he had three hits in the UK the other two being *A It Mek* (#7) and the Jimmy Cliff penned, *You Can Get It If You Really Want* (#2) found on the album *This Is Desmond Dekker.*

Israelites, on **Pyramid Records**, was two minutes and thirty-five seconds of musical brilliance. The song was sung in Dekker's native patois and by the summer of 1969, was number 1 in the UK and, more remarkably, made it to number 9 in the US.

Israelites, was a bouncy number that closely resembled the blues of the American south, and was a worldwide smash selling over a million copies, putting Dekker into the history books as the first Jamaican to have this level of success with an original song

The success of the song came about as several factors were aligned. In Dekker there was a talented artist, in Kong you had a good producer, and in addition an expansive marketing campaign and the distribution muscle of the UK partners. This was no coincidence as Leslie Kong and Chris Blackwell of **Trojan** were both original shareholders in **Island Records**. Kong was also a partner with Australian engineer Graeme Goodall, with whom he formed the **Pyramid** imprint.

On the heels of stardom, brought on by the success of the number one hit, Dekker toured the UK. On tour he was mobbed by adoring fans and became the darling of the British press gracing magazine covers and appearing on the BBC music show *Top Of The Pops*. Dekker was a star and looked the part, dressing in flamboyant costumes and on stage exhibiting moves like Rolling Stone front man Mick Jagger.

Dekker was a star in Britain and Jamaica, but not in the US. In the US he failed to take root or chart another single. This might have also been due to the fact that he never seriously concentrated on that market, in terms of promotion and touring.

Meanwhile back in Jamaica, Dekker topped the island's Festival Song contest by becoming the runner up in 1967 with *Unity* and went on to win in the following year with *Intensified*.

At the beginning of the 70s Dekker began sharing his time between Jamaica and the UK. As the decade progressed, he made a final decision to settle in Britain permanently. His reason was that it was less hectic to tour the country while living there, instead of flying all the way from Jamaica for each show.

In a cruel twist of fate Dekker seemingly at the peak of his career suffered a major loss with the untimely death of his manager Leslie Kong. Kong only in his thirties in the summer of 71 died suddenly of a heart attack. Dekker was devastated.

In the wake of this tragic event he felt somewhat lost and uncertain about his future. The role that Kong played in Dekker's professional life cannot be overstated and from that point forward he was not able to fully capitalize on his past successes. Kong's death also hit the singer where it hurt the most: financially. According to sources, Kong had formed a company into which he put most of Dekker's earnings which he could not get his hands on. Nevertheless, he had no choice but to soldier-on.

There was a power center that dealt with Jamaican artists at this time and anyone operating outside of it struggled. At its core was Chris Blackwell who owned **Island**. Also in it was the entrepreneurial class of Jamaican Chinese who owned the pressing plants and controlled distribution. The pioneering producers like Coxsone Dodd and Duke Reid had to deal with them. Blackwell had a plethora of smaller labels and distribution deals with the majors both in Britain and the US and was hard to get around unless you dealt with the majors directly. Unlike Jimmy Cliff, who was forward thinking and astute enough to know that in leaving **Island** he would have to stay within the major label structure, Dekker fell out of the power center and as a result below the radar.

Moving to England was also another factor that pushed him out of the genre's spotlight. As the 70s rolled on, there came the more militant strain of the music: dub and roots reggae. The ska and rocksteady period, as far as Jamaica was concerned, was passé and the Rastafarian invasion was underway. The Wailers spearheaded this movement. Much similar to the present time, the foreign markets fed off what was coming out of Kingston. And in his homeland Dekker was mostly forgotten.

Dekker it seemed was caught in a time

capsule; and survived by catering to a small but loyal fan base. His only other UK hit in this period was *Sing A Little Song*, produced by Tony Cousins and Bruce White on the **Rhino** imprint, which made it into the top 20.

At the end of the 70s, many white English bands influenced by Dekker ignited what became known as the 2-Tone craze. At its height, the groups that came to prominence practicing the subgenre were names like *The Specials*, *The Beat*, *Fun Boy Three* and *Madness*. Dekker hopped onto this train and rode this new wave considered as the second coming of ska. He then signed to punk label **Stiff Records**, delivering the satisfying *Black and Dekker* album. During this period he began to work with Graham Parker's backing band, *The Rumour*, both in the studio and for live performances.

The Robert Palmer produced *Compass Point* followed, but the singles issued from both offerings were not huge sellers, except for a reworked *Israelites* track that charted on the Belgian top ten.

It seemed that Dekker, as prolific as he was, would be forever tagged as the singer who did the song *Israelites*, which hit the charts on numerous occasions after its initial breakthrough.

Yet another comparison with his former label mate Jimmy Cliff was that Cliff had good business instincts and Dekker was a nice guy with managerial problems. This changed in 1981, when one of his background singers Leon Williams, with whom he had a long friendship as far back as 1969, started to manage him. In 1984, British courts declared Dekker bankrupt. This he said was due to mismanagement and theft on the part of his former handlers. He and Williams sued a number of labels and individuals for back royalties, and won a settlement that afforded the singer a decent living.

Dekker, faults and all, was not a quitter and continued to record and tour up to his last moment. He lived life to the fullest, never dwelling on past disappointments. While preparing for dates in Czech Republic, Ireland and Austria, on May 26th, 2006, he had a fatal heart attack.

He was buried at a private funeral in London and mourned by many. His obituary, found in many magazines, remembered him as a trailblazer and icon.

He defined the age of ska and showed that it was possible to break down racial barriers with the music. Dekker was a true legend and pioneer who paved the way for all of Jamaica's great stars and influencing a large number of other prominent musicians worldwide.

12. Alton Ellis

Christened: Alton Ellis
Born: September 1, 1938
Deceased: October 10, 2008

Mr. Rocksteady

When Jamaican music shifted from the frenetic big band sound of ska, it geared down to what would become known as rocksteady. Its biggest proponent and leading light was none other than Alton Ellis, O.D.

Rocksteady was the pre-incarnation of the music that the world would come to know as reggae. This was when its urky-jerky, Latin tinged predecessor ska was spurned by the masses. The reality of class distinction and the overwhelming poverty of the majority of Jamaicans led to more soul searching and a more realistic expression of what they were feeling. The music slowed. The lyrical content started to address the woes of ordinary people and document their everyday struggles. Alton Ellis was the voice of this new musical direction.

Born in Trench Town, he attended Ebenezer Primary and Boys Town Secondary Schools, and learned to play piano at an early age. There was always music around the young Alton as his family consisted of music lovers, and at least two siblings who were professional singers' brother Leslie and sister Hortense. Alton tested the waters at talent shows like Vere Johns Opportunity Hour, where he came out on top on more than one occasion.

In 1959 as part of a duo with singer Eddie Perkins, he scored his first hit *Muriel*. Like many, he started his career working with the stern musical patriarch Sir Coxsone Dodd owner of the legendary **Studio One**, for whom he would rack up several hits.

The group became history when Perkins

migrated to the US, leaving Ellis to carry on alone. The group's dissolution was somewhat of a setback and in the interim Alton found work as a printer. He tried again, with little success, to hook up with John Holt who chose instead to join *The Paragons*. But later would have more luck with brothers Leslie and Barry Gordon, Lloyd Charmers and Winston Jarret, forming a group called *The Flames*.

The early 60s saw the emergence of several gangs in Kingston's ghettos and with it a musical expression known as *rude bwoy music*. Artists of the time documented this phenomenon, one of them being Bob Marley's *Wailers* with the musical warning *Simmer Down*. Ellis's Flames recorded a group of anti-rudie tunes that also became popular most notably: *Dance Crasher*, *Cry Tough* and *Don't Trouble People*.

The group, more or less, evolved into a backing unit for Ellis and at the time bristling under harsh financial realities at **Studio One**, Ellis flew the coop and recorded for other producers. But before his departure he delivered the hits *Rock Steady, Girl I've Got A Date* and the aforementioned *Cry Tough*. At other times during his tenure at the label, he was paired up with his sister Hortense, a star in her own right, and the highly respected Phyllis Dillon on several recordings.

Moving on, the singer found a new home with **Treasure Isles**, owned by Duke Reid. Reid was an ex-policeman known for his intimidating presence. Reid a large man carried two guns on his person as part of his normal attire. At **Treasure Isles** Ellis did some of his finest work. The association brought forth classics such as *Breaking Up, Ain't That Loving You, You Make Me Happy, Why Bird Follow Spring* and *Willow Tree*, all included on his 1967 debut album, *Mr. Soul Of Jamaica*. Coxsone would rush out his own album with Ellis: *Alton Ellis Sing Rock and Soul* in the same year and later followed with *The Best of Alton Ellis*, in 1969.

This outpouring of original music and quality covers from the man described by his peers as having the "sweetest voice in reggae" would make him the main source of material in an era many considered to be the golden age of Jamaican music. The music was live and the primitive recording equipment, required perfection on the part of the singers and session musicians. On top of this, Reid and Coxsone drove performers to high levels of performances as both men shared the common characteristic of being hard taskmasters.

In 1967 Ellis toured the UK on a package with another star of the rocksteady era, Ken Boothe. He also fell in love with the place, and in the coming years would make it his home. Now on top of his game, Mr. Rocksteady was in heavy demand and sought after by all the leading producers. So he made his services available to the likes of Bunny Lee, Keith Hudson, Herman Chin Loy and Lloyd Daley. With Daley came two sizable hits *Lord Deliver Us* and *Back To Africa*.

The rock steady period was brief, dominating Jamaican airwaves for no longer than three years. From the beginning of the seventies onwards, newer stars would rise on the local scene, touting a more militant strain of the music centered on the themes of black identity and spirituality. This was due in large part to the influence and growth of Rastafarianism. It was around this time that rocksteady gave way to rockers, which when fully mature became known as reggae.

Ellis was a soft-spoken individual who never pretended to be a radical. The music was changing and Ellis was not feeling it. He responded to these developments by migrating. He first went to

Canada where he stayed briefly then to England where he permanently settled from 1972. This naturally ended his reign as the number one artist, but by this time his legacy was already firmly fixed.

This did not mean that Ellis resigned himself to a rocking chair. On the contrary, his focus turned to building up the reggae scene in Britain. The one-time tailor continued his working ways, starting his own label and record shop **All Tone** in South London and still recorded for star producers like King Jammy and Henry Junjo Lawes. His presence in England along with that of Sugar Minott helped to kick start the local scene that would thrive in later years with many homegrown British acts becoming reggae stars in their own right.

The consensus amongst his peers was that, as a singer, Ellis was the gold standard. Those regarding him as their main influence are too much to mention but includes in their own time, Bob Marley, Beres Hammond and Dennis Brown, who sang harmony on some of Ellis's records. The 2004 hit, a cover of Ellis's *I'm Still In Love*, which was a Billboard top five single for dancehall superstar Sean Paul and the little known Sasha, is evidence of how great he was as a songwriter as well. In 1994 the Jamaican Government conferred on him The Order of Distinction for contributions in music and culture.

In 2007 his manger Trish De Rosa was still busy juggling requests for recordings and concert bookings. At one of these live appearances the singer suddenly collapsed and had to be rushed to a nearby hospital. There the doctors had to deliver the grim findings to friends and relatives: that the artist had cancer. The following year, as he lay bedridden in Hammersmith Hospital in London he lost the battle. An obituary in the New York Times by Rob Kenner lauded *The Godfather of Rocksteady* for "profoundly influencing global pop music".

In an interview a few years before his passing, the legend spoke on the deterioration of reggae music and lambasted the pervasive "violent and materialistic content" of it. He went on to state that "the youth change the music and I accept the change", but "it's only that I want them to clean it up".

11. Burning Spear

Christened: Winston Rodney
Born: March 1, 1945

The High Priest

If Winston Rodney was Catholic, he would certainly be named Pope. As a reggae artist he is a purist in every sense of the word. His stance on his Rastafarian religion is unshakable and his style of reggae both musically and lyrically has remained the same, from the beginning to the present.

Spear has not been inducted into the *Rock and Roll Hall of Fame*, nor does he have the international standing of Marley or Cliff. However, he arguably deserves more respect than both for his commitment to preserving his musical integrity through thick and thin. If anyone can be accused of selling out, it couldn't be him.

Rodney was born in St Anne's Bay, St Ann, and the birth parish of other great Jamaicans, most notable Pan-Africanist Marcus Garvey and Reggae King Bob Marley. From a youth he was a man of the soil engaging in farming and stone masonry. In these formative years, he was captivated by strong black leaders who were in the forefront of the struggle against white imperialism. Men like Haile Selassie of Ethiopia, Jomo Kenyatta (aka Burning Spear) from Kenya, whose nickname he adopted, and Jamaica's own, the aforementioned Marcus Garvey.

During the days of laboring at his tasks, he began to write songs and sang to himself. His musical desires grew as time progressed. He was also taking note of the success of his fellow parishioner Bob Marley, who from 1964 with his group the Wailers started to hit the local charts. Rodney was proud of his neighbor, but yearned to start his own recording career.

As the story goes, one day while walking through Nine Miles, he ran into Marley who was on his way back from his farm. Rodney congratulated him on his recent achievements. As the conversation progressed, Rodney sought some advice on how to enter the music business. Marley pointed him in the direction of Coxsone and told him he could use his name as reference. Reggae Singer Larry Marshall disputes this account, as he claims that it was him who sent Rodney to Coxsone. Whatever the case may be, Rodney wasted no time acting on the advice and showed up in Kingston a few days later at Coxsone's **Studio One** headquarters to audition for the great man. This would prove to be an important first step in the development of a legendary career.

In Kingston he was joined by close friends Rupert Wellington and Delroy Hinds, so they moved forward as a trio. Rodney however was ever mindful to enforce that the name Burning Spear was his and ran the group accordingly.

The group's first set of singles beginning in 1969, were *Door Peep*, *Walla Walla*, *Morris Tuffest*, *The Population* and *New Civilisation*. These songs were released on several sub-labels that were owned by Coxone. The smaller imprints such as **Bongo Man**, **Supreme** and **Iron Side** was where Dodd put the B-List artists that were not yet considered as top commercial prospects. Two albums *Studio One Presents Burning Spear* and

Rocking Time, came to market in 1973.

The group's breakthrough single, *Marcus Garvey*, came in 1974 for producer Lawrence Lindo, aka Jack Ruby. Ruby was the only major producer at the time not based in Kingston. He operated out of the seaside tourist town of Ocho Rios and was one to champion a hardcore roots sound. Ruby was a larger than life figure, respected amongst the town's people. He ran his outfit on James Avenue, a street with a bad reputation.

The great acts have always had their fingers on the pulse of the time and Burning Spear was no exception. In tandem with Ruby, the group would make some of the most compelling records of the period.

The 70s was indeed the decade when black pride and militancy was at its peak. *Marcus Garvey* and the follow up *Slavery Days* captured the spirit that prevailed when the sayings of Garvey was on the lips of the masses with Rodney bellowing out the opening lines declaring, "*Marcus Garvey words come to pass*".

The songs grabbed the listener from the start with a catchy and distinctive horn sound; this was a signature of Ruby's style of production. And when Rodney sang, his purpose was to remind the people of their true heritage. It was men like Rodney and the message he purveyed through music that helped to shape the identity of Jamaican music, as Negro music. Sitting in the middle of the Caribbean, the tiny island would churn out songs that spoke of and for Africa.

The group flourished under Ruby. They stayed out in the country in a natural and peaceful environment existing on a diet of vegetables and fruits while smoking loads of marijuana. Theirs was a maverick movement, making the music that they wanted to make, regardless of what was popular.

The session musicians were a unit that went by the name *Black Disciples*. They contained future legends Robert Shakespeare (bass), Earl Chinna Smith (guitar), Valentine Chin (keyboards) and Leroy "Horsemouth" Wallace (drums).

Ruby put the singles out on two labels he owned – **Capo** and **Fox**. The partnership also produced two albums *Marcus Garvey* (1976) and *Man In The Hills* (1977). Both albums were critically acclaimed and commercially successful. These releases broke the group internationally, with distribution of them being handled by **Island** in the UK. After these two albums, Rodney emerged as a reggae star in his own right.

A tour of the UK gave his fans the opportunity to witness some of the most unorthodox performances of any reggae act. His was one where there was more showcasing of his band with long jamming interspersed with moans and chants far apart. On stage Rodney often times just flayed around like a whirling dervish and appeared to be in a trance like state, placing the audience under a kind of musical hypnosis.

During live performances, as well as in the studio, Rodney draped his voice around the instrumentals like a shroud. He smothered his compositions with mundane repetition, while overpowering each with his personality. What came out at the other end was less melody but more him. His recordings were different from what his contemporaries offered and his live appearances set him apart even more.

As fruitful as the partnership was with **Island Records**, Rodney was not satisfied with the mixes of his songs. He considered this a watering down of his sound. This spurred him to start his own label, **Spear Records**. So adamant was he about having total control of his vision with a sort of dictatorial zeal that he subsequently broke away from group-mates Wellington and Hinds.

Ruby was the next casualty. Rodney would permit no personality that could possibly exert a stronger viewpoint than his own and severed ties with his longtime producer.

He set about self-producing and releasing several albums, the first being *Dry and Heavy*, containing the hit *Throw Down Your Arms*. Then from 1977 to 1980 came others like *Social Living*, *Marcus Children*, *Living Dub Vol 1* and *Hail Him*. He was running his own show with his own label, but wisely retained **Island** for distribution.

The 1977 European tour on which he was backed by UK reggae upstarts *Aswad* yielded the concert album *Live* in 1978. In the early 80s he took his talents to British major **EMI**, but in later years also recorded for Massachusetts based **Heartbeat**, as well as **Slash Records** and French label **Nocturne**.

Rodney never looked back from the occurrence of international recognition. He continued to look outward and entertained no thoughts of regaining popularity in his native country. Rodney deemed himself to be above local stardom. The music coming out of Jamaica was way below his standards and would have resulted in stagnation or worse. From the outset, his commitment to quality has been firmly enforced and after jumping off the local springboard he made the world his playground.

In the company of giants like Marley and Tosh, he was indeed a part of an elite group of Jamaican artists that led an invasion of the pop world and made reggae into the international force that it is today.

A self-professed workaholic, he built a reputation of being one of the hardest working men in reggae, regularly undertaking over a hundred shows per year as well as releasing an album every two years up to the present time.

In 2000 he won the first of his two Grammy Awards for Best Reggae Album with *Calling Rastafari* and, then again, in 2009 for *Jah Is Real*. In 2002, when Rolling Stone magazine compiled an issue of musical legends, he was included along with Jagger, McCartney and other rock royalties. In 2007, he was honored with the Order of Distinction by the Jamaican government for his contributions to arts and culture.

Burning Spears is a living legend after a career spanning over four decades, and is now in semi-retirement. He lives in Queens, New York with his wife-manager Sonia and works when he wants to. At his age, that is an enviable position to be in.

10. Shaggy

Christened: Orville Burrell
Born: October 22, 1968

Diamond Kid

Shaggy holds the distinction of being the most successful living Jamaican artist. His albums have sold over 15 million units worldwide and he is one of a handful of Jamaicans that are international superstars.

Burrell's story differs from most. Similar to

Grace Jones, he migrated to the US in his teens, never having a musical career before then. Growing up in the US, he was influenced by rap, hip hop, and R&B. This background decided his target audience and from the get go what he traded in was a kind of commercial pop, albeit with an island flavor. Needless to say, it has been a very successful formula.

Living abroad also gave him an international perspective and helped him to have a more professional attitude. The music business in the US is a world away and much more organized than its Jamaican counterpart. An accurate description of what prevails in Kingston is a music scene rather than industry. An industry after all, contains highly specialized departments and is streamlined for cohesiveness to achieve certain goals. This is not so in Jamaica with its wild west, do-it-yourself approach. All this shaped Shaggy's worldview thus he saw his career through different lens.

He was born in a sleepy fishing village called Rae Town in Kingston and moved around quite often as a child, from place to place, and in between relatives. By his late teens, he was living in Portsmouth, St Catherine. This was his last stop before leaving for the US. There he joined his mother, a medical secretary, in the Flatbush section of Brooklyn in New York.

Several sources have cited that he did voice lessons in a music program at his alma mater Erasmus High School and otherwise spent his time on the streets with a group of friends. They came to be known as the *Rough Entry Crew* consisting of himself, Red Fox, Baja Jedd, Mr. Easy and Rayvon. In the early 90s they formed a movement as New York reggae artists trying to make a mark. Burrell got the nickname Shaggy from a member of the crew because of his high bushy hair, settling on it for his stage name.

He seemed, even in those early days, to be an extremely focused individual and started to frequent studios like **Don One** near White Plains Road. This was the period when he began to immerse himself in what one would refer to as street dreams but this carried with it a downside as well.

He was intent on making it as an artist but found the environment a little off putting because of the unsavory characters that hung around the studios. He loved the music, but at the time did not want to deal with all the extra negatives associated with it. He began to think about his future and with some pressure from his mother made a decision to join the army. In 1988 he enlisted with the Marine Corps.

Stationed in Camp Lejune, North Carolina, his location could have been an obstacle to continuing in music, but not for Shaggy. In between duties he used any amount of free time to make the long trek back to New York to record.

He cut a few unremarkable singles after meeting a young producer Shuan "Sting" Pizzona, who had as much passion as him for the business. The result was the song *Mampie*, a minor club hit in New York. It was then followed by another underground favorite called *Big Up*, and he steadily began building a name in the city.

In 1991 the Iraqi dictator Saddam Hussein invaded neighboring Kuwait, and set in motion a train of events that led to the first Gulf War. In response, the United States assembled an international coalition against Hussein. Burrell's company was ordered into action. Fortunately for him, the war ended rather quickly. Seven months later, he was back on American soil, in one piece.

Early in 1992 Pizzona and Shaggy did a remake of an old Jamaican song *Oh Carolina*. *Oh*

Carolina was first recorded in 1960 by the *Folkes Brothers*. The song is cited by musical historians as the first real reggae record. Its folk song melody and backbeat provided by *Count Ossie's* Rastafarian drum group was the first of its kind to Africanize the previously prevalent ska sound. Burrell and Pizzona used parts of the original and beefed it up with modern drum sounds and other hip-hop samples. Shaggy on top of the beat, established his personality right off the bat, toasting in his trademark baritone pitch, lustily and humorously. This came over as very refreshing and novel. It gained attention for the budding star.

The choice of *Oh Carolina* was instinctively keen as it had a long history of being revived and was still extremely popular as a party and club favorite right up to the mid-80s. Released on their label, **Sting International**, primarily for the New York market, it received airtime on KISS FM where Sting worked as a disc jock. The buzz around it started to build and by the summer of 1992 *Oh Carolina* was a number one record on the New York Reggae Charts.

Picked up for a UK release by independent **Greensleeves,** *Oh Carolina* charted in Britain and started to make inroads in Japan and other markets in Europe. The song gave Shaggy his first real taste of success but the fledgling artist needed a proper structure around him, if he was to see the next level. This help came by way of Robert Livingston.

Robert Livingston came up from the Kingston ghettos and knew the streets very well. He was familiar with the grimy side of life but was also ambitious and driven like Shaggy. He saw his salvation in music. Serving his apprenticeship in the music business as a roadie for reggae star Gregory Issacs, and ultimately ended up as an artist manager. Prior to meeting Shaggy, he handled the career of a volatile dancehall DJ on **Columbia Records** called Super Cat. That relationship was riddled with acrimony and they eventually parted ways.

Living in New York, Livingston was aware of Shaggy and the buzz surrounding him and his record. The introduction of the two came by way of Pizzona, and Livingston based on what he was already seeing decided to work with the artist. Livingston was still bruised by his previous experience with Super Cat but with Shaggy he felt that he was on to something special and observed that this artist was hungry for success.

Livingston made the connections for *Oh Carolina* to be released in Europe, where it charted in several countries. The success of the record then allowed him to book Shaggy as the opening act for reggae pop star Maxi Priest, at the time signed to **Virgin Records**. Virgin executives saw a winner in Shaggy and by 1993 a deal was done. *Oh Carolina* then became the lead single for Shaggy's debut album for the label, *Pure Pleasure* which went gold. The single was also a minor hit in the US, based mostly on the promotion it received by being included on the soundtrack of the hit movie *Sliver*, starring Sharon Stone.

With his next effort *Boombastic* and the album of the same name, Shaggy became a star. *Boombastic's* success made him one of the most recognizable artists in the world and he created his personal brand with the opening lines "*Mr. lova lova*". Using a strategy that was gradually being perfected, Burrell and Pizzona would this time sample Marvin Gaye's *Lets Get It On* for the song. Truth is, the version with the Marvin Gaye sample was a remix. The original cut was on a dancehall track called *Mavis*, which was a hit in Jamaica by dancehall DJ Merciless. The version of the song with the **Motown** sample however was the one that raced up the US charts reaching as high as Number 2 on Billboard's Hot 100.

Shaggy's vocal, which previously resembled that of other Jamaican dancehall stars alternating between the vocal sound of Lt Stitchie, Super Cat and Red Dragon, now took on a sound of its own. It became more nasal, and sounded like a sort of southern drawl which mimicked that of big band legends like Cab Calloway. The artist was now proving to be somewhat of a musical sponge soaking up myriad influences and letting them out as just.... SHAGGY!

Another thing about him worth mentioning was that from his first major hit, he marketed himself as a lady's man a sort of dancehall *Casanova* and would not deviate from such. With his image firmly set, he focused on building a brand instead of making the common mistake of many artists who try to be all things to all people.

The *Boombastic* album went on to sell over 4 million worldwide and yielded another hit, a clever remake of the Broadway classic *In The Summertime* (feat his pal Rayvon). This level of success made Shaggy into the biggest reggae DJ, surpassing a mark (two straight gold albums) previously set by that of fallen icon Shabba Ranks. The album also netted for Shaggy the prestigious Grammy in the category of Best Reggae Album.

The artist was now proving to the skeptics, ironically mostly his own countrymen, that his career was no fluke and that his appetite for success was gargantuan. Much like another crossover Jamaican artist, Sean Paul, Shaggy was ridiculed for his music. The venom came from other Jamaican acts mainly out of jealousy. They criticized him for not being hardcore and attributed his success to his racial features using the "*light-skinned*" argument that even Bob Marley in his time could not escape.

In perspective these arguments rang hollow. It was more accurate to reach the conclusion that Jamaican artists with an international outlook, who worked extremely hard, who were properly managed, who displayed above average intelligence and who aimed very high were usually more successful than others in crossing over. Can the light skinned argument be used against international icons Grace Jones and Jimmy Cliff?

For a while though, his detractors would have reason to gloat as after the huge success of *Bombastic*, Shaggy's career hit a bump. The follow up *Midnite Lover* was a poor seller and the single *Piece of My Heart*, featuring a young singer Marsha, flopped. **Virgin**, in a knee jerk reaction, dumped Shaggy from the label. In typical fashion the label then jumped on the bandwagon of hot reggae DJ Beenie Man, thinking that Shaggy's tide had ebbed.

By this time however, Shaggy was already a huge star that had broken out of the confines of the ethnic market to conquer the world of pop. *Bombastic* made him a big star in America but he was an even bigger draw in Europe. Over there he performed regularly to crowds totaling upwards of ten thousand. At this stage of his career, he was experienced in the vicissitudes of a musical career and was not overly surprised or discouraged by the turn of events. With all certainty, Shaggy would not stop and wanted more.

In 1998 his management was able to secure a spot on the soundtrack for the movie *How Stella Got Her Groove Back*. Part of the film was shot in Jamaica and a song by Shaggy *Luv Me Luv Me* and produced by Jimmy Jam and Terry Lewis was a perfect fit. *Luv Me Luv Me* featured pop icon Janet Jackson and became a hit. The song was a one off but served the purposes of keeping Shaggy from being forgotten.

For his next project, the artist shunned the big name producers and worked in his own studio in Long Island, surrounded by his own crew. On the team was, longtime producer Sting Pizzona, singing partner Rayvon, and members of his backing band, most notably keyboard player Christopher Birch, background singer and songwriter Rik Roc and others. What they came up with was a self-financed album called *Hot Shot*.

They shopped the project around and the floundering **MCA Records** was desperate enough to take the risk. In 2000 when the first two singles *Dance and Shout* and *Hope* failed to ignite, executives at the label were having sleepless nights. However, the third release would prove to be the charm when "It Wasn't Me", featuring Rik Roc, first caught on in Hawaii before exploding on stateside radio.

The catchy song lit up dance floors nationwide and the single raced up the Billboard Charts, ending up at number two. The fourth single, the more thoughtful *Angel*, was a clever merging of two classics Juice Newton's *Angel of The Morning* and Steve Millers *The Joker*. Layered with original lyrics by Burrell, the song featured

Rayvon on the hook and went all the way to number one. The album was an all-around strong musical statement with Shaggy rapping in his inimitable style and referencing a wide array of genres such as rock, Latin music, pop, disco and dancehall. *Hot Shot* was the result of the sponge being squeezed out in full force.

Hot Shot became the biggest selling album of any genre in this period with US sales of 6 million and equal amounts in the rest of the world, making it certified Diamond. This was Shaggy's *Thriller* and it was unrealistic for anyone to think that he could top it.

The album saved **MCA Records** from folding and made Shaggy wealthier beyond his wildest dreams. He again won the Grammy and garnered international awards and accolades too numerous to mention. He ascended to the mountaintop of international superstardom and toured venues reserved for the cream of the pop world, such as *Madonna* and *U2*. Indicative of the kind of moment he was having, he was even honored with a coveted spot in 2002 on *Michael Jacksons 30th Anniversary Special*.

The *Hot Shot* album turned Shaggy into the most successful living reggae artist. **MCA**

Records, in celebration of their biggest selling artist threw him a Platinum party in his native Jamaica and also gave his production company **Big Yard** a label deal to develop his own stable of artists. But as mentioned before, no one in their right mind expected this fantastic ride to last forever.

2003's *Lucky Day* with the leadoff single *Hey Sexy Lady* (feat. Bryan & Tony Gold), based on the budget **MCA** had to fork out was a disappointment. The album was only able to sell gold (500,000 units). Shaggy also overstepped his limitations on another cut on the album, *Strength of a Woman* which is a good composition, but one that needed a real singer and not him mimicking one. The label deal thus became a casualty of *Luck Day's* poor showing. The indefatigable Shaggy was traded off to the once mighty **Geffen** label that released his next album, the forgettable *Clothes Drop*.

Now feeling jilted by **MCA** and its treatment of him, in-spite of making the company a lot of money, he retreated from dealing with the majors. As he grew wearier of their corporate politics the artist and his management decided to regroup. This took the form of a kind of returning to their roots. They proceeded to set up shop in Jamaica, giving the **Big Yard** label its own headquarters. In Jamaica they acquired property on which they built a complex containing offices, two recording studios and a state of the art rehearsal facility.

But at the same time, a major shift at the very core of **Big Yard** was underway. Shaggy started to assume many responsibilities and began to make decisions previously left in the hands of his manager. Leaving behind the politics of the big record labels, he would indulge in some of his own. With this much success was the inevitable clash of wills and it was obvious that the balance of power had shifted.

Nevertheless, with this new direction established, the team went back to work. The result was the witty single *Church Heathen*. Again showing the eclectic tastes of the artist by merging dancehall with Gregorian Chants, it was another smash that returned Shaggy to the spotlight. This was significant, at least in a personal sense for Shaggy. The song was his first number one in his native Jamaica and the long sought after approval of his countrymen, like a void in his soul was finally filled. From the home grown acceptance garnered by *Church Heathen* would come a plethora of combination singles with veteran artists as well as with the younger generation of hot dancehall stars, who were now lining up to do a record with him. The single became the nucleus for the *Intoxication* album, distributed by **VP**, which was also nominated for a Grammy.

There is a song on the *Intoxication* album, *What Is Love* (feat. Akon) showing another side of the artist: a dark Machiavellian one. On it he sings of leaving his woman for no reason, "*I just want to mess around, though you're the best thing I found*". The song was maybe a cryptic message of the ruthless way in which his manager of twenty years Robert Livingston would be jettisoned.

The two parted ways in 2010. Robert on one hand seemed distraught about the break up, while Shaggy showed no emotion. When one can travel from "*girl you're my angel*" (*Angel*) to "*mi wan fi leave you long time*" (*What Is Love*), it speaks volumes as to the mental evolution that is sometimes brought about by success. It can sometimes turn us into little monsters.

On the other hand, the artist must be commended for the proper use of his celebrity status. The annual *Shaggy and Friends* concert, staged by the superstar benefiting The Children's Hospital in Kingston stands out as a remarkable feat of philanthropy. The charity has raised millions and has enabled the Hospital to undertake massive rebuilding and necessary modernization.

Shaggy really has nothing more to prove and is one of the few Jamaicans that are now a part of pop culture. His career has been remarkable for its achievements and resilience and his place in history is secure.

He is still a tireless worker, not for the money or fame, but because it's in his nature. After the split with Livingston, he gave up his stake in **Big Yard** to start his own company **Ranch Entertainment**. There is a feeling that his story still has more interesting chapters to be written.

9. U-Roy

Christened: Ewart Beckford
Born: September 21, 1942

The Originator

It is true that it is not the one who ran the race that counts but the one to be first over the finish line. This is apt in the case of U-Roy.

He followed in the footsteps of pioneers such as Count Machuki and King Stitt, as originators of toasting, but U-Roy was the first to gain both national and international fame in the new art form.

In 1971, after a decade of struggling mainly as a sound system selector U-Roy, exploded on the scene, locking down the top three spots on the Jamaican charts with *Wake the Town*, *Wear You To The Ball* and *Rule The Nation*, on Duke Reid's **Treasure Isle** label.

The early originators of toasting which in modern times would be called DJing or rapping was as a result of Jamaican sound system disc jockeys imitating the American radio personalities, who would talk over their records as a way of promoting both the discs and their show. Popular rock and roll jocks like Murray The K and Allan Freed spewed out glib anecdotes mixed with gibberish. While Jamaican sound hosts who were not on the radio and never far from what was happening in the United States, started doing their own interpretations in the island's dancehalls.

In the 50s when Jamaican music was in its infancy, two dominant players emerged: Coxsone Dodd and Duke Reid. Each owned the primary source of local entertainment, a sound system otherwise called a discotheque. The two were also record producers fighting over a pool of artists. Sworn enemies and bitter rivals they schemed and fought in a quest to outdo each other. The contests though drove the fledgling scene to level after level of creativity and innovation. One of these innovations would be the birth of the dancehall DJ that would grow to become a genre unto itself.

U-Roy was born in Trench Town, Kingston and by his teen years was active around the burgeoning music scene, starting out on *Dickies Dynamics* as a selector (one who plays the records and talks in between selections introducing the artist and the label).

In 1965 after four years at his maiden gig he moved to another sound, *Sir George The Atomic*. In 1968 he teamed up with Osbourne "King Tubby" Ruddock and took the controls at *Tubby's Home, Hi Fi,* as the number one selector.

This pairing would prove to be most fortuitous in U-Roy's professional life. Legend has it that Ruddock, who was a dub cutter (*one who used a machine to cut the acetate for an exclusive disc*) for Duke Reid, while tinkering with a mix before cutting, accidentally knocked out the vocal channel on a song. He however, did not discover this until he actually cut the disc. This left the song as an instrumental version. He played it at the dance anyway. As the version played it gave the selector, U-Roy, room to talk over it and the reaction from the crowd was instantaneously favorable. This was the beginning of what would become history making and groundbreaking for both U-Roy and Jamaican music.

U-Roy, with what was to follow, inadvertently became the father of the DJ movement and Tubby the originator of dub. What happened in those events resulted in the DJ being elevated to star status instead of a mere tooter of his employer's product. After U-Roy toasted over a version of The Techniques *You Don't Care*, his profile expanded. Duke Reid, ever the sharp businessman sought out the DJ to record for him. At first U-Roy was reluctant, but after being encouraged by King Tubby, he took the plunge.

Reid, the owner of a huge catalog of rocksteady hits, provided a treasure chest of material on which Roy could showcase his skills. Truth be told, this experimentation reached back to other sessions done by the U-Roy with producers Lee Perry (*Earth Rightful Ruler*), Bunny Lee *(King of The Road)*, Keith Hudson (*Dynamic Fashion Way*) and Lloyd Daily (*Secretly*), but it was through Reid that the cry of "eureka" would be heard.

In 1970 both Reid and U-Roy hit the jackpot. The artist scored toasting over Alton Ellis's *Girl I've Got A Date*, rechristened *Wake The Town* as well as The Paragon's hit *Wear You To The Ball*. Another single *Rule The Nation*, shot up the charts and barricaded U-Roy inside.

This style was a brand new invention and swept over the island like a tidal wave. One of his contemporaries Dennis Alcapone observed, "it felt like a new Jamaica". U-Roy became Jamaica's biggest star and spawned a legion of imitators. This flood of newborn DJs, with Alcapone and Scotty being the most successful, started a takeover of the market that heretofore was dominated by singers. Others, who came to the fore, as many producers engaged in a mad grab for anyone who could duplicate U-Roy's sound, were Charly Ace, Johnny Lover, King Sporty and I-Roy. This would set off the first of what would become cyclical waves in Jamaican music, where the market would alternate between singer-dominated and DJ-dominated phases.

Back then, the local market for music with both U-Roy and Alcapone was moving upwards of 60,000 units per hit. In those days, U-Roy recorded exclusively for Reid, and the producer wasted no time in putting the DJ's voice on versions of almost all of his rocksteady hits, releasing over 30 singles. The pioneer's throve of materials including hits and b-sides were compiled and released by Reid in three series under the title *Versions Galore from 1971 to 1973*.

In 1973 at the height of his popularity, U-Roy unhitched his wagon from **Treasure Isle** and freelanced with various producers. From his earnings, he also released a few self-produced singles on two labels he started **Mego-Ann**, named off his daughters, and **Del-Ma**, taken from the starting letters of his baby mother's names.

But after these heady times his career showed signs of burnout and his competitors began to overtake him. U-Roy, while sporting locks, did not overtly espouse Rastafarian themes in his music. In step with the rise of socialism and black militancy that was sweeping over the island, emerged Manley Buchanan aka Big Youth capturing the zeitgeist and overshadowing U-Roy in the process.

In this phase of his career Beckford recorded sparingly but in 1975 gained critical acclaim and international exposure from the album *Dread In A Babylon*. The album produced by Tony Robinson and released in the UK under license by **Virgin Records**, was lauded in the rock press as a musical statement of significance. On the heels of this release, the following year, the artist toured Europe, opening for Toots and The Maytals.

While continuing to record, albeit decreasingly so, U-Roy would now earn the title of "Daddy Roy The Teacher" when he directed his efforts into his own sound system *King Stur Gav* and, through tireless work, made it into one of the top sounds on the island.

In this entrepreneurial endeavor, he also cemented his greatness by helping to bring many disciples to prominence, artist that would come to dominate the early 80s dancehall scene. People like Ranking Joe, Josey Wales, Charlie Chaplin, Little Twitch, Admiral Bailey and Shabba Ranks as well as selectors Jah Screw and Inspector Willy.

Over the ensuing years both the DJ market, along with its sound system counterpart have changed and even while his fortunes have gone up and down, U-Roy remains a paragon of hard work and persistence. Now in the fourth decade of his career, he continues to tour the world.

U-Roy is one of the heroes of Jamaican music. Gale's artist profile says it best: "U-Roy's unique delivery helped to create an industry, alter the shape of Jamaican music and indirectly influenced the now international idiom of rap".

8. Shabba Ranks

Christened: Rexton Gordon
Born: January 17, 1966

Dancehall Emperor

It can be argued that the most well-known Jamaican second to Bob Marley is Shabba Ranks. Shabba most certainly did for dancehall reggae what Bob did for roots reggae. U-Roy is known as the father of all the DJs, Yellowman was named as King, but Shabba is the man that conquered; therefore, he has to be *The Emperor*.

He was the first of the dancehall DJs to earn gold certifications; the first to win, not one but, two Grammys and in the process became the first dancehall DJ to become an international star.

His story begins in a rural hamlet called Sturgetown, situated in the northern Jamaican parish of St Ann. St Ann is known for being a tourist parish, where Ocho Rios can be found; otherwise, it is a breadbasket region with a strong agricultural base.

Rexton was born to Ivan Gordon, known as Rasta Ivan, and Constance Christie (aka Momma Christie). He grew up in the Kingston 11 section of the city, to where his parents moved. In later years as a teenager, he would alternate between his mother's house in Seaview Gardens and friends in a ghetto known as Compound. He attended Seaward All Age School and later Dunoon Technical, and was an average student who, on discovering his musical talent, cared little for school.

In interviews he reveals that his love for toasting was inspired by artists like Yellowman, Charlie Chaplin, Brigadier Jerry and Josie Wales. He first started to venture out hanging around several area sounds, little known hi-fi's, like Studio Five, Love Bunch, and Roots Melody, and touching the mike.

In those early days he fraternized with a group of DJs who tried hard but never made it, names like Derrick Irie, Banana Man, and Kibba Ranks. He was closest to Kibba, who dubbed himself *The Navigator*, so Shabba took on the name *Co-Pilot*. When Kibba was arrested for rape and received a seven-year sentence, Shabba started to question the street life and began to take his gifts more seriously.

One of his mentors dancehall star Josie Wales took him under his wings and to "The Teacher" Daddy Roy for an audition. U-Roy heard what the rest of the nation would soon discover.

This kid had a voice.

In the beginning he had a problem with his delivery and timing but still, Shabba had *The Voice*. Daddy Roy, who owned one of the biggest sounds in the island King Stur Gav, took on Ranks as a junior DJ, one who warmed up the dances for the bigger talents. Just like an eager player on the bench, when put into the game, he would make sure he made a statement. He used his ruff bass vocals to good effect and toasted with manic intensity.

Shabba's first single *What A Heat* **(Roots**

Melody) showed promise, but was poorly promoted. When Josie Wales switched to sound system Jammy's Hi Power, owned by Lloyd "King Jammy", James who was also one of the top producers, he took his protégé with him.

At the time, Jammy was a power in the music business. He had all the top stars of the day recording on his imprint. His roster included Wales, Lt. Stitchie, Admiral Bailey and Chaka Demus, who were hit makers, but also a multitude of one hit wonders. This connection proved to be the most important of the aspiring DJs life. It is here Shabba would meet the people that would become pivotal to his future success.

Shabba Ranks was always known for his humility and likeability and these factors helped him to make and keep friends. Some of the people he befriended included engineer Bobby Dixon, who later formed his **Digital B** label on which Ranks would score numerous hits. Also songwriter, producer and singer Michael Bennett, then a member of vocal group *Home T*. Bennett would in later years have a hand in the songs that would help to bring Ranks international recognition. But all this came later on.

In 1987, he recorded and saw the release of a

cache of singles that would become dancehall favorites, all on the **Jammys** label. In prior years, he had proved his mettle on the sound system, holding his own alongside artists that were more popular than him. Night after night, he earned his respect amongst Admiral Bailey, the late Major Worries, John Wayne, Pampidoo, Don Angelo and Nitty Gritty. Chief amongst the dozens of songs he recorded were *Get Up Stand Up and Rock, Needle Eye Pum Pum, Love Punany Bad, Peenie Peenie* and *Original Fresh*.

Fans in the dances loved him, especially the women whom he seemed to always be paying compliments. Ranks developed into the *dean* of slackness, but did it in a clever way where it was never considered as degrading, but more like a celebration. He also struck a balance by recording cultural songs just as potent as his raunchy material: Just *Reality, Ah No Me Seh So*, and *Poor People*.

The following year he continued his fine form with the last major hit on the **Jammys** label, a cool collaboration with singer Coco T and Bennett's group Home T, *Who She Love.*

He then turned his affections to another hot producer, Augustus "Gussie" Clarke. Gussie owned the **Music Works/Anchor** imprint and was known for his more musical and progressive approach to record production. This was in contrast to the quantitative style of Jammy, who piled hundreds of artists unto one riddim, usually basic and bare. With Clarke, whose label was distributed in the UK by indie **Greensleeves**, the artist scored hits that would start to build his name overseas.

His previous songs with Jammy were mainly dancehall staples and often times too slack for radio play, but his new songs would correct that. He scored chart-topping songs in Britain and Jamaica, namely *Be Good To Me* (feat. Rebel Princess and Coco T), *Pirates Anthem* (feat. Home T) and the mainstream hit *Twice My Age* with Krystal. *Twice My Age* was Shabba's break out hit and brought him to national prominence.

From 1989 into the new decade, Shabba would have other big singles. This time for the **Digital B** label, these included *Best Baby Father* and *Roots & Culture*. It must be noted that the arrangement for *Roots & Culture* with the background vocals reply of "murderer" after each line uttered by Shabba was copied in the mid-90s international hit *Here Come The Hotstepper* by singer Ini Kamozi.

In 1990 Ranks was on top of his game as a top tier DJ along with Ninja Man, Super Cat and Cutty Ranks. In that year he had another big hit the ode to female cheaters, with his trademark intro *"x-rated"*, on *Caan Dun* (**Steelie & Cleevie**). By this time Shabba had seven albums on the market that were steady sellers, the most popular of the lot being *Best Baby Father* (**Blue Mountain**), *Holding On* (**Two Friends/Greensleeves**), *Just Reality* (**VP**) and *Rapping With the Ladies* (**Greensleeves**).

It seemed that Ranks could do no wrong. His gruff bass tone and original style created a new vocal sound in the dancehall. In the same way that U-Roy was the first coming of the DJs, Shabba was the second. As all the early DJs used U-Roy as the template, Shabba would become the mold for those succeeding him. His vocal dexterity, going from hard to soft and fast to slow would be imitated by the next generation of toasters who became stars. The next icons: Buju Banton, Bounty Killa and Vybz Kartel.

In the 90s there was one artist that was intent on knocking Ranks off his perch Ninja Man. At the year-end Sting Concert, the two met in a much-anticipated clash. Shabba drew first blood crying, "*Ninja bow*", much to the delight of the eager crowd. However, he was no match for the *King of Stage*, the original *Don Gorgan*, who used Shabba's style of dress to ridicule him, pulling up lyrics on the spot, not Shabba's strong suit. Ranks was shot down by the first volley of verbal assaults by his opponent. There is a popular rumor that Ranks wept backstage after the humiliation. But in the subsequent fortunes of both artists, Shabba would have the last laugh.

In 1990 with Ranks at the zenith of local stardom and making a growing impact overseas, he met Clifton "Specialist" Dillon. Dillon, a Jamaican who had migrated to the US and a self-made hustler, dabbled in the music business and was looking to further his ambitions of becoming a music mogul. At this time Michael "Mikey" Bennett was writing a lot of songs that featured Shabba. Bennett also headed a label called **Two Friends** with another music business insider Patrick "Shadow" Lindsay. Through this network a connection was made. Dillon immediately saw something in Shabba and thought the time was right to make a move on the US market. He then assumed responsibilities as manager and signed the artists to his company, **Shang Music**. Ranks was the biggest Jamaican act at the time, and was pitched to **Epic** A&R Vivian Scott, who made the deal happen.

The first single off the debut album *As Raw As Ever* (**Epic**) was a duet with red-hot singer Maxi Priest called *Housecall*. The Mickey Bennett composition kept Ranks' thick patois in check and gave him lines that could be easily understood by the audience they were aiming to win over. The chorus and verses sung by Priest were also carefully crafted. Adding other ingredients was the legendary Sly Dunbar, and a remix by David Morales would prove to be the proverbial icing on the cake. *Housecall* was on target, cracking the US Top 40 and going Top 5 in the UK.

Where Yellowman, with his international foray on **CBS** had failed, Ranks's was a major success. The follow up single was *Mr. Loverman* (feat. Chevelle Franklin) and proved an even greater triumph, topping several international charts. *Mr. Loverman* became his signature tune and was responsible for cementing the artist in the annals of pop culture with a single word that he hollered on it, his name: "*Shabba*"!

The DJ was now the biggest Jamaican international success story since Bob Marley. More significantly, Shabba did something that Marley, in his brief lifetime never achieved –

winning Black Americans over to reggae. His following in the US was largely urban and he was as big a star as the rappers and R&B artists of the time. The label, being aware of this, was quick to pair Shabba with top stars like KRS One, Queen Latifah, Chubb Rock and Johnny Gill, with whom he scored the hit *Slow and Sexy* on the second album *Xtra Naked*. Both albums went gold and the artist copped back-to-back Reggae Grammies in 1992 and 1993. Shabba was the toast of the music world, even appearing in *Time* magazine.

Dillon and his team at his management company, now renamed **Specs/ Shang**, had done a tremendous job in marketing Ranks. Offers for features on other star's records and for tours began pouring in. Back in Jamaica, the native press hailed him as a national hero and described him as a megastar.

Then the bottom fell out.

The events leading up to what came next is nothing short of bizarre. They also exposed Ranks and his management team to have been woefully unprepared for the scrutiny that the star would come under as a result of international success.

In 1992 Ranks manager had released a song by

newcomer Buju Banton called *Boom Bye Bye*. It was a war cry that advocated killing of homosexuals. The tune came to the attention of several gay rights groups in the US who mounted a campaign against it and Banton.

Dillon was quietly delighted, since Banton was seen as Shabba's rival at the time. The episode resulted in Banton being kicked off the **Mercury** label, and as a result, slowing his international career significantly. But you know what they say about the digging of holes.

In early 93, Ranks went on a British television show called *The Word*, and was asked if he shared the view point expressed by Banton on *Boom Bye Bye*. Incredulously, Ranks quoted from the Bible saying homosexuals should be "*crucified*".

It would have been more intelligent to keep your opinion about the matter private and the question could have been easily sidestepped with proper coaching but that did not happen. His public pronouncement however, was tantamount to career suicide and everything came to a halt.

The darling of the music world was now it's most hated. A tour in progress on which Ranks shared billing with Bobby Brown, Guy and TLC gave him the boot. Then many other shows were cancelled as well as several pending TV appearances. More crucially his records were pulled from retail, as gay rights activists turned up the heat. The power of influential homosexuals within the music industry came to bear and Shabba felt the full brunt of it. A statement was issued through his management, tantamount to an apology but had little effect on the outcome of things.

In 1994 **Epic** released *A Mi Shabba*, the final album owed under the artist's contract. It stalled in the lower rungs of the charts as by this time, Shabba mania was officially over.

Back in Jamaica, the news that the artist issued a written apology for his anti-gay sentiments was met with equal venom by local fans. The Jamaican populace did not take kindly to him fessing up to who they described as "*batty men*". The artist suddenly found himself in the middle of the ocean and not knowing where to go. The loss of prestige, at home and abroad, was too much for the artist and his management team. By the late 90s, they acrimoniously parted ways.

The once powerful **Specs /Shang,** who also had Patra, Mad Cobra and Richie Stephens on their roster, still could not remain solvent in the wake of the loss of their top money earner. The market had also moved on to embrace newer stars like Shaggy.

In the aftermath, Ranks retreated from the music business and literally disappeared from public view. After his career free-fall, he became more of a family man, spending more time with his wife Michelle and their children.

In the 2000s, he crept back into the business, now older and wiser and this time around, being extremely cautious in his dealings with producers and promoters. He resumed recording, though sparingly, and only if the price was favorable. Ranks also performed occasionally, being notoriously known for his very high asking price.

As the cycle of time came full circle, his achievements have come to be appreciated for the impact they had on breaking barriers for the dancehall genre. He paved the way for those who went on to even greater success like Sean Paul, Shaggy and Junior Gong. In terms of respectability, there is no one that comes even close to him.

In 2011 just to show the younger heads a thing

or two, Shabba showed who had the voice with a blistering vocal on the hit *None A Dem* (**Di Genius**). The song also returned him to the top of the Jamaican charts.

There is a verbal war between Yellowman and Beenie Man as to who is The King of the Dancehall. But none can challenge Shabba for a title given to him in a glowing tribute in *Fader* magazine that dubbed him as the *Dancehall Emperor*.

7. Marcia Griffiths

Christened: Marcia Griffiths
Born: November 23, 1949

First Lady of Reggae

The lone-living female Jamaican artist with legendary status is the Hon Marcia L. Griffiths, O.D.

With a career now approaching its fifth decade, the First Lady of Reggae has thrived and survived through all the changes in Jamaican music. She now stands as a giant amongst all Jamaican artists, male or female. She has, for over the past forty years, been the most successful, most influential, most consistent and most revered of any woman from this little island.

Her story begins in West Kingston, where she was born to Joseph and Beatrice Griffiths. She attended Kingston Senior School, and loved to sing. She started out by singing at school concerts and in the church choir. Her parents were churchgoers and may not have approved of the fact that their tall, wispy daughter often times could not be found, as she sneaked out to be with her friends. As a beautiful young lady, who knows where she might have been and what she might have been doing. As it turned out, she was with friends who sang for their own amusement. After all, this was Jamaica in the late fifties to early sixties and poor folks did this sort of thing as there was no money to spend on outside entertainment.

On one such occasion she met a singer from the *Blues Busters*, Phillip James, who took her to audition for a talent show ran by Byron Lee. She made it into the show and immediately made an impression with the Carla Thomas original *No*

Time To Lose. Her raw talent and unique vocal sound thrilled the audience and warmed Lee on the prospects of wanting to work with her, which he did for a short while. However, she never recorded for the producer-band leader, as he was too busy with his own group, The Dragonaires, at the time.

Marcia's recording career began at **Studio One** on Coxsone's "B" label, **Downbeat**, with the unreleased *Wall Of Love*. But in 1964 she had her first taste of success with a song penned by her future lover and singing partner, Keith Anderson aka Bob Andy, *Feel Like Jumping*.

Andy, an excellent songwriter, sensed chemistry with Griffiths and brought her songs to record. She remarked, *"luckily for me Bob was strong and wise and in those early years he was really there for me"*. She scored again for Coxsone with *Truly* and quickly moved up to be regarded as one of the top female vocalists, becoming even more popular than say the likes of Phyllis Dillon and Hortense Ellis.

In 1970 she officially became a duo with Andy under the name *Bob and Marcia*, and started to make inroads into the international market. The pair charted in 1971 both in Jamaica and the UK with two singles for producer Harry J, *Young Gifted and Black* (# 5 UK) and *The Pied Piper* (# 11 UK) both title tracks of albums handled in Britain by **Trojan**. Other albums by the pair included *Sweet Memories* in 1976 and *Kemar* in the following year. These were their last two releases, even though they had already called it quits a few years earlier for, according to sources, "financial reasons". They however continued to work together in an arrangement where Andy still wrote for her.

Another chapter of a remarkable career began to take shape even before the demise of Bob and Marcia. She invited two friends of hers, Rita Marley (formerly of the Soulettes) and Judy Mowatt (formerly of the Gaylettes) to sing harmonies on some of the Bob & Marcia sessions. Pleased with the way their voices seamlessly blended, she further engaged their services for her live shows.

Rita's husband Bob Marley began working on the *Natty Dread* album. It would be the first release under a new name Bob Marley & The Wailers (following the departure of Bunny Wailer and Peter Tosh). Marley indicated to his wife that he liked the sound of the three and wanted to use them on the record.

Their voices on the songs for the album became an indispensible part of the sound. A sound that was hard to duplicate by other singers. It wasn't just background singing, but more like group vocals arranged where they led on some parts. So from 1975, they went on tour with the future *Reggae King*, and were now officially named The I Threes.

Marcia Griffiths, already a star in her own right, now became a supporting player in a grander scenario. The I Threes became just as important in a musical crusade, which would allow Bob Marley to conquer the world, both as a recording artist and live performer. Marcia, as a member of the I Threes, made history of her own. Later The I Threes would be lauded as the most influential Jamaican female group ever. This move also gave her financial stability. Before then, in spite of all her solo success she had little to show for it. This thing with Marley was her main gig, and she stayed with it right up to the time of his passing in 1981.

But Griffiths, with all she had on her plate, never really abandoned her solo career, as she managed to turn out several classics that were recorded in between tours

In 1978 she harnessed womanpower and worked with the female" Coxsone" of Jamaican music, Sonia Pottinger. Pottinger was the first successful female record producer in Jamaica and released her first records starting from 1966. Sonia was married to record producer Lloyd Pottinger and together they owned several labels: **Gay Feet**, **Tip Top**, **Rainbow** and **High Notes**. It was on **High Notes** that Marcia found a brief home and had the massive hit *Stepping Out A Babylon*, which was included on the brilliant album *Stepping*. With *Stepping* the artist proved that she could conquer every area of music. This classic was as hard as the roots sound being delivered by the Rasta artists of the 70s.

Marcia's versatility and vocal range allowed her to move effortlessly from ballads to roots reggae, putting distance between her and others. Talent wise, it was obvious that divine providence had given her the edge. *Stepping* the single was also Marcia's first hit that was her own original composition and proved to be effective because of the personal nature of the lyrics. On it she confides, *"When I think of all the bitter times I've had"* and further down *"give thanks to the almighty God He showed me what I am"*. This was Marcia at her very best, both vocally and creatively. The *Stepping* album also contained other popular tunes like "*Peaceful Woman*" and "*It's Impossible*". Marcia followed *Stepping* with *Naturally* another classic album, featuring "*Tell Me Now*", "*Truly*" and "*Dreamland*".

In the early 80s after Bob Marley passed away, Griffiths concentrated on work with the I Threes and her solo career. In '85 she did the album *Rock My Soul* with producer Sydney Crooks, as well as *I Love Music* with Chris Stanley. But for the most part, her career went through a dry spell.

In 1982 Bunny Wailer got an idea, after hearing the smash hit *Electric Avenue*, by Guyanese singer Eddy Grant. Based on this inspiration he wrote a tune called *Electric Boogie*. He brought in Marcia to record it and by 83 released the single in Jamaica on his own **Solomonic** label. The song was a hit in Jamaica, but seemed to have died right there.

In 1989 Bunny re-recorded *Electric Boogie* singing on it himself and released his own version of the song. In that same year, a radio jockey from Washington, DC picked up Marcia's version and played it extensively on his show. This caused the song to become popular enough to enter the US charts peaking at # 51. But this relatively low chart position however does not tell the whole story. Marcia's *Electric Boogie* kept growing and growing mainly based on the fact that it inspired its own dance craze, *The Electric Slide*. It acquired the status of a modern classic, becoming a favorite at cook-outs, line dance parties, tourist resorts, on cruise ships and karaoke gatherings. The *Electric Boogie* song became a part of pop culture. Capitalizing on the song's success, an album titled *Carousel*, on which it was included, was rushed out by **Island** subsidiary **Mango** in 1990.

The decade of the 90s saw Marcia becoming more popular than ever and is a textbook case of how to survive in the fickle music industry. At this time, she teamed up with hot producers like Donovan Germaine (**Penthouse**) and Phillip "Fattis" Burell (**Xterminator**) and had a number of hits. Here she exercised flexibility and plain old common sense by working with a number of the hot young DJs who were dominating the scene. Scoring with *Half Idiot* (featuring Cutty Ranks), and on other dancehall hits with Tony Rebel, Mad Cobra and Buju Banton. Charting with the singles *Fire Burning*, *I Shall Sing* and *Closer To You* (feat. Beres Hammond), she saw the release of the aptly titled *Indomitable* album on **Penthouse**.

In 1994 she received official recognition for her contributions to Jamaican culture when the government conferred on her the prestigious medal: The Order of Distinction. **VP Records**, to mark her 35th year in the business, released the *Certified* album in 1999.

If there is anything to critique about Marcia's illustrious career, it is an absence of, and/or poor management. Case in point is that her biggest crossover hit, *Electric Boogie*, was not properly capitalized on. The song is much bigger than her, as many people who enjoy it, still don't know the singer by name.

Griffiths however, has set the bar in many areas. Her style of dress has made her a fashion icon. Her influence on a whole generation of singers would make up a list too long to be mentioned. Her professionalism and commitment to quality is a lesson in itself. It says that one does not have to stoop to the lowest and cater to the basest nature of one's character in order to achieve success.

Today, more than ever, the legend is in demand as a live performer. She is being booked as Bob and Marcia, The I Threes and as Marcia Griffiths. This proves that no work goes unrewarded, regardless of time. Marcia is a giant and the only Jamaican female singer deserving of the title Queen of Reggae.

6. Gregory Isaacs

Christened: Gregory Isaacs
Born: July 15, 1951
Deceased: October 25, 2010

Cool Ruler

There is an elite group of Jamaican artists of international stature. One of the names you will find there is Gregory Isaacs. He is one of the legends of reggae music and one of the most beloved by the people of his native country.

The news of his passing in 2010, after a yearlong battle with lung cancer, put the nation in a somber mood. Few musical artists are like close relatives the way he was, and due to the impact he had on people, most felt the lost in the most intimate way.

Isaacs was born in the Fletchers Land section of Kingston. He was the first son of Lester Isaacs and Enid Murray. As a youth, he acquired vocational skills and later practiced as an electrician and cabinetmaker. His heart however, was somewhere else and he longed to trade singing in the furniture shop for the recording studio. More than anything else he wanted to be on records like his heroes Alton Ellis, Delroy Wilson and Ken Boothe. At age 17 he made the first steps toward realizing this goal, though success did not come quickly.

The first single was released in 1968, *Another Heartache* (a duet with Winston Sinclair) and flopped. The following year he joined with singers Penroe and Bramwell to form The Concords. But after only a year the trio disbanded as they failed to ignite.

Gregory was undaunted and, by 1971, was a solo artist recording for Rupert Edwards and Prince Buster, but to no avail. After six frustrating years, he started working with a producer who finally got it. You see, Gregory Isaacs was not the typical singer. He did not have what you would describe as a pleasant singing voice. His was nasal and weird, and may have proved too unconventional for some producers. With Alvin "GG" Ranglin, there was an obvious chemistry and he finally had a hit with *Love is Overdue* in 1974. The single jump-start a career that would be the most prolific of all amongst Jamaican artists, resulting in hundreds of albums and singles. The Discogs website credits the crooner with 150 albums and close to 400 singles, but the music grapevine rumors that Gregory over, his long career, did an estimated 500 albums.

This entry into the popular arena also revealed a singer with a sound that people had never heard before. As previously mentioned, his voice was easily recognized for its startling peculiarities. He also sang slow and flat but over the years this apparent vocal disability would come to be appreciated for its uniqueness.

Another point, evident early on, was his talent as a songwriter. Gregory was a poet in the true sense, using phrases and prose that were superior to what his contemporaries were offering. He wrote a lot of love songs but not the syrupy, *baby, I love you,* kind. His text fleshed out the real issues in relationships. He dealt with the drama that came with the matters of the heart: personality conflicts, infidelity, infatuation, love found and love lost. Also noteworthy, is that he wrote most of his songs as close to Standard English as possible. It would not be an exaggeration to say Isaacs was Jamaica's musical Shakespeare. On the heels of *Love is Overdue* were more hits that were placed on his first album *In Person* that sold a whopping 75,000 copies when it came out.

In 1973 Isaacs and another singer Errol Dunkley started a label **African Museum** on which he released a lot of self-produced material. Throughout the 70s, he quickly took his position as one of the top Jamaican artists and outworked others to do so. In this decade, the hits were numerous: *All I Have Is Love, Top Ten, Loving Pauper, Extra Classic, Black a Kill Black, Mr. Cop, Mr. Brown, Border and Number One*. His albums also sold well. In 1977 he put out the album *Cool Ruler* on his own label, which would become the nickname that would stick to the future legend.

So successful was he in this period that the major labels came. In 1978 Isaacs signed to **Virgin** subsidiary **Frontline**, and gained major exposure with an appearance in a movie now regarded as a cult classic, *Rockers*. His international debut *Soon Forward* did not set the world on fire. When his contract with **Frontline** ran out, he then signed to **Charisma**, releasing the disc *More Gregory*, which fared no better. It would take another label, one that understood the genre, to give him the breakthrough he sought.

In 1982 Isaacs emerged from Tuff Gong studios with what would be considered a masterpiece, the album *Night Nurse*. Under a new contract with **Island**, the album went as high as # 32 on the UK Charts, with the title track becoming a major hit locally and beyond.

This victory was bitter sweet as Isaacs, who had been going to court on gun and drug possession charges was convicted and sentenced to six months.

Indicative of his darker side, this would be a tragic result of his many run-ins with the law and a bad side effect to what was increasingly becoming public knowledge of the singer's cocaine habit. He documented this with the 80s hit *The More Them Get It*.

These personal issues extended into financial problems and led to a blitz of recordings done for almost any producer with the cash resulting in a barrel of hits and misses. Nevertheless, some of the songs that made it were killer tracks, especially in partnership with riddim twins Sly & Robbie. Sly & Robbie had some big ones with Issacs *Soon Forward*, *Don't Want To be Lonely*, *Mary* and *Top* Ten which they released on their **Taxi** label.

For the road he used the legendary band Roots Radics and made a sizable impression on the international scene. Issacs became one of the artists who were now stepping into the vacuum created by Marley's passing. The rock press at this time hailed Issacs as one of reggae's great hopes.

As the music began to turn towards the harder dancehall style led by the rise of the DJs Isaacs fell right into the mix. He not only recorded on the new riddims but also paired up with the DJs on many singles. Record shops in Jamaica overflowed with product with Issacs's name.

In 1989 another significant partnership was forged by Gregory with producer Augustus "Gussie Clarke" for whom he delivered the massive single that took him straight into the digital era, *Rumours*. Clarke also produced an equally potent follow up, *Red Rose For Gregory* and, at the beginning of the 90s, paired the singer with another legend, Dennis Brown, on the *No Contest* album featuring the hit *Raggamuffin*.

As the 90s progressed, drug problems and all, the artist kept up an unbelievable work pace by delivering more hits, namely: *Rough Neck, Mind You Dis, Too Good To be True* and *Report To Me*. In 1997 his financial position vastly improved when a Simply Red cover of his classic *Night Nurse* topped the British Charts.

Isaacs however, because of his personal issues, continued to collect advances from and made commitments to various parties at a rate that defied logic. On many new recordings he simply covered his own past hits. As his drug problem worsened, he also dodged promoters, from whom he had taken deposits. Sometimes he didn't care and sometimes he was just too zoned out to travel. The addiction also wearied heavily on his overall health with the singer losing all his teeth due to incessant freebasing, a fact that contributed to a decline in his vocal abilities. But he never stopped working.

One thing that Issacs was consistent with was his ever-dapper mode of attire: jacket and pants, along with his trademark felt hat.

He soldiered on right up to the very end, even as his health failed and at the time of his passing was a four time Grammy Nominee. His last two releases *Brand New Me* (**Tads**) and *Isaacs Meet Isaacs* came out the same year that he died.

Gregory Issacs transitioned while receiving treatment at a London Hospital, capping off a remarkable life and career and in Jamaica was given a state funeral, complete with a musical tribute by his peers.

5. Toots Hibbert

Christened: Frederick Hibbert
Born: December 8, 1945

History Personified

Reggae music can be defined as: Jamaica's interpretation of all musical genres of the world. The man who reinforces this definition is the living legend Toots Hibbert.

Referred to by historians of the art form as a Godfather of Ska and a founding father of reggae itself, Toots epitomizes the soul of Jamaican music and is one of its foremost ambassadors.

He is larger than the narrow constricts that those outsiders try to fit reggae into. He unabashedly presents his native music in a free-form narrative that includes blues, rock, country, soul and pop. He has outlived and outran most of his contemporaries and is still one of the most booked artists on the live music circuit, in any genre.

The story of the man who is breathing history began in the central parish of Clarendon in the town of May Pen. His father was a Seventh Day Adventist minister, and the young Frederick began to take part in the services from the age of seven. This ingrained in him a passionate love for gospel music while, his observance of his father's preaching would influence the revival style performances that he would come to be known for.

Migrating to Kingston around age 15 he forgo any further schooling and instead went straight into the working world as a barber. Some sources also said he tried his hand at boxing, not a surprise as he possesses a stocky muscular frame. At his place of employment he would sing incessantly to ward off boredom, due to the mundane nature of his job. Patrons at the shop grew tired of him singing "*over their head*" and advised him to become an artist.

In Kingston, around 1961, he met two aspiring

singers Nathaniel Mathis and Henry Gordon both, born in 1945 and hailing from the eastern parish of Portland. On hearing Hibbert's voice, they were smitten and immediately wanted to be in a group with him. Mathis already had some recording experience, but they started to rehearse together in order to hone a sound. They decided on a name for the new unit: The Maytals.

After practicing for close to a year, they went to Coxsone's **Studio One** compound for an audition. They had to sing for, then in house producer and all-rounder, Lee Scracth Perry, who had the power to say yes or no. Perry liked them but, along with other Studio One session players, did not approve of the way The Maytals were trying to sound like an American R&B group. They were thus encouraged to find their own sound. This is where Hibbert, who sang lead, asserted his leadership and dug deep into his church background and molded the sound of the group by melding gospel with ska.

Hibbert, commonly known as Toots, also incorporated the sound style and persona of the soul singers he admired like James Brown, Little Richard and Otis Redding. This outward looking need, coupled with an inward desire to set a standard of being like those artists, instead of being obsessed with his local competition would set him apart from many of his contemporaries.

The Maytals first records were *Hallelujah*, *Matthew Mark* and *Six and Seven Books*. But due to Coxsone's penny pinching mentality, which extended to not properly compensating the acts recording for him, The Maytals left in 1963 to work with a Coxsone protégé, a former amateur boxer called Prince Buster. The singles *Broadway Jungle*, *Dog War* and *Pain In My Belly* were very successful but could not help to prevent another falling out this time with Buster, also over money. The group then moved on to Byron Lee, owner of the **Dynamic Sounds** imprint and recorded an album.

In 1966 The Maytals suffered a near fatal blow when Toots was arrested, charged and subsequently convicted of marijuana possession. The harsh sentence of 18 months left Mathis and Gordon in a dilemma, but they waited patiently for their leader.

An interesting back-story of the whole sordid affair is that in 1966 The Maytals won the Festival song competition. Winning this most coveted prize meant national exposure for the victor and after the group captured it with the anthem, *Bam*

Bam, their popularity skyrocketed. It is said that Toots was framed by others who were jealous of his and the groups achievements. Of note is that the success of *Bam Bam* caught the attention of Reggae's grand patron, **Island Records** founder Chris Blackwell, who started to make overtures to the group. Toots' ode to his incarceration, *54-46 That's My Number,* was released in 1968, becoming an instant smash. The group with Toots now a free man was right back in the thick of things.

Along its evolutionary path, Jamaican music went from mento to ska, and then on to what became known as *rocksteady*. Rocksteady became the accepted form of the music from around the mid-sixties. But It would soon acquire a new name. In 1968, The Maytals released a catchy up-tempo tune named *Do The Reggay* that spoke of a fashionable dance. The "*reggay*" in the song's title would become the new moniker for the island's music.

The origins of the word reggae, the name of the genre of music indigenous to Jamaica, are myriad. The 1967 edition of The Dictionary of Jamaican English lists the word "rege" as an adjective meaning "rags, ragged clothes or a quarrel". Other sources cite producer Bunny

"Striker" Lee as one of the first to use the term. It is said that during one of his recording sessions while listening to the "skank", which was a section of the instrumentals played on the organ and guitar, he verbalized the word *regge* because that was what the "skank" sounded like. Lee said the skank sounded like sheke skeke, a close rhyme that evolved into the name. There is also the social condition that existed in the island at the time, along with cultural peculiarities that may have contributed. There was a local term "streggae" that referred to a loose, immoral woman or for an untidy person from which the word may have also had its genesis. Toots gives his own take on the word alluding to the Leslie Kong produced *Do the Reggay* saying, "*the reggae was like a kind of dance that was for the poor*". Poor people were being described as "regular" people with the prefix "reg" playing off the word "regular". *Enough of the history lesson let's get back to the story.*

Toots and his Maytals, now around 1969, found a home with Kong and entered their most prolific phase by recording close to a hundred titles. Over the next three years, the trio reaped a bounty of success. In 1969 they were again victorious in the Festival Song Competition with *Sweet & Dandy* and, in 1972, triumphed with

Pomps & Pride.

Two albums for **Trojan**, *Monkey Man* (69) and *From The Roots* (71), were then released in Europe. The group also gained much needed international exposure with their cameo in the 1973 motion picture, *The Harder They Come* and two of their tracks *Sweet and Dandy*, and *Pressure Drop* were included on the film's soundtrack album.

The Maytals, at the end of the 60s, was the biggest group in Jamaica both in terms of sales and popularity. It was from this point that the group was rebranded as *Toots and The Maytals,* to capitalize on Hibbert's captivating stage presence. Their growing popularity in Europe encouraged Blackwell to sign them which he did in 1975. Unfortunately for them, this period also marked the ascent of Bob Marley, and for all intent and purposes, he was the label's top priority.

But before the ink was put to paper for **Island**, the workaholic Toots would deliver two more albums to **Trojan**: *In The Dark* and the masterpiece *Funky Kingston*. These two items showed the group in its most eclectic form, pushing the boundaries of island sound towards a continental one that included New Orlean's jazz and blues, while overtly gospel. Funky Kingston featured the timeless classic "Country Roads", on which The Maytal's reggaefied the John Denver original, which became the group's signature song.

Their first album for **Island** Reggae *Got Soul*, featured a young Steve Winwood playing keyboards on some tracks. Along with backing-band The Dynamites, they embarked on their first official US tour. On this trek encompassing both the east and west coast, they played some small venues; while, in the bigger ones they were the opening act for the *J Giels Band* and *The Who*.

Toots made every appearance count and his high energy performances allowed him to pick up fans that would stay with him over the years. The Maytals had a full aggregation on stage with horns and Toots dressed like a rock star, always in leather, and mimicked his idols like Otis Redding and James Brown. Live, Toots is an animal that gives one hundred percent and as the years progressed the ageless wonder continued to push his body to the limit.

In 1979 he started his own label **Righteous Records**, which he used to put out songs that **Island** didn't want. Working at **Island** would allow The Maytals to be produced by the legendary duo of Sly & Robbie, which would help to steer them in a new musical direction and modernize their sound. Between the years of 1979 and 1981, **Island** released three more worthwhile discs: *Pass The Pipe*, *Just Like That* and *Knock Out*. Also of note is the live offering *Live at The Hammersmith Palais* which made the **Guinness Book of World Records** for the fastest album to be made available commercially, with it being recorded mixed and released in 24 hours.

In 82 Hibbert called time out on the group, embarking on a solo career though still touring the world under the group's name and would fly like this for a decade, after which Mathis and Gordon resumed a working relationship with him.

During his solo years, he intensified his working relationship with Sly & Robbie. As a result, the Grammy nominated *Live In Memphis* (88) came out. On this album Hibbert did his own renditions of timeless Stax/Volt classics such as *Knock On Wood*, *Love and Happiness* and *Dreams to Remember*.

The Maytals, under Toot's leadership, keeps chugging along and is now in their fifth decade of existence. In the 2000s they inked a deal with **V2**

Records, and their long illustrious career earned them the privilege of having an anthology of their recordings *Times Tough* being released. The anthology chronicles their survival through all the stages of Jamaican music from ska, rocksteady, roots dub, reggae and dancehall.

Toots and his musical brothers Nathaniel and Henry are not only a vital piece of Jamaican musical history, but also black musical history. They are one of the few Jamaican musical acts to be listed in the *Rolling Stone's Encyclopedia of Rock and Roll*.

As for the man, Frederick "Toots" Hibbert, his influence is seen in countless other artists spanning the globe. He is respected by artists such as Daryl Hall, the late Robert Palmer and the late Joe Strummer and has collaborated with the likes of Bonnie Raitt, Willie Nelson, and Sheryl Crow. Influential music magazine *Rolling Stone* also listed him at number 71 on their *100 Greatest Singers of All Time* survey.

The man is Jamaican musical history in the flesh and is still not done yet.

4. Dennis Brown

Christened: Dennis Brown
Born: February 1, 1957
Deceased: July 1, 1999

Crown Prince

The most influential Jamaican singer of all time is the Crown Prince of Reggae Dennis Brown. It is his style that spawned a cottage industry of emulators that came to prominence. The late icon was the most loved and, in spite of his tragic decline towards the end of his career, he remains a giant amongst the musical heroes of his native country.

Dennis Brown was a child prodigy, born in the heart of the musical scene. His home was located at Orange Street, downtown Kingston, where most of the early recording studios were within walking distance. One of thirteen children for Arthur and Yvonne Brown, his father was an amateur singer, playwright and actor. His mom was a homemaker. A vacuum however, was created in the young man's life with the tragic loss of his beloved mother who succumbed to illness when he was just a teen.

His talent was evident from as early as age nine and impressed members of his community so much that they would dish out money, just to hear him sing. It was obvious to everyone around that he was blessed with a golden voice and he was already being dubbed "the boy wonder" of Jamaican music. So mercurial was he that his popularity began to eclipse that of one of his main influences Delroy Wilson.

By age eleven he scored his first hit *No Man Is An Island* for **Studio One** and in the 70s other smashes arrived like the flood. Following his maiden hit were *If I Follow My Heart, Your Love Is Amazing, Ride On feat Big Youth, No More Will I Roam, Money In My Pocket, Silhouette* and, a haunting cover, Santana's *Black Magic Woman*. The single *Money In My Pocket* apart from topping the Jamaican charts was a huge hit in the UK, reaching #14, and would pave the way for subsequent success in this market.

From the mid-seventies Dennis was a star and, in effect, one of Jamaica's first teen idols. Most of his early hits were love-type songs but his eclectic musical tastes led him to covering material that ranged from R&B, folk and rock. Songs like *Black Magic Woman*, Carole Kings' *You're No Good*, Burt Bacharach's *Rain Drops Keep Falling* and The Chilite's *How Could I Let You Get Away*.

Brown had a definitive vocal sound and made these songs into his own. In many interviews he credited his unique singing style to his penchant for improvising. After Dennis covered a song, you almost forgot about the original.

In 1977 the single *Wolfs and Leopards* (**Third World**) and the album of the same name was a game changer. As stated in an All Music review, this heralded Brown to be a full-fledged Rasta man and marked a shift towards "cultural and political themes".

The album was more or less a compilation of

singles; nevertheless, in a thematic sense, held together as a cohesive body of work. It was stacked with hits namely, the title track, *Stop Fussing and Fighting Brother*, *Whip Them Jah Jah, Children of Israel, Lately Girl* and the song that would become both his signature tune and also a perennial fan favorite the irresistible *Love and Hate*, aka *Here I Come*.

This also marked him as a composer of note, since on the album he wrote or co-wrote all the songs, except for the lone cover the Burt Bacharach/ Hal David penned *Rolling Down*. Its deep roots sound also came about, in part, due to the fact of it being recorded at Lee Perry's *Black Ark Studio* the site of many groundbreaking roots albums.

Brown, much like one of his contemporaries Gregory Issacs, surged passed his competitors by out recording them. His prolific ways resulted in hundreds of singles on the market.

The Jamaican music scene was and is to this day fiercely competitive. In an atmosphere where the artists are not usually under contract to any one-label, producers scoop down on the popular ones like vultures. But with producer Winston Holness, Brown did some of his best work. In tandem they turned out three of the biggest albums of his career: *Westbound Train, Wolves and Leopards* and *Just Dennis*.

Holness was a few years older than Brown and, on meeting, the two clicked and the chemistry was undeniable. The producer was a sort of wise man known as Niney The Observer (Observer was also the name of his label) and Brown submitted to his mentoring as a son would to a father. So close were the two that they even shared a house together in the Kingston suburbs of Pembroke Hall.

This coupling was very advantageous to the singer as under Niney's stewardship, he emerged more confident in his powers as both a composer and performer. Moreover, the songs they worked on were instant classics. The *Just Dennis* album alone contained the most loved of Browns legion of hits; *Cassandra, Some Like It Hot, Westbound Train, Love Jah* and, the repatriation, anthem *Africa*.

This firmly established Brown as the undisputed champion and, by 1978 even Bob Marley was calling him the best reggae singer and his personal favorite. As the saying goes "all good things come to an end" and 1978 was also the last year Brown worked with his mentor recording the album *Tribulation*. This ended what was then considered as a partnership "made in heaven". In an interview with UK magazine *Black Echoes* Brown explained, "I was going along with one man's ideas for too long" and "now I know I can produce myself".

In light of his phenomenal success the barely 21 year old singer pumped some of his earnings into his own label **DEB** (the initials of his full name) and released many singles, with *So Long Rastafari* being a standout cut and the album *Joseph Coat of Many Colors* coming to market. **DEB** was however, shuttered after only one year in operation as Brown was not as talented a businessman as he was a singer. The label that was a partnership with producer Castro Brown (no relations to Dennis) suffered, as a result of so called duplicitous dealings on the part of Castro and overall poor management by both.

He immediately ran back into the waiting arms of producers longing for his talents. Those who mainly benefited were Bunny Lee, Ossie Hibbert, Tad Dawkins and, but especially, Joe Gibbs.

Under Gibbs, as with Holness Brown flourished and transcended stardom moving into greatness. With the *Visions of Dennis Brown* album for Gibbs, his was the voice of the people crying out like a dreadlocked *John the Baptist*. On cuts such as *Concrete Castle King* he lambasted the slumlords who kept tenants in deplorable conditions. On others he touched themes pertaining to black pride, *Deliverance* and *Malcolm X*. There were also deeper kind of love songs and uplifting advice with the cuts *Say What You Say* and *Sister Stay At Home*. *The Words Of Wisdom* album, also for Gibbs, gave his fans another timeless classic *Should I*.

While Bob Marley was busy colonizing the world, Dennis had Jamaica firmly on lock. But with this much success he was already being eyed by the scouts at several major overseas labels which would rob the island albeit for a short while, of the services of their most precious son.

At the peak of his powers he made an appearance at the Montreux Jazz Festival in Switzerland. Here Brown was backed by the legendary Lloyd Parkes and The We The People Band. His high-energy stint matched those of other great's ala Peter Tosh and Bob Marley, and resulted in the live set, *Dennis Brown Live At Montreux* on **Atlantic Records**.

In the years during Marley's reign and immediately after his death, labels were hungry for other reggae stars to fill the demand in the growing market. In 1980 Brown delivered *The Spellbound* album again for Joe Gibbs, which was the first disc that deliberately aimed for an international audience.

By 1981 the ink was dry on a contract with **A&M** with Brown becoming label mates with reggae influenced group *The Police* and the singer relocated to England. The first release of a three-album deal was *Foul Play* produced by Gibbs and Clive Hunt. It contained typical Brown offerings like *If I Had The World* and *If I Follow My Heart*, as well as crossover style attempts: *On The Rock* and the funky title track. But the album was a poor seller and the problem, it seems, was that the tracks that the label was pushing were much weaker than others that was more organic to Browns style.

Love Has Found Its Way (82) was an improvement on its predecessor. Standout cuts were the mellow lover's rock sounding title track and the Black Uhuru, style *Halfway Up Halfway Down*. But it too failed to spark as the label was at a lost as to how it should be marketed. If any album could have broken through it would have been this one. With that opportunity lost, the release of the third album *The Prophet Rides Again* was just a formality and marked the end of Browns association with **A&M**. The whole affair seemed to have been a misadventure and also soured the relationship between Brown and Gibbs.

When Brown returned to the local scene around late 1983, Jamaica was in the throes of a musical revolution. The singers were being swept from power by the DJs led by a slack-talking albino called Yellowman. This spurred Brown to join with the other leading singers Gregory Issacs, Freddie McGregor and John Holt, forming a kind of singer's militia to combat their dj adversaries. They embarked on a campaign where they voiced and released singles at a merciless pace. As for Brown himself he played a sort of double game by teaming up with leading dancehall producer King Jammy and the DJs as well. Survival was his primary interest and took precedence over any so-called crusade.

The workaholic set out to overwhelm the local market with products and the hits started to flow as if he never went away. When he combined forces with rhythm legends Sly & Robbie, the renaissance was in full bloom.

Sly & Robbie, in previous years, had played on sessions featuring Brown on vocals for other producers. When they worked with him on their own **Taxi** label, the result was pure gold. With **Taxi**, Dennis scored three of his biggest hits in the 80s: *Sitting and Watching*, *Have You Ever* and *Revolution*.

His restless nature led him to trying his hand at another record label – **Yvonne's Special**, named after his wife. On it he released some good self-produced material with *Promised Land*, featuring UK reggae outfit Aswad, being most notable. In the nineties he maintained a high profile with another impressive string of hits: *Slow Down*, *Raggamuffin* (feat. Freddie McGregor); *Let Off Supm* and *Big All Around* (both with Gregory Issacs); *Wild Fire* with John Holt; *Ababa Jan Hoi*, *Death Before Dishonor*, *To The Foundation*, and *Stop the Fighting*.

As a performer he also exceeded all expectations, being one of the most exciting and consistent. He holds the record for the most appearances on Reggae Sunplash gracing its stage a record seventeen times in its twenty-one year existence. Throughout his illustrious career he gave many legendary performances all over the world and even had his own annual show in Jamaica dubbed *Dennis Brown and Friends*, aka *The Inseparable Concerts*. Brown never failed to give his all under the bright lights and it was typical of him to prance around the stage like a stalker, for the entire length of his set.

All geniuses it seems have their vices and his was addiction to cocaine. In the final years of his life his most precious instrument his voice, due to the abuse, was severely damaged. This impaired his ability to do quality work and his appearance became harrowing to say the least. Many Jamaican artists dabbled in hard drugs and survived, but Brown deteriorated rapidly under its might.

While touring Brazil in May 1999 the singer became severely ill and doctors there diagnosed him with pneumonia. Shortly after returning home, he was again hospitalized after suffering a heart attack.

On the morning of July 1st *The Crown Prince* took his last breath due to what was described as a complication due to pneumonia. Rumors swirled that the artist died of AIDS, but there was no medical evidence to verify these claims.

On July 17th Brown received a state funeral in The National Arena and was fittingly laid to rest in National Heroes Park. He left a rich legacy, matched by only a few.

Bob Marley came to be loved by the world at large, but at home he was not as appreciated as Dennis Brown. Brown's vocal style came to be imitated by a whole generation of younger artists, successful in their own right. The list includes Luciano, Richie Stephens, Tony Curtis, Bushman, the duo Brian and Tony, Jack Radics, Coco Tea and others, too numerous to mention.

Most remarkable is the wealth of classical songs that are like everyday hymns to Jamaican people. The song *Love and Hate*, with its Biblical lyrics taken from David's Psalms, is probably the most loved reggae composition ever.

Brown was one of those rare humans to come along. His somewhat unfortunate last days, cannot overshadow the brilliance of his life and his immense contribution to reggae, the people and his country. He still remains the Crown Prince of Reggae.

3. Peter Tosh

Christened: Winston McIntosh
Born: October 19, 1944
Deceased: September 11, 1987

Reggae Rebel

"He will be a wild man who will be hostile to everyone and everyone will be hostile to him". So goes the description of the Biblical Patriarch Ishmael in the Book of Genesis. This prophecy could also be applied to reggae great Peter Tosh.

Musically, he was the most militant of all that came out of Jamaica, with an equally volatile personality to match. Peter was a hard man to deal with, but no one, at least from a distance, expected him to die at the hands of ruthless killers in his own home. He was cut down, on a muggy September evening, in 1987 at the ripe age of 43.

His rebellious image earned him the nicknames Stepping Razor and Rebel Wailer. The media and the powers that be may have only anointed one as the king of reggae but amongst the kings of reggae, Peter *The Great* ruled in his own right.

Born in the parish of Westmoreland, in the district of Belmont to Alvera Morris and James McIntosh, the lad never knew his father and his father claimed he wasn't aware of his birth. He was Alvera's only child. At around age six, due to financial hardships, he was taken to an uncle, Uriah Campbell, who raised him until his early teens.

Winston was unusually tall for his age group, and had a deep, dark complexion. His mother recalled that he started to sing at an early age, and before he was ten he already was somewhat proficient on the guitar, and then by thirteen on keyboards.

His uncle was a disciplinarian and church-man, and may have been very harsh on the young Tosh, who had to attend church every Sunday and twice during the week. This overly strict home life seemed repressive to the young McIntosh and, coupled with the absence of his father, probably started to foster in him contempt for authority and authoritarian figures. He would spout a lot of religious symbolism in his music but would take a very anti-Christian, anti-church position on his path to success.

Alvera left the country and ended up in the Kingston slum of Trench Town, and was shortly after joined there by her 15-year-old son. School was not a priority and he developed a rough exterior, but not in pursuit of gangster glory, but to facilitate his one and only passion: music.

This passion led him to Joe Higgs, a Trench Town based musician and mentor to those who were interested in developing their craft. In 1961, at Joe Higg's Third Street residence, he met other aspiring artists, which included Robert Marley and Neville Livingston.

This became the school where he and others were being taught how to play instruments and learning vocal techniques, including the rudiments of harmonizing. Tosh had a head start, as he already knew the basics on keyboards and guitar, even proceeding to teach Marley the guitar.

The friendship and camaraderie that was built up led to the formation of the pre-Wailers group, the Teenagers, some say The Juveniles. Whatever name it was, the group consisted of the three, plus Beverly Keslo, Junior Brathwaite and Cherry Green. When the group started to make a name as the Wailers, it whittled down to a trio of just the future legends.

Peter was clearly the most talented of the three, and his rich baritone voice betrayed the fact that he had a wide vocal range, where the highest notes were easily within his ability. He stood out as the leader of the outfit and, when they auditioned for Clement Dodd, was the one whose persistence persuaded him to record them after their earlier attempts failed to impress the legendary producer.

The Wailers were amongst a new wave of groups trading in the popular ska style of music. Their releases on Coxsone's **Studio One** started to dominate the music scene from around 1964. Their first hit was a Marley original *"Simmer Down"*, followed by more smashes in the ensuing years.

By 1966 the group appeared doomed when

Marley migrated to live with his mother in the US, and Peter began his long-hate affair with the authorities by getting arrested for a short while for possessing marijuana. However, the group continued under Tosh until Marley's return in 1967.

In 1971 Tosh began a solo career, parallel to his work with the Wailers. The single *Maga Dawg*, for Joe Gibbs was followed by others *Dem Haffi Get A Beating*, *I'm The Toughest* and *Nobody's Business* which gave a hint to his strident world-view. Around this time, he also started his own label **Intel-Diplo**, which stood for *Intelligent Diplomat*.

By 1972 the Wailers inked a deal with Chris Blackwell's Island Records and began work on the album that would permanently stamp reggae as a musical force on the international scene: *Catch A Fire*. The album featured two of Tosh's original compositions *400 Years* and *Stop That Train*. It received critical acclaim, but did not move big units. So, in order to draw attention to the international neophytes, the label put them on the road.

The label had to dole out tour support, as they were not yet a big concert draw hence, no money was being made. The rigors of touring in these early days also exacerbated tensions that were already simmering below the surface. Conflicts over money aside there were also other factors.

Weather by design or through natural process, Marley moved to center stage in the group and became the dominant figure. This did not sit well with Tosh. Peter reacted in a manner that would come to typify his behavior; with extreme emotion, by lashing out at those around him. To him, this was a conspiracy to relegate him to the backbench and imputed favoritism being shown to the half-white Marley by the white Chris Blackwell, whom he started to refer to as Chris "Whiteworst.

By 1974 Peter quit after a fistfight between himself and members of the group, while touring in the UK. He later remarked that "Bob Marley was my student" and he would never play "backup" to him. His departure hardened his resolve to succeed on his own, but it also entrenched his feelings of resentment towards his former group mate and the gatekeepers in the music industry.

A determined Tosh kicked his solo sojourn into high gear after having success with several singles, most notably, *Brand New Secondhand* and the classic marijuana advocate anthem, *Legalize It*.

Columbia Records a rival label to the **Warner Bros Group**, which handled distribution for Marley's label **Island**, signed him and released the album *Legalize It*, in 1976. This according to producer Lee Jaffe, after struggling financially to make the record and it being rejected by several other labels that he said were "scared" of dealing with Tosh.

It was a fine debut for the ex-Wailer and was praised by the critics, delivering hits like the title track, *Ketchy Shuby* and *What Cha Gonna Do*. The deal also granted him the rights to local distribution on his label.

With *Equal Rights* in 1977, he burnished the image of an uncompromising militant and gained a new alias, *Steppin Razor*, from the number four track on the disc. On the song he warned "*I'm a stepping razor don't you watch my size I'm dangerous*". Marley reasoned with his adversaries, but Tosh cursed them mercilessly. Marley's modus operandi employed logic, Peter's anger. *Equal Rights* established Peter as the number one agitator with other numbers, *African*,

Apartheid, *Downpressor Man* and *Get Up Stand Up*.

In an overeager thrust towards mainstream recognition, the most anti-establishment artist in the world left **Columbia Records** and signed with a label owned by musicians who epitomized debauchery. In 1978, Tosh inked a deal with **Rolling Stones Records**, owned by the legendary British rock group, The Rolling Stones. This was an odd marriage to say the least, as Tosh was known for his belligerence towards the vices of the western world and Rolling Stones front man Mick Jagger and its guitarist Keith Richards, the so-called *Glimmer Twins*, were the poster children of them. This was evident in a live performance video of Tosh and Jagger performing their hit song the Temptations cover, *Walk and Don't Look Back*, with the very masculine Tosh being visibly uncomfortable with Jagger's clown like and almost effeminate movements.

However, the deal did make Peter a known commodity with the single becoming a mild hit in the US. The promotion also gave him major exposure while appearing on many national TV shows and an opening spot on the Stones's world tour.

Three albums came out of this association: *Bush Doctor*, *Mystic Man* and *Wanted Dread and Alive*, but many critics said Peter did his worst work under the label. This however holds little merit, as some of his most well-known works are on them: *Buck In Ham Palace, Mystic Man, Reggae My Litis, Pick Myself Up, Coming In Hot* and, the soulful duet with American singer Gwen Guthrie, *Nothing But Love*.

From the moment Tosh embarked on a solo career it was evident that there was no way he could have remained a Wailer. He was a colossal talent with an ego to match, and this proved too combustible.

His musical output was just as potent as Marley's and his live shows just as electric. Assembling a stellar lineup of musicians under the name of *Word Sound and Power*, he conquered everywhere he went and at the height of his career played to very large audiences, especially in Europe and Africa. His stage attire went with his colorful personality and borrowed from the standard dress of eastern cultures particularly the Middle East. His brand of reggae borrowed from country, blues, rock and R&B. It was palatable to international tastes.

But there was something about Tosh that prevented him from becoming the huge star. It had nothing to do with his music because Peter did not compromise when it came to quality.

Tosh, it seemed, was a deeply troubled individual. Stemming from his dislike of authority from his youth days of being forced to go to church, he rejected advice and eschewed instructions. Peter, throughout the years, developed a serious victim complex where he felt someone was out to get him. Personal responsibility was not something he readily accepted. It was always something or someone that was trying to stop him.

He lambasted Blackwell for allegedly sidelining him during the Wailers years with **Island** and equally excoriated the Rolling Stones, **Columbia** and **EMI** for not promoting his records, charging all with *racism*. In 1978 on the One Love Peace Concert in Kingston, a show staged to calm political tensions running high in Jamaica, he used it instead as a platform to pour venom on both The Prime Minister and Leader of the Opposition. He had many brushes with the law to the point of physical clashes, and was nearly beaten to death on at least one occasion. He trashed a house on loan to him owned by Keith

Richards and was evicted by the police. He also had difficulty in acknowledging the contributions of others to his development. He told Roger Steffens in an interview that Joe Higgs, a man widely regarded as his mentor, "did not teach me to sing harmony". There is also the apparent bitterness of heart that he reserved for his fellow Wailer, Bob Marley, which could only emanate from deeply-seated jealousy. On hearing the news of Marley's passing, according to **Island** publicist Valerie Cowan, he remarked, "at least it leave a little space for all of us to go through now". Others saw it more as righteous indignation against an evil system, and journalist Vonnie McGowan said Peter became "overzealous and was taken over by his own spirituality".

On the other hand, this could've just been Peter being Peter, whose habit was to speak impulsively and without thinking, as in other interviews he said that Bob's death brought back "sad memories". In his zeal to right the wrongs of society, he might've become obsessed with *being right*, instead of *doing right.*

In 1983 his popularity was at an all-time high with the release of the *Mama Africa* album, containing the US top 50 hit *Johhny B* Goode his own take on the Chuck Berry classic. Included were also *Glasshouse*, as well as some of his earlier songs like *Stop That Train* and *Maga Dawg*, and the cynical *Peace Treaty*, a swipe at detractors who criticized his behavior at the 1978 peace concert. Tosh, then seemingly at the peak of his powers disappeared from public view.

At the end of December 1983, he performed at a concert in Kingston then went to Africa. For some time, the singer was suffering from an ulcerated stomach with bouts of excruciating pain. In Africa he sought to rest and seek the aid of so-called "medicine men", in an attempt to cure his condition. These medicine men were sometimes equated with those in Jamaica known as obeah men, practicing spiritual mediums. Tosh was apparently getting too close to the same forces, the agents of evil he condemned so frequently in his music.

In addition, Tosh's new girlfriend, Andrea Marlene Brown became the dominant force in his life assuming many of his business affairs. Many of his associates hinted that she had a huge influence, mostly negative, over the artist and that since meeting her, he was a changed man.

The artist emerged from his self-imposed exile in 1987 with a brand new album *No Nuclear War*.

Marlene was credited as the producer. He was also anxious and eager to resume touring, as the three-year layoff left him in dire financial straits. However, instead of 1987 being the year of his big comeback, it would be the last one of his life.

Tosh had a childhood friend Dennis Lobban. Whilst he took to the musical highway, Lobban went in the direction of criminality, earning a long rap sheet that included wounding police officers, for which he did jail time. One of his jail stints, according to rumor, was one for gun possession allegedly found in a car in which him and Tosh were the only occupants. It is said that in this matter Lobban took the fall, sparing Peter from jeopardizing his musical career. After his release he reunited with Tosh, who opened his home to him and helped him out financially.

This did not sit well with Marlene who was openly contemptuous of Lobban and advised Peter to get rid of him. The feelings of animosity between the ex-convict and Tosh's girlfriend were mutual and Lobban, feeling that Tosh was indebted to him for his lost years, started to stew internally with hatred. One day, when Lobban was in Peter's presence, he heard the artist talking on the phone about money for some upcoming shows. He decided right then and there that he would rob his old friend at the first opportunity.

In September 1987 Tosh returned to his Plymouth Avenue residence, in the upscale Kingston suburbs of Barbican, after a brief trip abroad. On the evening of September 11th, the singer and Marlene played host to a number of friends. In the house were Michael Robinson, Santa Davis and Wilton Doc Brown. But more visitors were on the way.

In the vicinity of the Carib Theater at Cross Roads, Dennis Lobban and two other men chartered a taxi, driven by one Steve Russell. They made way to Tosh's home. Lobban, a regular acquaintance showed up, at the door and was welcomed by Michael Robinson. Lobban and his two sidekicks entered and immediately brandished firearms, ordering everyone to the ground. Shortly after Jeff "Free I" Dixon and his wife arrived and walked straight into a crime scene in progress. Lobban pressed Peter for money, with the artist replying that there was none. Not getting what they came for, the three men unleashed hell, peppering the room and its terrified occupants with bullets, and then made their escape into the waiting cab. When the smoke cleared, all were wounded and lay in a sea of blood: three mortally – Doc Brown, Jeff Dixon and the reggae superstar. Within minutes the news spread across the island like wildfire and the nation shivered in shock, at the loss of another beloved artist.

A manhunt was immediately ordered to find the killers. Lobban, in a matter of days, turned himself in to police, accompanied by a Catholic priest. His two accomplices were never caught. Lobban, in a historically speedy trial was convicted of triple murder and sentenced to death. The cab driver was also charged, but later acquitted. Lobban's sentence was subsequently commuted to life in prison without the possibility of parole. He was carted off to the infamous General Penitentiary, where he remains to this very day.

Jamaica again had lost another cultural giant and mourned for the reggae icon that was given a state funeral at the National Arena. He was also honored with a posthumous win for the *No Nuclear War* album in the reggae category at the 1988 Grammy Awards.

Peter Tosh for all his shortcomings played a major role in colonizing the world with reggae music, and the manner of his death in no way has diminished his stature as one of the all-time greats of Jamaican music.

2. Jimmy Cliff

Christened: James Chambers
Born: April 1, 1948

Hall Of Famer

He's the first international reggae star, first Jamaican movie star and the second one to be inducted into the prestigious Rock & Roll Hall of Fame.

Jimmy Cliff, the living legend, transcends the genre of reggae; moreover, he is an international pop star and overall musical icon who sits in the company of the living legends like Dylan, Springsteen and, his own countryman, Toots Hibbert.

Jimmy Cliff is one of a handful of Jamaicans that still enjoy regular rotation on pop radio. His cover of Johnny Nash's *I Can See Clearly Now* is one of those evergreen recordings that adult contemporary stations in America just can't resist playing. Consequently, only the songs of Marley and Shaggy are featured on this same level.

In addition, Cliff is one of the great singer songwriters that have given the world classic compositions *Wonderful World Beautiful People*, *Harder They Come* and *Vietnam* (called the best protest song ever by Bob Dylan).

Cliff was born in the rural community of Somerton, located twelve miles out of tourist mecca Montego Bay in the western parish of St. James. His mother was a homemaker while, his father a farmer and tailor. Chambers was bit by the musical bug very early in his life and, from the first grade; he was already performing in front of friends in school and in church. His single most defining trait would be his drive. This led him to literally run away from home to escape the trappings of small town country life, which was rife with stagnation and failure.

At age 13 he arrived in the capital city, where he enrolled at Kingston Technical High School and took up barbering as a trade. But his only intention was to sing. The young man knew what he wanted and that was not to, in his own words, "*work in a banana field or to cut cane*".

No one is certain of its origins, but on embarking on a serious musical journey, he adopted the stage name *Jimmy Cliff*. The young aspirant made the rounds of most of the producers in the city and was rejected by all, except a man called Count Boysie, for whom he did his first song *Daisy Make Me Crazy*.

By age 14 he made even more progress when he barged into a record shop on Orange Street, owned by producer and his future manager Leslie Kong, and convinced him to give him a chance to audition. Other accounts state that he was taken to Kong by singer Derrick Morgan.

A couple of failed releases followed, but the teenager hit with *Hurricane Hattie*, which topped the islands charts in 1962. This was followed by a number of other popular releases most notably *Dearest Beverly* and *King of Kings*.

This was the era of ska and Cliff's polished and disciplined approach to his craft, along with a sweet sounding high tenor vocal, endeared him early out as one that could appeal to audiences across the entire class spectrum. An association with the venerable musician and record man Byron Lee proved prodigious, as this helped him to travel to the World's Fair, in New York in 1964. The World's Fair was an expo where Jamaican music was being displayed. Cliff made his next big move when he met up with **Island Record's** Chris Blackwell, and subsequently signed a deal with his label.

After scoring a massive hit with Mille Small, via the single *My Boy Lollopop* in 1964, Blackwell knew that the island's music could have mainstream success if it was presented and marketed in a particular way. In Cliff, Blackwell saw someone with the talent and work ethic to go beyond the success he already had in Jamaica. **Island's** headquarters was in London, and Cliff was encouraged to move there, which he did.

This was the first step that indicated how forward-thinking he was, as he took the plunge in order to pursue an international path to success instead of resting on his laurels.

Britain however did not have streets paved in gold and the artist struggled and often time was in dire financial straits. The singles that were released on **Island** at this time were not big sellers and Cliff turned to session work to get by.

A turn in the road came in 1968 with the success of a Beatles like composition called *Waterfalls*, not in the UK but in Brazil of all places. The tune was a far cry from the music of his native country, and was another indication of the eclectic tastes of Cliff.

However, the following year would be the one when all the suffering and hard work began to pay off. In that year, the release of his self-titled album, on another label owned by Blackwell and partner Lee Gopthal, **Trojan** was a smash. It yielded the top five, British chart hit *Wonderful World Beautiful People*, as well as *Vietnam* and the classic that would become his signature song and ode to his struggles, *Many Rivers To Cross*. The album also was strategically licensed for release in the US on **A&M Records**, under the title *Wonderful World Beautiful People*, and to **Phillips** for South America. It was an all-around success, both critically and commercially.

This distinguished Cliff as the first reggae star to come out of Jamaica. Only Desmond Dekker trumped Cliff, with a bigger hit, *Israelites*. Dekker had the first original hit but Cliff was a bigger star in general.

It became evident from this stage that Cliff was not really a Jamaican reggae singer, but a Jamaican pop singer who also did reggae. The follow up, *Another Cycle*, recorded at the infamous Muscle Shoals studio in Alabama, was a further departure from the music of his homeland. It also contained the classic *Sitting In Limbo*.

In 1970 he had two UK hits: a cover of Cat Stevens, *Wide World* and *You Can Get It If You Really Want*, found on the album *Goodbye Yesterday*. *You Can Get It If You Really Want* was also a hit for Desmond Dekker, when he covered it in later years.

In 1971 Cliff, who said in many interviews that, "acting was my first love", was offered the lead role in a Jamaican movie with the working title *The Harder They Come*. Also in that year Cliff lost his manager Leslie Kong who died suddenly after a brief illness but pressed on with his career regardless.

The film *The Harder They Come* was the handiwork of a white Jamaican, Perry Henzell, and Jamaican playwright Trevor Rhone. Henzell went to school in the UK and Canada, where he majored in film studies. Henzell returned to Jamaica in the 1950s and embarked on a career as a director of commercials until he met playwright Trevor Rhone. Rhone developed the idea for the film and Henzell, looking for a new challenge, agreed to produce and direct it.

As for Cliff's involvement, it would be more accurate to say that Blackwell placed him in the movie. According to reliable sources, Blackwell served as a shadow executive producer for the film. This was Blackwell pulling the necessary strings to bolster name recognition of his artist.

More importantly, the soundtrack to the movie reignited interest in a number of Cliff's past releases namely, *Many Rivers To Cross, Sitting In Limbo, You Can Get It If You Really Want* and gave birth to a new classic the title track *The Harder They Come*. The success of the movie and album transformed Cliff into an international sensation and a bankable star.

But for all the investment into the artist's career and maneuverings by Blackwell to bring about this state of affairs, he would be repaid with disloyalty as Cliff refused to re-sign with **Island**. The star instead cashed in on his newfound popularity. He gave the label one more disc,

Struggling Man, and then departed for the **Warner Brothers** subsidiary **Reprise Records**.

Thus began a remarkable run of albums on which Cliff's pop sensibilities were explored to the fullest extent. He never professed to be a reggae artist in the strictest sense, but the critics wanted him to be one. So in their state of being confounded by his eclecticism savaged his albums in the press.

He further went on to blow up the stereotype of what Jamaican artists usually subscribe to, the Rastafarian religion, by becoming a Muslim. His conversion to Islam in 1973 raised the ire of his countrymen and he was even spat upon by Rastafarians at a Wailers concert in 1975.

He moved from **Reprise** to **MCA**, trading in funk, soul and rock and seemed to be all over the musical map, not making any of them real big sellers but enough to keep him in the forefront on the international scene.

In the US after *The Harder They Come* and *Another Cycle*, he lost ground but gained in other vital markets in Europe, South America and Africa. The two countries where he subsequently had his biggest following were Nigeria and Brazil.

When he continued on his label hopping ways which was Jimmy, the businessman always searching for a better deal, he landed at **Columbia Records**. He then delivered two of his best albums, starting in 1982 with *Special* and, in the following year, *Power and The Glory*. This pair of albums produced the strongest results for the artist in the US after a prolonged lull.

He structured the deal so he could release them in Jamaica on his own label **Oneness** and with a number of singles started to reconnect with his native audience. On *Special* were the hits *Treat The Youths Right* and *Rub A Dub Partner* and on the latter were favorites: *We All Are One, Sunshine In The Music, Reggae Night* and the title track. In spite of this, he still avoided touring the US in support of them concentrating on the markets in which he was a certified superstar.

His thirst for real success in the US market remained unsatisfied and he finally teamed up with Ronald Bell of Kool & The Gang to produce two albums, with the intent of carving out a sound more palatable to the tastes of stateside audiences. But the pairing lacked chemistry and the production was stale and a mere rehash of the Kool and The Gang sound. *Cliffhanger*, the first of the two was not a big seller but garnered Cliff the consolation prize of a Grammy win in the best Reggae Album category in 1985. The second, *Hanging Fire*, feared no better.

His appearances in movies, more of a side trip, saw him starring alongside Peter O Toole and Robin Williams in *Club Paradise* (86) and a smaller role in 1990, *Marked For Death*, did not hurt his cause.

In 1995 he was somewhat vindicated when a cover of Johnny Nash's *I Can See Clearly Now*, off the *Cool Runnings* movie soundtrack, made top ten on the US singles chart. Since then Jimmy's voice has never left the American airwaves making his version of the classic song, the definitive one.

Cliff consistently releases albums even after over forty years in the spotlight. The overwhelming respect he enjoys by his peers came to the fore with the *Black Magic* album with features from a whos whos of the rock world including Sting, Joe Strummer of the Clash, Annie Lennox and Wyclef Jean .

One of his compositions, *Trapped*, originally found on the *Images* album furthered his acclaim as a songwriter of note, when it was covered by Bruce Springsteen for the *We Are The World* album.

In 2003, the Jamaican government with its third highest medal – The Order of Merit, honored him. And in 2009 he was inducted into the prestigious *Rock and Roll Hall of Fame*. Not bad for a poor country boy from Jamaica.

His love for all styles of music served him well but left him out of the reggae mainstream. Cliff does not have the political or social gravitas usually associated with most legendary reggae artists regarded as champions of Third World causes, but this does not diminish his stature as one of the all-time greats. What's important is that his songs have stood the test of time, and his groundbreaking role in the movie *The Harder They Come* preceded the rise of Bob Marley as an international superstar. This means he is Jamaica's first international star.

His life's work, commitment to quality, stamina, and longevity as well as a professional approach to his craft are testaments to his character. His penchant for taking musical risks and his adventurous spirit has made him an influence for many musicians all over the globe.

Cliff is one of the fathers of World Beat, a musical category of its own that stands separate from reggae.

On top of all this, he is still going strong with no sign of retiring any time soon, made evident by a 2012 release and Grammy winning album, *Rebirth*, supported by a US tour.

His musical contribution is a part of Jamaica's proud heritage. And his pioneering role in opening the doors for international recognition of the island's art form makes him a standard bearer for Jamaican artists of every generation.

1. Bob Marley

Christened: Nesta Robert Marley
Born: February 6, 1945
Deceased: May 11, 1981

King Of Reggae

There are personalities in history that are inextricably linked to their countries of origin, for better or for worse – Hitler to Germany, Stalin to Russia, Moa to China, Selassie to Ethiopia, Castro to Cuba and Marley to Jamaica.

In Marley everything came together. His story is one of greatness personified. He remains the foremost ambassador of reggae music, having put Jamaica on the world stage. Marley also became the main voice and primary agent that turned a little known Rastafarian religion into a worldwide movement. Jamaica is not an economic power but is certainly culturally relevant, thanks to their native son Nesta Robert Marley, popularly known as Bob Marley, the King of Reggae.

A romance between a 16 year-old black, country girl Cedella Booker and a white, ex-soldier, Norval Marley, in the 1940s, resulted in the birth of a mulatto child named Nesta.

Norval worked in the colonial office for the British government and his primary duty was to convince local farmers to stay on the land and work their farms with the assistance of the authorities. His was an intimidating presence with him usually dressed in his regimental attire, on horseback, riding through the area of Nine Miles, St Ann. This was where he met Cedella.

The couple married in 1944, but by the time the young Marley arrived his father had already exited the scene. Norval reportedly visited Cedella maybe once or twice after the boys birth and then disappeared from their lives permanently.

The young Marley existed in a world of dire poverty, but in rural Jamaica surrounded by relatives he could at least be sure of his meals. Hard life would become more acute once on his own

Next, his mother entered into a relationship with a man called Thaddeus, who was the father of another youngster living in Nine Miles, Neville Livingston. Nesta and Neville both attended Stepny All Age and became close friends.

When Marley's mother decided to seek work opportunities in Kingston he was left in the care of his grandfather Omeria, from whom he learnt a lot of Jamaican folk songs. He also became curious about the guitar by observing one of his mother's cousins Clarence Martin, a noted mento guitarist in the 40s. It was evident that the musical talents rested on his mother's side.

Growing up as a so-called "half breed", in those days, was tough. Fair skinned people were supposed to be amongst the privileged class. On the other hand, in pre-independent Jamaica, wealth belonged to the white rulers who also looked down on mulatto children as inferior. Here he was, caught in the middle. This bothered him. But would help to toughen and hone his mind with an uncommon introspection and a lifelong search to find himself, including his place in society. This reality could have broken him and, it would a lesser man. But Marley was no ordinary fellow. Instead, he focused. He was determined to be somebody.

His father's absence would open him up to accommodating many fathers. These men would play critical roles in his life and he would learn from them and use these lessons as fuel for his ambitions.

At age 12, he joined his mother in the Kingston slum of Trench Town. It was a volatile situation where he was shuttled between her friends and relatives, as she was constantly on the go looking for work. In those days he went to school intermittently, spending the rest of his time on the streets, where criminality and violence were the norm. Then he found or was found by music. By no choice of his own, he was living in a part of the city that was giving birth to new musical expression that would give the island its own identity.

From the 30s upward, the richer-class of Jamaica was playing a copy of the big band music from North America that became known as mento, or in the other islands calypso. When the sound rippled down into the lower rungs of society, it became ska. By the late fifties when Marley was a teenager, ska gave way to another sound called rocksteady. This all took shape in Trench Town.

One of the biggest stars of rocksteady was Alton Ellis. Marley looked up to Ellis and ventured out, doing talent shows like The Vere Johns Opportunity Hour. Music was it and from then on music it was. This led him and his stepbrother Neville to the home of one of the first of his substitute fathers, Joe Higgs.

Higgs was born Joseph Higgs, June 3rd 1940. By the late 50s, he became popular as part of a duo Higgs and Wilson, with Roy Wilson and had a number of hit singles. The first of them was *Oh Manny*, which sold a major 50,000 copies. Over time, he became the Godfather of Reggae and one of the first among many to address social issues in the music. His lasting legacy is due to the fact that he opened up his home to aspiring artists, whom he mentored and molded on their way up.

This is where the most influential group in the history of Jamaican music, The Wailers, would be born. At this location, Marley and Livingston would meet Winston McIntosh (aka Peter Tosh) as well as Junior Braithwaite, Beverly Kelso and Cherry Green. At Higgs' residence, friendships solidified and they became a group that was initially named the Teenagers (some say The Juveniles). Higgs was also a stabilizing force in their lives keeping them grounded in the harsh realities of the music business. When their friends would tell them that they were ready Higgs, according to sources, would chase them away saying *"they are not ready they are just getting ready"*. The group would rehearse for nearly two years before doing a record.

While the group was in gestation, each member survived by doing day jobs. Marley worked in a welding shop. At his job was a want to be singer Desmond Dacres, later to be famously known as Desmond Dekker, who came to work one day boasting about his recent recordings. Marley told his coworker that he too wanted to be on records. So Desmond took him to **Beverly's Records**, ran by Leslie Kong. But first he had to get past the listening ears of Jimmy Cliff and Derrick Morgan, who themselves were singers but doubling as talent scouts for Kong. If they were not impressed, Kong would not be interested. He sang and both men listened and nodded in approval. The results were two singles: *One Cup of Coffee*, released under the name Bobby Martell; and the more radical *Judge Not*, under Robert Marley and The Beverly All Stars. The year was 1962.

After their two-year apprenticeship was served, Higgs took the group now known as The Wailers to Clement Coxsone Dodd, the most established of all the producers of the time.

Clement Dodd was born January 26th 1932. At school he became a well-known cricket player and was given the nickname Coxsone, based off the English cricket star Alec Coxon. Apart from the Chinese and Syrians who engaged in the music scene, Dodd was one of the first black entrepreneurs who took his love for music to another level. He built several successful sound systems and later his own record label and studio. He was also keen to see the value of copyrights and music publishing from early out. Dodd mainly made records that were covers of American music, mostly soul and doo wop, but subsequently originals of the artists who insisted on writing their own material.

By the mid-60s, Dodd's **Studio One** label was the place you could not afford not to be. The Wailers' first single for Dodd *Simmer Down*, a Marley original, went straight to number one. When the group came to the producer's attention, Marley was homeless. Dodd took a liking to him and provided a room, which was shared with a handyman working for the producer. Marley was also given a bicycle, becoming like a son to Dodd.

The Wailers continued their hot streak in 1965 with favorites like *Put It On, Lonesome Feeling, Love and Affection* and *Mr. Talkative*. But in-spite of these hits the group was broke. Bob then made the decision, in 1966, to go to America, specifically Delaware, where his mother had migrated to a few years earlier.

Before departing he had met and was deeply in love with a young woman named Alpharita Anderson.

Alpharita Anderson was born in Cuba and was a year younger than Bob, but came to Jamaica with her parents as a child. Alpharita's parents settled in the Greenwich Road section of Kingston, which was like a pass through community for people living in Trench Town travelling from the east of the city. It is said that she first became acquainted with Peter Tosh, but really liked his much shorter light skinned friend. Alpharita, nicknamed Rita, was also interested in music and eventually became part of a group called the Soulettes. They all became a part of the scene at the time and the romance between Rita and Bob blossomed.

Bob, shortly before leaving for Delaware under Coxsone's advice on February 10th 1966, took Rita as his bride. Along with Rita's first child Sharon, whom Bob adopted as his own, they would have other children David, Cedella and Stephen.

While in the United States, Marley got a job at the Chrysler automobile plant in Wilmington. His new life however, was like running from one frustration to the next as he quickly fell into a state of unhappiness, pining for the former days when music was the only thing. In Wilmington, his daily routine consisted of going to work then retreating into the basement to play his guitar and write songs. Not having time to spare and feeling his dream fading from view, after ten *long* months, he kissed his mother goodbye and flew back to Jamaica.

On his return to the group, now down to three,

himself, Livingston and Tosh resumed working together. They formed their own label **Wail m n Soul Em**, but still recorded for Coxsone and others.

Shortly after the three friends met a priest by the name of Mortimer Planno, and began to learn and practice the teachings and rituals of a sect called Rases, later known as Rastafarians.

Planno was born September 26th 1929 in Cuba and came to Jamaica with his parents at around the age of three. In his adolescent years, he honed in on the teachings of Pan-Africanist Marcus Garvey and a shaman known as Bedward. His main achievement, propelling him to the forefront of the Rastafarian movement, was being a part of a delegation that went to Ethiopia in 1961. The Rasta's creed had as its central theme black superiority. Their manifesto included repatriation of the Negro Diaspora to Africa and the belief that the Ethiopian Emperor Haile Selassie was the reincarnated Christ, and therefore a god. They believed in a black government, the Nazarene vow of not cutting the hair or shaving of the face and subscribed to a natural living of vegetarianism and the smoking of marijuana as a sacrament.

This new path being taken by The Wailers did

not sit well with Coxsone, but was welcomed by an eccentric music producer called Lee Perry.

Perry also embraced Rastafarianism and, years earlier had ceased, working for Coxsone. He started his own label **Upsetter** and built a studio that he named Black Ark. With Perry, The Wailers indulged in their newfound beliefs. This is when they came into their element and traded in the dance oriented rocksteady groove for the more meditative vibe of a new sound called roots rock reggae. The lyrical content reflected their state of conversion and, just like their religion, promoted antiestablishment themes.

In 1970 under Perry's direction they delivered the *Soul Rebel* album, a potent collection of songs. The album would be licensed to UK imprint **Trojan**, which would build the initial buzz for the group in Britain.

However, Perry, for all his musical kinship would prove no better than Coxsone and allegedly gave none of the proceeds from the deal to the group. On discovering what he had done, the trio beat him up. This aside, *Soul Rebel* and another release *Soul Revolution* were works that showed the brilliance of Marley, Tosh and Livingston containing the instant classics *400 Years, African*

Herbsman, Kaya, Keep On Moving, Duppy Conquerer and *Dont Rock My Boat*.

Perry stole their money, but The Wailers stole his musicians when they swiped most of The Upsetter band, which included the brilliant rhythm section of brothers Aston and Carlton Barrett. The whole Lee Perry affair though was not as straightforward as it might have seemed.

Around 1968 or 1969, American singer Johnny Nash was in Jamaica recording an album. Whilst there he went to a Rasta ceremony led by Planno, where he was introduced to Marley. In a state of marijuana induced haze, on hearing Marley sing, he became smitten.

On his return to the States, Nash convinced his partners Danny Sims and Arthur Jenkins, with whom he owned a label **JAD**, to sign The Wailers. This they did for recording and publishing. Unlike Nash, Sims was a more hardened businessman and was only interested in the group as songwriters who could supply material for their artists, which along with Nash included Betty Wright and Gloria Gaynor. Sims doubted the commercial appeal of reggae and, when Blackwell showed interest in 1972, **JAD** cashed out by selling the recording contract to

Island. **JAD** however, wisely kept a share of The Wailers publishing. Perry saw everybody getting paid and therefore made his own side deal. *Ah the music business.*

There are encounters which are like hinges on which the doors of history turns and the day the Wailers walked in to the London offices of **Island Records** to see Chris Blackwell is one of them.

The white Christopher Blackwell was born in England on June 22nd 1937 to aristocratic parents, who were plantation owners in the British colony of Jamaica. At age ten he came to the island where he attended school. In his early twenties he became deeply interested in the music business and started to buy and bootleg the island's music. Back in Britain he sold the records to shops, catering to Caribbean immigrants. In 1958 he started **Island Records** with Australian recording engineer Greame Goodall. The label hit pay dirt in 1964 with the worldwide smash *My Boy Lollipop*, sung by the Jamaican teenager Millie Small. Blackwell acted as Small's manager and this took him deep into the heart of the music business. He then built the label into an indie powerhouse signing Cat Stevens, Grace Jones, Traffic and of course The Wailers. Later on he would bring to the world U2, who would become one of the most successful groups of all time.

The Wailers, being allegedly robbed by both Coxsone and Lee Perry, realized that the *"mystery man"* in England doing all the deals was Blackwell. On a tour of England, while opening for Johnny Nash, their road manager, a Trinidadian named Brent Clarke, took them to Blackwell's office. So the group turned up at Blackwell's office to discuss their missing royalties. Whatever was said, at the end of the day, they walked out with 4,000 pounds but only as an advance for an album. Blackwell was no slouch, but he knew how much he made off the Perry and Coxsone's deals and pivoted towards the future while soothing the irate Rasta men. When **JAD** sold their contract to **Island**, Blackwell had The Wailers lock stock and barrel.

Blackwell was a dual citizen and the Jamaican side made him knowledgeable of the islands music. With the success of Millie Small's record and subsequently those of Desmond Dekker and Jimmy Cliff, Blackwell was a firm believer in the product. On the other hand, he sold millions with his white acts and figured that if he could market his Jamaican roster in a similar fashion he could experience the same with them. After all he could make or acquire the Jamaican records for less money therefore making a larger profit.

At first his sights were set on Cliff, but the artist left **Island** when his contract expired. Exit Cliff enters The Wailers.

In Marley he saw an artist with multicultural appeal. Peter and Bunny were right in believing that Blackwell had his game plan all figured out. He was not thinking Wailers. For him the only way was *Bob Marley and The Wailers*. Right or wrong it was the only marketing strategy that made sense.

In 1973 the brilliant *Catch A Fire* album was released. The Wailers was immediately dispatched to promote it. At first the numbers were not great, but it showed promise, moving around 14,000 copies. Then problems arose.

Bunny Wailer quit the group after the first leg of touring. Some say he could not stand cold weather and Livingston himself blamed Blackwell for booking the group in "freak" clubs that did not measure up to his religious beliefs. Another ground breaking album, *Burning,* came shortly after and, their mentor, Joe Higgs replaced Bunny on the road.

In 1974 Peter Tosh scuffled with his band mates on the tour bus and, in a fit of anger, abandoned the tour and quit. In the aftermath, he peppered Chris Blackwell with vitriol, calling him Chris "Whiteworst". Tosh also made claims of favoritism that benefited Marley and that Tosh's potential was being stifled. From then on, Tosh ceased communicating with Marley and seemingly resented him up to the very end.

This could have been it but Marley did not have "born to lose" tattooed on his forehead and courageously soldiered on. The whole affair, more than anything refocused him. With the infighting and negativity now out of the way, Marley could now become the leader that he was meant to be. This was now his show to run and he was ready to go to the next level and beyond.

For the next album *Natty Dread*, Bob assembled a lineup that would assist him in conquering the world. The Wailers, before the break up, was essentially a vocal group. With Peter and Bunny gone, Marley needed new voices as reinforcement. For this he called upon his wife Rita and the friends she sang with, Marcia Griffiths and Judy Mowatt. Rita and Judy previously backed Marcia, who at the time had a respectable solo career albeit one that was financially unrewarding. When Bob called, they answered and dubbed themselves as the I Threes and were on their way to greatness.

The contingent also consisted of Aston Barrett (bass), Carlton Barrett (drums), Alvin Anderson (lead guitar), Alvin Patterson (percussion), Bernard Harvey (keyboards), Marley (lead vocals & guitar),and Lee Jaffe (harmonica). In later years, some members would leave to be replaced by new ones namely Junior Marvin, Donald Kinsey, Earl Smith and Tyrone Downie.

This album would mark the point from which Marley would begin a rapid ascent to the heights of stardom, becoming the first genuine superstar from the so-called Third World. *Natty Dread* charted in Britain, most of continental Europe and the US. The break out single was *No Woman No Cry*, which was certified gold when it was also included on the concert album *Live*.

Blackwell, in his role as producer added overdubs, using outside musicians to give the records that "international" appeal. The tour supporting *Natty Dread* set the world on fire and audiences were being hypnotized with the first strains of the riff-heavy Led Zeppelin like sound of *Lively Up Yourself*. In the coming years,

Marley could do no wrong and never put out an album that disappointed his growing legion of fans.

This new genre called reggae, through sweat was now taking its place alongside other mainstream music. It was potent in all its glory, being everything that rock wanted to be but could not. Reggae had all the right ingredients. It was rebellious, spiritual, political and socially relevant.

Marley possessed youth, electricity and truth that galvanized the oppressed on a wider scale than his forebears such as Woodie Guthrie, Bob Dylan and Joan Baez. Now, the downtrodden of all races had a spokesman. This made him powerful but it also made him a target.

Rastaman Vibration released in 1976 was his most political album yet. It was also an election year in Jamaica, and political tensions between the governing left leaning Peoples National Party and the opposition Jamaica Labour Party was at an all-time high. Marley, by this time, was living at the upper-class residence at 56 Hope Road, where his red BMW motor car could be seen in the driveway. Success had brought him wealth and many, many friends. Gone was the shy reticent young man that hardly spoke. Now Marley was being looked upon as the great man and this was where he held court as a central figure. At Hope Road there was a beehive of activity with characters of every persuasion, including a lot of criminal types, going and coming with alarming frequency.

As the Rolling Stone Encyclopedia of Rock &Roll states *"Marley's pronouncements on public issues"* were being accorded the attention *"usually reserved for political and religious leaders"*. In the song Rat Race he named dropped the United States's spy outfit, the Central Intelligence Agency (CIA). Marley, it seems, was at least aware that he was been monitored.

The ruling government at the time held to the so-called doctrine of "democratic socialism", but Prime Minister Michael Manley's cozy relationship with Cuban President Fidel Castro, in the eyes of Washington, was no laughing matter.

Many Rastas, including Marley, shared the ideals of socialism, which advocated a classless society and what Manley, the self-styled "Joshua" was trying to do. Manley took an anti-Imperialist stance by nationalizing a lot of foreign owned businesses raising the ire of the United States. As a consequence, Henry Kissinger, America's Secretary of State under Presidents Nixon and Ford, travelled to Jamaica to deliver a stern warning to the Jamaican leader. When Marley agreed to do the *Smile Jamaica* concert, largely regarded as a political vehicle to boost Manley's re-election, the die was cast.

As to who did what still up to this day remains a mystery, but sources claim that Marley was singled out in CIA communications as being "pro-PNP". Marley was also being followed by a character, Carl Colby CEO of Colby Films and son of former CIA director William Colby, obtaining footage of the singer for a documentary. In addition, it is no secret that enforcers on the side of the opposition party were ready to carry out any order given by their masters. On December 3, 1976 gunmen stormed Marley's residence in a bold assassination attempt. This offensive wounded the artist, his manager Don Taylor and his wife Rita.

In the early part of 1977, in the wake of the attempt on his life, Marley and his band relocated to Britain. The attempt on his life seemed to give him a new sense of urgency and a deeper understanding of his own mortality. He now worked even more feverishly, delivering one brilliant album after another, beginning with the masterpiece *Exodus*. He then went on to break one record after the other, in terms of concert attendance, on his many tours.

Then another messenger came, a harbinger, an omen of impending misfortune, one that would succeed where the assassin's bullet failed. In that same year he hurt his left big toe in a friendly soccer game, while on tour in France. The diagnosis given by the doctors was that the toe was cancerous and should be immediately removed.

A rumor about the illness is that it was the result of covert operations by sinister forces. It is said that shortly after the shooting at Hope Road, Marley was visited by a white man who gave him a gift, a pair of cowboy boots in which cancerous agents were placed. As the Jamaican proverb goes that "belief kills and belief cures", Marley sought advice from his Rastafarian brethren who opposed the first doctor's advice. A second opinion was then sought.

In hindsight, it is apparent that his religious beliefs in this case, proved to be a liability. The second physician played ball with Marley's yes men and instead, removed a part of the toe claiming that it was only a portion that contained the tumor. From that time forward the toe was a constant source of pain and irritation, but not regarded as life threatening and Marley went about life, business as usual.

Marley's stellar run continued unabated. His fame grew larger and larger as he scaled unimaginable heights, both creatively and commercially.

He returned to his homeland in 1978 to do the *One Love Concert* where on stage he joined the hands of Prime Minister Michael Manley and Leader of the Opposition Edward Seaga. This was Marley's cry for peace as the island was in the throes of a full scale political civil war.

But apart from this brief visit he ceased to call Jamaica home on a permanent basis, as the very thought that his own countrymen tried to kill him was too much to bear. Marley, from then on, would love Jamaica from a distance.

The *Exodus* album, with the feel good classic *Jamming*, as well as the Curtis Mayfield reworked *People Get Ready*, now titled *One Love* was another milestone for the Jamaican as with this disc the biggest music market; the United States started to open up. Marley already broke reggae in a big way in Asia, Africa and Europe and was now calling a resistant America.

In quick succession came the albums *Kaya* (78), *Survival* (79) and *Uprising* (80).

In 1980 Marley had already gotten rid of long time manager Don Taylor and came full circle, rehiring the man who knew the US market best, Danny Sims. This was a part of Marley's plan to go on the offensive in the US, where his albums sold poorly in comparison to other markets.

In that same year, he had a two-night-stand at Madison Square Gardens, in New York City. Both were sold out affairs. On one of these he opened for R&B legends The Commodores and upstaged them. Days after the concerts, while jogging in Central Park in New York City, Marley collapsed.

In the ominous halls of the hospital the news was bad, very very bad. The tumor, which began in his toe, had now metastasized and was present throughout his entire body. He courageously did the next date, his final one, in Pittsburgh then came off the road to seek treatment.

What is incredulous is the collective amnesia

of everyone who surrounded Marley concerning his health, and the necessity to stay on top of it with regular checkups.

The star had become big business and no one seemed to want to slow the train. In this regard the failure to act doomed him as a casualty of his profession.

Eight months later, on May 11, 1981, he died.

The posthumous release, *Confrontation*, came in 1983. Years later, a greatest hits collection *Legend* would become one of the bestselling albums of all time moving upwards of 20 million copies worldwide.

The corporate machinery kicked into high gear and kept the cash registers ringing, making Marley one of the highest money earners even in death.

Many awards came from his native country, some say, too late, and from around the world. But they pale in comparison to the genuine love that the downtrodden of this world has for one of the most potent voices of the Twentieth Century. The world's accolades, he could do without. His gift to mankind was music.

Marley took a little-known genre by the name of reggae mainstream, and made his native Jamaica into a star whose magnet attracts millions of tourist every year. His musical legacy is one of the richest of all the icons, and his bloodline the most celebrated with his sons Ziggy, Damian, Stephen, Kymani and Julian all having successful solo careers.

Bob, in his brief life and career, did more than most in several lifetimes. He was truly special, and remains the one and only *King Of Reggae*.

DEDICATION & THANKS

For my parents Sylvia and my late father Ray, all my brothers and sisters, my grandparents, the late Lucia and Sydney Whyte and the Grant clan in general.

And for my wife Andrea and all my children: William, Russell, Tavan, Megan, Shakira and Aaron.

Also to Clarence "Ben" Brodie who saw something in me when he took me on as a trainee reporter at The Boulevard News.

Thanks

In addition to my father God, I would like to thank Janice Ross for editing and formatting and Dave Grant for the cover design. I also would like to thank my business partners and brothers in arms Benton Dunn and Marcello Johnson.

AUTHOR'S BIO

Roger Grant is a Jamaican author, songwriter, record producer and artist manager. He attended Seaward All Age and Calabar High School. He holds a Diploma in Entertainment Management from The Institute of Management and Production and a Certificate in Public Relations from The University of the West Indies. Grant is The CEO of 619 Entertainment Group and lives in Philadelphia, with his wife and some of his children.

ORGANIC BASE BOOKS
Contact Roger Grant

1 (267) 407-6262
Facebook: Roger Grant
Linkeden: Roger Grant
Emails: sixonenine52@yahoo.com
or organicrecordsus@yahoo.com

www.ingramcontent.com/pod-product-compliance
Lightning Source LLC
Chambersburg PA
CBHW050847160426
43194CB00011B/2059